ASSESSMENT IN THE CLASSROOM

ASSESSMENT IN THE CLASSROOM

PETER W. AIRASIAN
Boston College

McGraw-Hill, Inc.

New York • St. Louis • San Francisco • Auckland • Bogotá • Caracas
Lisbon • London • Madrid • Mexico City • Milan • Montreal • New Delhi
San Juan • Singapore • Sydney • Tokyo • Toronto

This book was developed by Lane Akers, Inc.

ASSESSMENT IN THE CLASSROOM

Copyright © 1996 by McGraw-Hill, Inc. All rights reserved. Printed in the United States of America. Except as permitted under the United States Copyright Act of 1976, no part of this publication may be reproduced or distributed in any form or by any means, or stored in a data base or retrieval system, without the prior written permission of the publisher.

This book is printed on acid-free paper.

1 2 3 4 5 6 7 8 9 0   FGR   FGR   9 0 9 8 7 6 5

ISBN 0-07-000772-1

This book was set in Veljovic by The Clarinda Company.
The editor was Lane Akers;
the designer was Wanda Siedlecka;
the production supervisor was Richard A. Ausburn.
Project supervision was done by The Total Book.
Quebecor Printing/Fairfield was printer and binder.

Photo Credits

Chapter Opener 1: Elizabeth Crews. **Chapter Opener 2:** Joel Gordon. **Chapter Opener 3:** Elizabeth Crews. **Chapter Opener 4:** Cary Wolinsky/Stock, Boston. **Chapter Opener 5:** Joel Gordon. **Chapter Opener 6:** Arthur Grace/Stock, Boston.

Library of Congress Cataloging-in-Publication Data

Airasian, Peter W.
    Assessment in the classroom / Peter W. Airasian.
        p.   cm.
    Includes index.
    ISBN 0-07-000772-1 (text).— ISBN 0-07-000773-X (I.M.)
    1. Educational tests and measurements—United States.
    2. Examinations—Validity—United States.   3. Grading and marking
(Students)—United States.   I. Title.
LB3051.A5626   1996
371.2′6—dc20   95-20310

ABOUT THE AUTHOR

Peter W. Airasian is Professor of Education at Boston College, where he is Chair of the Educational Research, Measurement, and Evaluation Program. His main teaching responsibilities are instructing pre- and in-service teachers in classroom assessment strategies. He received his Ph.D. from the University of Chicago, with a concentration in testing, evaluation, and assessment. He is a former high school chemistry and biology teacher. He is co-author of *Minimal Competency Testing* (1979), *School Effectiveness: A Reassessment of the Evidence* (1980), *The Effects of Standardized Testing* (1982), and *Classroom Assessment* (1994). He is a past Chair of the American Educational Research Association's Special Interest Group on Classroom Assessment. Currently, he is studying the processes classroom teachers use to assess themselves.

For Lynn, Greg, and Gwen

CONTENTS IN BRIEF

PREFACE   XVII

CHAPTER 1
THE CLASSROOM AS AN ASSESSMENT
ENVIRONMENT   1

CHAPTER 2
ASSESSMENT IN PLANNING AND DELIVERING
INSTRUCTION   29

CHAPTER 3
FORMAL ASSESSMENT: TEACHER-MADE TESTS   81

CHAPTER 4
PERFORMANCE ASSESSMENT   131

CHAPTER 5
GRADING PUPIL PERFORMANCE   183

CHAPTER 6
STANDARDIZED ACHIEVEMENT TESTS   227

GLOSSARY   266

INDEXES   270

CONTENTS

PREFACE   XVII

CHAPTER 1
THE CLASSROOM AS AN
ASSESSMENT ENVIRONMENT   1

SOME DEFINITIONS: TESTING, MEASUREMENT,
ASSESSMENT, AND EVALUATION   4

PURPOSES OF ASSESSMENT   5

Diagnosing Student Problems   6
Judging Academic Learning and Progress   6
Providing Feedback and Incentives   6
Placing Pupils   6
Planning and Conducting Instruction   7
Establishing Classroom Equilibrium   7

BEHAVIOR DOMAINS ASSESSED   9

Cognitive Domain   9
Affective Domain   10
Psychomotor Domain   11

METHODS OF COLLECTING ASSESSMENT
INFORMATION   12

Paper-and-Pencil Techniques   12
Observational Techniques   13

STANDARDIZED AND UNSTANDARDIZED
ASSESSMENTS   14

Standardized Assessments   14
Unstandardized Assessments   15

INDIVIDUAL AND GROUP ASSESSMENT   15

Individual Assessment   15
Group Assessment   16

CHARACTERISTICS OF GOOD ASSESSMENT: VALIDITY AND RELIABILITY   17

Validity   19
Reliability   20

ETHICAL ISSUES AND RESPONSIBILITIES   22

CHAPTER SUMMARY   24

CHAPTER 2

ASSESSMENT IN PLANNING AND DELIVERING INSTRUCTION   29

THE INSTRUCTIONAL PROCESS   31

Purpose of Planning Instruction   32

LEARNING ABOUT PUPILS: SIZING-UP ASSESSMENT   33

Pupil Characteristics   34
Sources of Information   35
Forming Descriptions of Pupils   36
Features of Sizing-Up Assessments   37
Quality of Sizing-Up Assessments   39
Improving Sizing-Up Assessments   42

CHARACTERISTICS CONSIDERED IN PLANNING INSTRUCTION   46

Pupil Characteristics   46
Teacher Characteristics   46
Instructional Resources   47

LESSON PLANS   48

EDUCATIONAL OBJECTIVES   49

Stating Educational Objectives   50
Questions about Educational Objectives   52

TEXTBOOK OBJECTIVES AND LESSON PLANS   54

IMPROVING PLANNING ASSESSMENTS   59

ASSESSMENT DURING INSTRUCTION   61

Teachers' Tasks during Instruction   62

Teachers' Thinking during Instruction 63
Assessment Indicators 64

THE QUALITY OF INSTRUCTIONAL ASSESSMENTS 65

Problems That Affect Validity 66
Problems That Affect Reliability 67

IMPROVING ASSESSMENTS DURING INSTRUCTION 68

CHAPTER SUMMARY 72

CHAPTER 3

FORMAL ASSESSMENT: TEACHER-MADE TESTS 81

THE LOGIC OF FORMAL ASSESSMENT 84

PREPARING FOR ASSESSMENT 85

An Example 85

PREPARING PUPILS FOR FORMAL ACHIEVEMENT TESTING 91

Issues of Test Preparation 92
Provide Good Instruction 92
Review before Testing 93
Familiarity with Question Formats 93
Scheduling the Test 94
Giving Pupils Information about the Test 95

PAPER-AND-PENCIL TEST QUESTIONS 95

Types of Test Items 96
Higher-Level Test Items 99

GENERAL GUIDELINES FOR WRITING AND CRITIQUING TEST ITEMS 102

Cover Important Objectives 102
Write Clearly and Simply: Six Rules 103
Review Items before Testing 113

ASSEMBLING THE TEST 114

ADMINISTERING THE TEST 115

Physical Setting 115
Psychological Setting 116
Cheating 116

SCORING TESTS   118

Scoring Selection Items   *118*
Scoring Short-Answer and Completion Items   *118*
Scoring Essay Items   *119*

DISCUSS TEST RESULTS WITH PUPILS   123

CHAPTER SUMMARY   123

CHAPTER 4

PERFORMANCE ASSESSMENT   131

PERFORMANCE ASSESSMENT IN SCHOOLS AND
CLASSROOMS   135

Performance-Oriented Subjects   *136*
Early Childhood and Special Needs Pupils   *137*

DEVELOPING PERFORMANCE ASSESSMENTS   138

Define the Purpose of Assessment   *139*
Identify Performance Criteria   *140*
Cautions in Developing Performance Criteria   *142*
Developing Observable Performance Criteria   *144*
Provide a Setting to Elicit and Observe the Performance   *146*
Scoring or Rating Performance   *147*
Anecdotal Records   *148*
Checklists   *149*
Rating Scales and Rubrics   *151*

USES OF PERFORMANCE ASSESSMENTS   158

Self-Assessment and Peer Review   *158*
Linking Assessment and Instruction   *161*
Grading   *161*

PORTFOLIO ASSESSMENT   162

Purpose of Portfolio   *164*
Performance Criteria   *165*
Setting   *166*
Scoring and Judging   *166*

VALIDITY AND RELIABILITY OF PERFORMANCE
ASSESSMENTS   170

Clarity of Purpose   *170*
Preparing Pupils for Performance Assessment   *171*
Improving Performance Assessments   *172*

CHAPTER SUMMARY   175

CHAPTER 5
GRADING PUPIL PERFORMANCE 183

GRADING: ITS RATIONALE AND DIFFICULTIES 184

Why Grade? 185
The Difficulty of Grading 190

GRADING AS JUDGMENT 192

STANDARDS OF COMPARISON 193

Comparisons with Other Pupils 194
Comparison to Predefined Standards 195
Comparison to a Pupil's Ability 199
Comparison to Pupil Improvement 201
Grading in Cooperative Learning 202

SELECTING PUPIL PERFORMANCES 203

Academic Achievement 203
Affective Considerations 205

SUMMARIZING DIFFERENT TYPES OF ASSESSMENT 206

What Should be Included in a Grade? 208
Selecting Weights for Assessment Information 209
Combining Different Assessment Information 210
Computing Pupils' Overall Scores 212

ASSIGNING GRADES 214

A Criterion-Referenced Example 214
A Norm-Referenced Example 216

OTHER METHODS OF REPORTING PUPIL PROGRESS 217

Parent-Teacher Conferences 218
Other Reporting Methods 221

CHAPTER SUMMARY 221

CHAPTER 6
STANDARDIZED ACHIEVEMENT TESTS 227

TEACHER'S PERCEPTIONS OF STANDARDIZED TESTS 230

COMMERCIAL ACHIEVEMENT TESTS 231

Test Construction 232

ADMINISTERING COMMERCIAL ACHIEVEMENT
TESTS 236

INTERPRETING COMMERCIAL ACHIEVEMENT TEST
SCORES 237

Percentile Rank Scores 238
Stanine Scores 239
Grade Equivalent Scores 239
Three Examples of Test Interpretation 241

THE VALIDITY OF COMMERCIAL ACHIEVEMENT
TESTS 250

Content Coverage 250
Test Norms 251
Test Administration 252
Interpreting Commercial Test Results 252

STATE-MANDATED ACHIEVEMENT TESTS 254

Group-Based, State-Mandated Tests 254
Individual-Based, State-Mandated Tests 257
An Example of State-Mandated Assessment 258

CHAPTER SUMMARY 260

GLOSSARY 266

NAME INDEX 270

SUBJECT INDEX 273

PREFACE

Curriculum revision has become commonplace in teacher education programs over the past few years. In most cases the new curriculums that are emerging are streamlined versions of their predecessors, having fewer credit hours in which to teach a professional knowledge base that continues to expand. This tightening of the professional curriculum together with increased amounts of field experience has resulted both in restructured core courses and, in some cases, in an array of narrower courses that have only one or two credit hours attached to them. Whatever curriculum design is used, the results usually have one thing in common: the new courses, which often vary considerably from one school to another, don't map well with the large survey texts that were produced for the old curriculum. Consequently, instructors are increasingly moving toward the use of customized course packets composed of one or more modestly priced texts often accompanied by a collection of readings.

In view of this curriculum variation, it seems sensible to offer a new, more flexible type of Assessment and Evaluation text, one that can be mixed and matched to fit a variety of curriculum arrangements. *Assessment in the Classroom* has been expressly designed for this purpose. Because of its modest length and price, and its focus on the assessment needs of regular classroom teachers, this text is ideal for any of the following situations:

- To be the core text in either brief or full-length assessment courses for teachers.
- To teach the assessment "unit" in educational psychology courses.
- To teach the assessment component of those integrated methods courses (course blocks) which combine formerly separate content areas and often last a full year.

The special mission of *Assessment in the Classroom* is to show how assessment principles apply to the full range of teacher decision making: from organizing the class as a social system to planning and conducting instruction to the formal evaluation of learning and, finally, to grading. The goal is to show students that assessment is an everyday, ongoing part of their teaching, not some esoteric affair that is divorced from their daily routine. With this in mind, the following features have been built into this text.

- ◆ *Realistic assessment* The focus throughout is on the realities of classrooms and how assessment techniques can serve those realities.
- ◆ *Validity and reliability* These two central concepts are introduced in Chapter 1 and then linked in later chapters to each specific type of assessment information. In this way the particular validity and reliability problems of informal assessment, performance rating, and paper-and-pencil tests are identified. Practical strategies for improving the validity and reliability of various assessment techniques are also presented in each chapter.
- ◆ *Practical guidelines* A good portion of each chapter is devoted to practical guidelines to follow and common errors to avoid when conducting the type of assessment under discussion. The dangers of ignoring recommendations are also described.
- ◆ *Teacher thinking* Interspersed throughout the text are excerpts from interviews with real teachers that add the wisdom of practice to the text discussions.
- ◆ *Up-to-date coverage* Such current topics as portfolio assessment, grading cooperative learning activities, and ethical issues in assessment are thoroughly covered.

ACKNOWLEDGMENTS

With great appreciation I would like to acknowledge the following reviewers whose initial support encouraged my undertaking this project: Kay Alderman, University of Akron; Hilda Borko, University of Colorado; CarolAnne Kardash, University of Missouri; Paul Pintrich, University of Michigan; and Gary Stuck, University of North Carolina. I would also like to acknowledge those reviewers of my larger text, *Classroom Assessment,* whose experience with that text provided much useful guidance in designing this one. Principal among these are Jane Canner, Hunter College; Greg Hancock, Auburn University; Mary Ellen Harmon, Boston College; Robert Hoehle, Drake University; Paul Jons, University of Nevada, Las Vegas; Robert Kanoy, University of North Carolina; Audrey Kleinsasser, University of Wyoming; Rosalyn Malcolm-Payne, University of Alabama; Alan Moore, University of Wyoming; Susan Nolen, University of Washington; Kim Schulze, St. Cloud State University; Donna Siegel, University of the Arts and Sciences of Oklahoma; Richard Stiggins, Lewis and Clark University; Catherine Taylor, University of Washington; Dale Wittington, Cleveland State University; Peter Wood, Bowling Green State University; and Wenfan Yang, Gonzaga University.

I have dedicated this book to Lynn, Greg, and Gwen who provide the support and inspiration for all my endeavors. I also wish to again thank Lane Akers, my editor, for his foresight, encouragement, and advice. Thanks also to Kate Scheinman, who so ably guided the manuscript through the production process. Lastly, I acknowledge my mother and father, who made education an important focus in my life; John Walsh, who was responsible for starting me on my career; and Ben Bloom, who provided guidance and perspectives that still influence my thought and work.

Peter W. Airasian

ASSESSMENT IN THE CLASSROOM

CHAPTER 1

THE CLASSROOM AS AN ASSESSMENT ENVIRONMENT

SOME DEFINITIONS: TESTING, MEASUREMENT, ASSESSMENT, AND EVALUATION

PURPOSES OF ASSESSMENT
Diagnosing Student Problems
Judging Academic Learning and Progress
Providing Feedback and Incentives
Placing Pupils
Planning and Conducting Instruction
Establishing Classroom Equilibrium

BEHAVIOR DOMAINS ASSESSED
Cognitive Domain
Affective Domain
Psychomotor Domain

METHODS OF COLLECTING ASSESSMENT INFORMATION
Paper-and-Pencil Techniques
Observational Techniques

STANDARDIZED AND UNSTANDARDIZED ASSESSMENTS
Standardized Assessments
Unstandardized Assessments

INDIVIDUAL AND GROUP ASSESSMENT
Individual Assessment
Group Assessment

CHARACTERISTICS OF GOOD ASSESSMENT: VALIDITY AND RELIABILITY
Validity
Reliability

ETHICAL ISSUES AND RESPONSIBILITIES

CHAPTER SUMMARY

1

Today was a typical day in Ms. Lopez's classroom. In addition to preparing her room for the day's instructional activities, writing the homework assignments on the blackboard, reviewing her lesson plans, taking attendance, passing out a new textbook, and reminding pupils of next Thursday's field trip, Ms. Lopez also:

- Assigned grades to her pupils' science test
- Selected Martha, not Matt, to deliver a note to Mr. Henderson, the school principal
- Decided on topics to cover in tomorrow's lessons
- Recommended that Robert spend extra time this weekend rewriting the first draft of his report
- Completed the monthly school progress report on her pupils
- Referred Aaron to the Special Education Department because of his poor gross motor skills
- Stopped the planned language lesson halfway through the period in order to review the previous day's lesson
- Placed pupils who were below the accepted cutoff score on the state-mandated basic skills test in a special remedial group
- Rearranged the class seating plan to separate Bill from Leroy and to put Monroe in the front of the room so he could see the blackboard better
- Moved Jennifer from the middle to the high reading group
- Called on Kim twice even though her hand was not raised
- Praised Anne for her B grade, but encouraged Tim to work harder in order to improve his B grade
- Switched instruction from discussion to individual seatwork when the class became bored and unruly
- Previewed and selected a film strip on astronomy for next week's science unit
- Determined that she should construct her own test for the science unit on physical and chemical changes rather than using the unit test provided with the textbook
- Sent Randy to the school nurse when he complained of a headache
- Corrected her pupils' projects for the unit on the three branches of American government
- Decided to spend an extra two days letting her students reread and evaluate their poetry portfolios
- Judged that Rose's constant interruptions and speaking out in class warranted a note to her parents about the problem
- Assigned homework in science but not in social studies
- Checked with the school counselor regarding possible reasons for Joshua's increasingly inattentive class behavior

- ◆ Paired Kim, a class isolate, with Mary, a class leader, for the group project in social studies
- ◆ Sent Ralph to the school principal because he swore at a teacher and fought with a classmate
- ◆ Held a parent-teacher conference with Tim's parents in which she told them that Tim was a capable student who could produce better work than he had thus far
- ◆ Consulted last year's standardized test scores to determine whether the class needed a review of the basic rules of capitalization

As you can see, Ms. Lopez's day in the classroom, like those of teachers at all grade levels, was filled with situations in which decisions had to be made—decisions about grading, planning instruction, judging the success of instruction, providing for pupils' needs, interacting with and encouraging pupils, testing, assigning homework, and dealing with parents. Some decisions were about individual pupils and some about the class as a whole. Some were about instructional matters, some about classroom climate, some about pupil personalities, and some about pupil learning. Some, like the decision to change Jennifer's reading group or refer Aaron for screening, are decisions made infrequently during the school year. Others, like planning topics for instruction, calling on pupils during class, and assigning grades to pupils, are made many times each day.

Teacher decisions and the evidence that guides them are the lifeblood on which classrooms function. Taken together, all these decisions help teachers to establish, organize, and monitor classroom features such as interpersonal relations, social adjustment, instructional content, lesson pace, and pupil learning. Evidence gathering and decision making are necessary and ongoing aspects of life in all classrooms; and classroom decisions should be made on the basis of good evidence.

The decisions Ms. Lopez made were based upon many different kinds of evidence that she collected. Why, for example, did Ms. Lopez praise Anne for her B grade but encourage Tim, who attained the same grade, to do better next time? How did she know that the way to settle down her bored and unruly class was to switch from discussion to seatwork, when there were many other things she might have done to settle the class? What made her decide to move Jennifer to the high reading group? Why did she finally decide that Rose's parents needed to be notified about their child's behavior? Why did she think pairing Kim with Mary for the social studies project was better than pairing Kim with Martha, Rose, or Joshua? Why did she feel that letting pupils spend two extra days reflecting on their poetry portfolios would be more useful than using the time to introduce some other topic? Why was Martha, but not Matt, trusted to deliver a note to the principal? All of these decisions were based upon information Ms. Lopez had gathered to help her select appropriate courses of action in her classroom. This book is about the process of gathering, evaluating, and using such information to help make good classroom decisions.

Teachers are constantly gathering information to make classroom decisions.

SOME DEFINITIONS: TESTING, MEASUREMENT, ASSESSMENT, AND EVALUATION

Assessment is the process of collecting, synthesizing, and interpreting information to aid in decision making.

Assessment is the process of collecting, synthesizing, and interpreting information to aid in decision making. When many people hear the word *assessment* they think of pupils taking paper-and-pencil tests to determine how much they have learned. While paper-and-pencil tests are important components of assessment, the preceding list of Ms. Lopez's decisions makes clear that there is much more to assessment in classrooms than administering tests to pupils. Assessment, as we will use the term, includes all the information teachers gather in their classrooms: information that helps them understand their pupils, plan and monitor their instruction, and establish a viable classroom culture, as well as test and grade.

There are differences between assessments, tests, measurements, and evaluations. Assessment is a general term that includes all the different ways teachers gather information in their classrooms. A **test** is a formal, systematic, usually paper-and-pencil procedure to gather information about pupils' behavior. Tests provide only one of the many types of assessment information teachers deal with, and thus, testing is only one strategy for assessment. Other important assessment strategies are observations, oral questions, projects, and portfolios.

A test is a formal, systematic, and usually paper-and-pencil procedure for gathering information.

Measurement is the process of quantifying or assigning numbers to performance.

Measurement is the process of quantifying or assigning a number to performance. The most common example of measurement in the classroom is when a teacher scores a quiz or test. Scoring produces a numerical description of performance: Jackie got 17 out of 20 items correct on the biology test; Dennis got a score of 65 percent on his math test; Rhonda's score on the creative essay was 85 percent. In all these examples, a numerical score is used to represent the individual's performance.

Evaluation is the process of judging the quality or value of a performance or a course of action.

Once assessment information is collected, teachers use it to make decisions or judgments about pupils, instruction, or classroom climate. **Evaluation** is the process of making judgments about what is good or desirable, for example, deciding about the quality of pupils' performance or the desirability of a particular instructional activity. Evaluation occurs after assessment information has been collected, synthesized, and thought about, because this is when the teacher is in a position to make informed judgments.

Imagine a teacher who wishes to *assess* the mathematics readiness of a pupil in order to decide where to start instruction for that pupil. Notice that the reason for assessing is that a decision must be made. First, the teacher gave a grade appropriate paper-and-pencil *test* of mathematics readiness. The pupil's score on the test, 25 percent of the items right, provided a *measurement* of his math readiness. Of course the teacher used other forms of assessment to determine the pupil's readiness. She talked to the pupil about math, watched him while he did math exercises, and

---

TABLE 1.1   DEFINITIONS OF COMMON ASSESSMENT-RELATED TERMS

Assessment. The collection, synthesis, and interpretation of information to aid the teacher in decision making.

Test. A formal, systematic, usually paper-and-pencil procedure for gathering information.

Measurement. Quantifying or assigning numbers to performance.

Evaluation. Judging the quality or goodness of performance or a course of action.

---

checked prior grades and test scores in his school record file. The teacher then thought about all the assessment information she had collected. She *evaluated,* or made a judgment about, the pupil's current stage of readiness in math. Her final decision, based on this assessment and evaluation, was to recommend a tutor for the pupil to help him catch up to the rest of the class. Table 1.1 summarizes the definitions of assessment, test, measurement, and evaluation.

While the focus in this book is on teacher-centered classroom assessment, it is important to note that other types of assessment also go on in classrooms. Just as teachers constantly assess their pupils, instruction, and classroom climate, so too do pupils constantly assess the teacher, instruction, and classroom climate. Just as teachers want to know whether pupils are motivated, hard-working, academically able, and adjusted to the culture of the classroom, so too do pupils want to know if the teacher is fair, gives hard tests, enforces rigid discipline, can be swayed by a "sob story," and likes them as individuals (Brophy and Good, 1974; Jackson, 1990). Moreover, in all classrooms, pupils are being constantly assessed by their peers. The classroom is a public place and it does not take most pupils long to learn where they stand, both in the teacher's pecking order and in the academic, athletic, and social pecking orders established by their peers (Jackson, 1990; Rist, 1970). Assessment in the classroom is as likely to come from classmates as from the teacher. Discussion of these pupil-teacher and pupil-pupil assessments is interesting and important, but beyond the scope of this work. It is useful, however, to bear in mind the pervasiveness of classroom assessment and its consequences for both pupils and teachers.

In classrooms teachers constantly assess their pupils, and pupils assess the teacher, instruction, and each other.

PURPOSES OF ASSESSMENT

Teachers assess for many purposes because they are required to make many decisions. If we review Ms. Lopez's decisions during her classroom day, we can get a sense of the many purposes teachers have for assessment.

Diagnosing Student Problems

Teachers are constantly on the lookout for pupils who are having learning, emotional, or social problems in the classroom. Having identified such problems, the teacher can sometimes carry out the remedial activities needed, but at other times the pupil must be referred for more specialized diagnosis and remediation outside of the classroom. Thus, Ms. Lopez set up her own, in-class group for basic skills remediation, but she recommended that Aaron be screened by a specialist for his apparent gross motor skills deficiency. She reviewed last year's standardized test performance to determine whether her pupils had a special need for remedial work in capitalization, but she also checked with the school counselor about possible reasons for Joshua's inattentive behavior. Much of the assessment data teachers gather is used to identify, understand, and remediate pupils' problems and learning difficulties.

Teacher assessments are used to identify and remediate student problems.

Judging Academic Learning and Progress

A number of Ms. Lopez's decisions had to do with judging pupils' academic learning and progress. She assigned grades to her pupils' science tests, completed a monthly progress report on each pupil, decided to construct her own test for the science unit rather than to use the test provided in the textbook, corrected pupil projects on the American government unit, and conducted a parent-teacher conference with Tim's parents. Much of a teacher's time is spent collecting information that will be used to grade pupils or provide information about their academic progress.

Providing Feedback and Incentives

Another important reason for classroom assessment is to provide feedback and incentives to pupils. For example, Ms. Lopez praised Anne for attaining a B grade but suggested that Tim could work harder and do better in the future, even though he received the same grade. She used assessment information from Robert's first draft report to suggest that he review and improve what he had written. In both of these cases, information about academic performance was used to provide feedback to pupils about their performance and, in Tim's case, provide incentive for improving his performance. In order to provide such feedback, teachers must constantly assess student learning and behavior.

Accurate feedback about academic performance is needed in order to provide students with incentive to improve.

Placing Pupils

Most classroom teachers must make decisions about the placement of pupils in their class. Whenever a teacher divides pupils into reading or math groups, organizes groups for cooperative learning, pairs pupils up for class projects, or recommends that a particular student be placed with a particular teacher next year, assessment for placement purposes has taken place. Ms. Lopez made a placement decision when she moved Jennifer from the middle to the high reading group. She made another placement decision when she identified pupils who were below the cutoff score on the state-mandated basic skills test and placed them into a remedial group. Finally, when she paired Kim, the class isolate, with Mary in the social studies project group, she made another placement decision. Note that Ms. Lopez's placement decisions were made for both academic and social reasons.

Placement decisions are made for social as well as academic reasons.

Planning and Conducting Instruction

Many of the decisions that Ms. Lopez made were focused on planning and conducting instruction in the classroom. This should not be surprising, since instruction is the central classroom activity. The instructional decisions that Ms. Lopez made can be divided into two types: planning decisions and process decisions. When Ms. Lopez selected the topics to be included in tomorrow's lessons, previewed and selected the astronomy film strip for next week's science unit, decided to spend two extra days on the poetry portfolios, and assigned homework in one subject but not another, she was planning future instructional activities. In addition to planning decisions, the actual process of teaching or delivering instruction to a class also requires constant assessment and decision making. At two points during the day, Ms. Lopez altered her instruction in the middle of the lesson because her pupils were confused and unruly. Once she stopped her language lesson to review the prior day's lesson because pupil responses to her questions indicated that the class did not understand the content of yesterday's language lesson. Another time she switched her method of instruction from discussion to seatwork when the students became silly and unruly. A great deal of teacher assessment is for the purpose of planning and delivering instruction.

Establishing Classroom Equilibrium

A final, often overlooked purpose of assessment is to establish and maintain the social equilibrium of the classroom. Classrooms are complex social settings where people interact with one another in a multitude of ways. For classrooms to be positive social and learning environments, order, discipline, and cooperation must be present. Thus, helping pupils learn and maintaining order in the classroom are closely related; some amount of orderliness is needed if teaching is to be successful. When Ms. Lopez selected Martha instead of Matt to deliver a note to the school principal, and when she changed the class seating plan to move Bill and Leroy farther apart, she was making decisions to preserve classroom order and

An often overlooked purpose of assessment is to establish and maintain the classroom society.

stability. The fact that she allowed Randy to go alone to the school nurse indicated her trust in him. On the other hand, Rose's constant interruptions and speaking out necessitated sending a note to her parents, and Ralph's swearing and fighting led to his being removed from the classroom. Ms. Lopez's efforts to make Kim a part of the classroom society by calling on her even though her hand was not raised was another attempt to create and maintain a viable social and learning environment.

All of Ms. Lopez's decisions and all of the purposes of assessment just described can be grouped into three general types or areas of assessment (Airasian, 1989). Table 1.2 compares these three assessment types. Some classroom assessments help teachers carry out their official responsibilities as members of the school bureaucracy. Decisions such as grading, grouping, assessing progress, interpreting test results, conferencing with parents, identifying pupils for special needs placement, and making promotion recommendations are part of the official responsibilities a teacher assumes as an employee of a school system. These assessments can be termed **official assessments.** Other assessments are used to plan and deliver instruction and include decisions about what will be taught, how and when it will be taught, what materials will be used, how a lesson is progressing, and what changes in planned activities must be made because of pupils' reactions to instruction. These assessments can be termed **instructional assessments.** A third kind of assessment is used by

Teachers perform three types of assessment: sizing-up assessment, instructional assessment, and official (administrative) assessment.

Instructional assessments are used to help plan and deliver instruction.

TABLE 1.2   COMPARISON OF THREE TYPES OF CLASSROOM ASSESSMENTS

	Sizing Up	Instructional	Official
Purpose	Provide teacher with a quick perception and practical knowledge of pupils' characteristics	Plan instructional activities and monitor the progress of instruction	Carry out the bureaucratic aspects of teaching such as grading, grouping, and placing
Timing	During the first week or two of school	Daily throughout the school year	Periodically during the school year
Evidence-gathering method	Largely informal observation	Formal observation and pupil papers for planning; informal observation for monitoring	Formal tests, papers, reports, quizzes, and assignments
Type of evidence gathered	Cognitive, affective, and psychomotor	Largely cognitive and affective	Mainly cognitive
Record keeping	Information kept in teacher's mind; few written records	Written lesson plans; monitoring information not written down	Formal records kept in teacher's mark book or school files

teachers early in the school year to learn about their pupils' social, academic, and behavioral characteristics so as to enhance instruction, communication, and cooperation in the classroom. These assessments allow teachers to set up and maintain an effective classroom society and are called **sizing-up assessments.** Succeeding chapters will describe these three general types of assessment in greater detail. At this point it is only necessary to recognize that assessment serves many classroom purposes.

Teachers size up their students in the first weeks of school so that they can organize their classrooms into learning communities.

BEHAVIOR DOMAINS ASSESSED

In addition to having different purposes, classroom assessments also differ in the types of behavior they describe: cognitive, affective, or psychomotor.

Classroom assessments cover cognitive, affective, and psychomotor behaviors.

Cognitive Domain

The most commonly assessed school behaviors are in the **cognitive domain**. Cognitive behaviors include a range of intellectual activities such as memorizing, interpreting, applying, problem solving, reasoning, analyzing, and thinking critically. Virtually all the tests that pupils take in school are intended to measure one or more of these cognitive activities. Teachers' instruction is usually focused on helping pupils attain cognitive mastery of some content or subject area. A weekly spelling test, a unit test in history, a worksheet on proper use of *lie* and *lay,* an essay on supply and demand, and an oral recitation of a poem all require cognitive behaviors. The Scholastic Aptitude Test, the American College Testing Program Test, the written part of a state drivers' test, an ability test, and standardized achievement tests such as the Iowa Test of Basic Skills and the Stanford, Metropolitan, SRA, and California Achievement Tests also are designed to assess pupils' cognitive behaviors.

Cognitive assessments cover intellectual activities such as memorizing, interpreting, applying, problem solving, reasoning, analyzing, and thinking critically.

Ms. Lopez was relying primarily upon cognitive information about her pupils when she made the following decisions: assigned grades, moved Jennifer from the middle to the high reading group, planned instruction, suggested that Robert spend extra time working on his report, identified pupils for remedial work in basic skills, graded pupils' American government projects, and consulted last year's standardized test scores to find out whether she needed to review the rules of capitalization for the class. In each case, Ms. Lopez was assessing her pupils' thinking, reasoning, memory, or general intellectual behaviors.

The many behaviors in the cognitive domain have been organized into general categories. One organization is called the *Taxonomy of Educational Objectives: Cognitive Domain* (Bloom, Englehart, Furst, Hill, and Krathwohl, 1956), but it is most frequently referred to as Bloom's Taxonomy or the

Cognitive Taxonomy. Bloom's Taxonomy is widely accepted and used in describing different types of cognitive behavior.

A taxonomy is a system of classification. Bloom's cognitive taxonomy is organized into six levels, with each level representing a more complex type of cognitive thinking or behavior. Starting with the simplest and moving to the most complex, the six levels are: knowledge, comprehension, application, analysis, synthesis, and evaluation. The type of cognitive behavior exemplified by each level of the taxonomy is illustrated below.

1. *Knowledge:* Memorization behaviors such as memorizing formulas, poems, spelling words, state capitals

2. *Comprehension:* Understanding behaviors such as summarizing what one has read or explaining an idea in one's own words

3. *Application:* Behaviors such as using information to solve unfamiliar problems; for example, predicting the outcome of actions

4. *Analysis:* Behaviors such as breaking a large body of information into smaller parts; for example, analyzing the tone, style, form, and meaning of a poem

5. *Synthesis:* Behaviors such as combining smaller bits of information into a generalization or conclusion; for example, formulating a general principle based upon a series of laboratory observations

6. *Evaluation:* Behaviors such as judging the merit or worth of a person, object, or idea; for example, weighing the pros and cons of a course of action and deciding what to do

Quellmalz's (1985) taxonomy of cognitive behaviors is similar to Bloom's and includes five categories: recall, analysis, comparison, inference, and evaluation.

Although taxonomies differ in the particular levels or categories they include, their most important function is to remind teachers of the distinction between higher- and lower-level thinking behaviors. In general, any cognitive behavior that involves more than rote memorization or recall is considered to be a **higher-level cognitive behavior.** Thus, the knowledge level of Bloom's Taxonomy and the recall level of Quellmalz's represent **lower-level cognitive behaviors,** since their focus is on memorization and recall. All succeeding levels in these taxonomies represent higher-level behaviors which call for pupils to carry out thinking processes more complex than memorization. There is a growing emphasis in classroom instruction and assessment to focus on teaching pupils the higher-order thinking skills (HOTS), that go beyond rote memorization.

Lower-level cognitive behaviors involve rote memorization and recall; cognitive behaviors that involve more than rote memorization or recall are termed higher-level behaviors.

Affective Domain

A second domain of behavior is the **affective domain**. Affective behaviors involve feelings, attitudes, interests, preferences, values, and emotions.

Emotional stability, motivation, trustworthiness, self control, and personality are all examples of affective characteristics. Although affective behaviors are rarely assessed formally in schools and classrooms, teachers constantly assess affective behaviors informally. Teachers need to know who can be trusted to work unsupervised and who can't, who can maintain self-control when the teacher has to leave the classroom and who cannot, who needs to be encouraged to speak in class and who doesn't, who is interested in science but not in social studies, and who needs to be prodded to start classwork and who doesn't. Most classroom teachers can describe their pupils' affective characteristics, based on their informal observations and interactions with the pupils.

Affective assessments involve feelings, attitudes, interests, preferences, values, and emotions.

Ms. Lopez was relying mainly upon her assessment of pupils' affective behaviors when she selected Martha, not Matt, to deliver a note to the school principal and when she changed the class seating plan to separate Bill and Leroy, who were unable to control themselves when seated together. When she switched instruction from discussion to seatwork to avoid unruliness, decided to send a note home to Rose's parents about her interruptions in class, paired Kim with Mary in the hopes of overcoming Kim's shyness and reticence, and kept Ralph in from recess for swearing and fighting, she also was making decisions based upon the affective characteristics of her pupils.

Teachers rarely make formal affective assessments but are constantly making them informally.

In contrast to the cognitive domain, there is no single, widely accepted taxonomy of affective behaviors, although the taxonomy prepared by Krathwohl, Bloom, and Masia (1964) is the most commonly referred to and used. In general, affective taxonomies are all based upon the degree of a person's involvement in an activity or idea. The lower levels of affective taxonomies contain low-involvement behaviors such as simply paying attention, while the higher levels contain high-involvement behavior characterized by strong interest, commitment, and valuing.

Psychomotor Domain

A final domain of behavior is the **psychomotor domain**, which includes physical and manipulative behaviors. Playing a sport, setting up laboratory equipment, building a bookcase, acting in a school play, typing, holding a pencil, buttoning a jacket, brushing teeth, and playing a musical instrument are examples of activities that require psychomotor behaviors. Although psychomotor behaviors are present and important at all levels of schooling, they are especially stressed in the preschool and elementary grades where tasks like holding a pencil, opening a locker, and buttoning or zippering clothing are important to master. Similarly, with certain special needs pupils a major part of education involves so-called "self-help" skills such as getting dressed, attending to personal hygiene needs, and preparing food, all of which are psychomotor accomplishments.

Psychomotor assessments involve physical and manipulative behaviors.

Psychomotor assessments are particularly important with very young or some special needs students.

There are a number of taxonomies of the psychomotor behavior domain (Hannah and Michaels, 1977; Harrow, 1972). Like the affective domain, however, no single taxonomy has become widely accepted and used by the majority of teachers and schools.

Ms. Lopez was concerned with her pupils' psychomotor behavior when she moved Monroe to the front of the room so that he could see the blackboard better, sent Randy to the school nurse because he felt ill, and referred Aaron to the special education department because he continued to exhibit poor gross motor skills. In each case, Ms. Lopez's decision was based upon assessment evidence that pertained to some aspect of a pupil's physical or motor behavior.

METHODS OF COLLECTING ASSESSMENT INFORMATION

Teachers gather most of their assessment information using paper-and-pencil and observation techniques.

Teachers use two primary methods to gather assessment information: paper-and-pencil techniques and observational techniques. Each method is relied upon heavily by teachers to help them obtain the assessment information they need to make classroom decisions.

Paper-and-Pencil Techniques

Paper-and-pencil assessments involve pupils writing down their responses to questions or problems.

Paper-and-pencil techniques refer to assessment methods in which pupils write down their responses to questions or problems. When pupils take a multiple-choice test, complete a written homework assignment, turn in a written report, draw a picture, write an essay, or fill in a worksheet, they are providing paper-and-pencil evidence to the teacher. Paper-and-pencil assessment techniques are of two general forms: supply and selection. **Supply,** or production, **techniques** require the pupil to construct a response to a question. An essay question, for example, necessitates the pupil's construction of a response in order to answer the question. Similarly, a short-answer or "fill-in-the-blank" question requires that a pupil construct an answer. Book reports, journal entries, and class projects are all examples of supply-type, paper-and-pencil techniques.

There are two forms of paper-and-pencil assessment: supply and selection.

Other paper-and-pencil procedures require the pupil to select the correct answer from a list of presented options. Multiple-choice, true-false, and matching questions are called **selection techniques** because, as the name implies, the pupil responds to each question by selecting an answer from choices provided with the question. Notice that a selection-type question provides the maximum degree of control for the person who writes the question, since that person specifies both the question and the answer choices. In supply-type questions, the person who writes the question has control only over the question itself, and responsibility for constructing a response resides with the pupil.

Supply techniques require pupils to construct a response to a question or problem; selection techniques require students to select an answer from choices that are provided.

Observational Techniques

Observation is the second major approach classroom teachers use to collect assessment data. As the term suggests, observation involves watching or listening to pupils carry out some activity (observation of process) or judging a product a pupil has produced (observation of product). When pupils mispronounce words in oral reading, interact in groups, speak out in class, bully other pupils, lose their concentration, have puzzled looks on their faces, patiently wait their turn, raise their hands in class, dress shabbily, and fail to sit still for more than three minutes, teachers become aware of these behaviors through observation. When pupils submit a science fair project, produce a still-life drawing, set up laboratory equipment, or complete a project in shop class, the teacher observes and judges the product they have produced.

Observation techniques are applied to student activities and to student products.

Thus, Ms. Lopez observed that Monroe often squinted when she was writing on the blackboard and decided to move him to the front of the room so he could see the blackboard better. She noticed Randy with his head on his desk and a grimace on his face and sent him to the school nurse for examination. During the language lesson she saw blank looks on her pupils' faces and got no raised hands when she asked questions, so she stopped to review the lesson from the previous day. Ms. Lopez observed Ralph swearing at another teacher and fighting with a classmate, actions that earned him a trip to the principal's office. These examples show how observations produce information that leads to classroom decisions.

In most classrooms, the teacher's desk faces the pupils' desks; and during instruction, the teacher faces the pupils. The fact that teachers and their classes are located in a confined space, facing and interacting with one another from one to six hours per day, means that teachers can observe a great deal of their pupils' behavior, appearance, and reactions.

Some observations are formal and planned in advance, as when teachers assess pupils reading aloud in reading group or presenting an oral report to the class. In such situations, the teacher wants to observe a particular set of pupil behaviors. For example, in reading aloud the teacher might be watching and listening for clear pronunciation of words, changing voice tone to emphasize important points, periodically looking up from the book while reading, and so forth. Because such observations are planned, the teacher has time to prepare the pupils and identify in advance the particular behaviors that will be observed.

Some teacher observations are formal and planned in advance while others are informal and spontaneous.

Other teacher observations are unplanned and informal, as when the teacher sees Bill and Leroy talking while they should be working, notices the pained expression on a pupil's face when a classmate made fun of his clothes, or observes the pupils fidgeting and looking out the window during a science lesson. Such spontaneous observations, based on what is often called "kidwatching," reflect momentary unplanned happenings which the teacher observes, mentally records, and interprets. Both formal and informal teacher observations are important information-gathering techniques in classrooms.

Paper-and-pencil and observational techniques complement each other in the classroom. Imagine classroom decision making without being able to observe pupils' appearances, reactions, performance, and interactions. Now imagine what it would be like if no paper-and-pencil information could be obtained in classrooms. Both types of information are needed to carry out meaningful assessment in classrooms, so a teacher's mastery of both evidence-gathering approaches is important.

Supplementary assessment information can be obtained from previous teachers, school staff, and parents.

Although paper-and-pencil and observational techniques are the primary methods by which teachers gather information, helpful supplementary information can also be obtained from the pupils' prior teachers, school nurses, and parents. Teachers routinely consult previous teachers to corroborate or reinforce current observations. Parents frequently volunteer information and respond to teacher queries. While useful, each of these supplementary sources of information has its limitations, and should be treated with caution when making decisions.

STANDARDIZED AND UNSTANDARDIZED ASSESSMENTS

The information teachers collect and use in their classrooms comes from assessment procedures that are either standardized or unstandardized.

Standardized Assessments

Standardized assessments are intended to be administered, scored, and interpreted in the same way for all test takers.

Standardized assessments are intended to be administered, scored, and interpreted in the same way for all test takers, regardless of where or when they are assessed. Standardized assessments are meant to be given to pupils in many different classrooms, but always under identical conditions of administration, scoring, and interpretation. The main reason for standardizing assessment procedures is so that scores can be compared across pupils without the conditions of administration, scoring, and interpretation distorting the comparison.

The Scholastic Aptitude Test (SAT) and the American College Testing Program Test (ACT) are examples of standardized tests. So are national achievement tests like the Iowa Tests of Basic Skills and the Stanford, Metropolitan, California, and SRA Achievement Tests. Regardless of where a pupil is taking the test, that pupil will be administered the same test, under the same conditions, with the same directions, in the same amount of time as all other students who are taking the test at that time. Moreover, the results of the test will be scored and interpreted the same way for all test takers. When Ms. Lopez identified pupils below the cutoff score on the state-mandated basic skills test for remedial work and consulted the previous year's test scores to determine if the class needed a review of capitalization rules, she was examining information from standardized assessment instruments.

Unstandardized Assessments

Few teacher-made assessment instruments are standardized. Most are constructed for use in a single classroom with a single group of pupils. Most reflect the particular areas of instruction focused on in that particular classroom. The teacher has no intent or desire to administer the same assessment to pupils in other classes for comparative purposes and so does not need to standardize the conditions, administration, and scoring beyond his or her particular class.

Unstandardized (teacher-made) assessments are developed for a single classroom with a single group of students and are not used for comparison with other groups.

When Ms. Lopez assigned grades to her pupils based upon her science test and decided to construct her own test for the science unit, she was relying upon assessment information that was **unstandardized**. Many of Ms. Lopez's unplanned observations of her students' behavior also are classified as unstandardized assessments. These fleeting, infrequently occurring, unpredictable, seldom-repeated classroom observations represent a rich and important, though unstandardized, form of assessment data. Teachers use these observations to make decisions about individual pupils and the class as a group.

It is important to note that standardized assessments are not necessarily better than unstandardized ones. Standardization is important when one desires to make comparisons among pupils in many different classrooms and locations. If comparison beyond a single classroom is not desired, standardized assessments are not needed.

Standardization is important when pupils are compared across different locations and classrooms.

INDIVIDUAL AND GROUP ASSESSMENT

Assessments can be administered to one pupil at a time or to a group of pupils simultaneously. The former are called individually administered assessments, and the latter group administered assessments.

Individual Assessment

Individual assessment information is collected from one pupil at a time, either under formal conditions or from teacher observation and interaction. Standardized tests like the Stanford-Binet Intelligence Scale (Terman and Merrill, 1973) or the Wechsler Intelligence Scale for Children (WISC)

(Wechsler, 1974), two commonly used school ability tests, are given under controlled conditions to one pupil at a time. As with most individually administered assessments, they are given orally and require that the examiner pay constant attention to the pupil, since how the pupil interacts with and responds to the examiner provides information just as important as the score he or she attains.

One-on-one assessment provides opportunity for clinical observation and clarification.

One major advantage of individual assessments is that in a one-on-one situation there are many opportunities for clinical observation of the pupil. For example, the administrator can observe the pupil's attention span, listening ability, speech, frustration level, and problem-solving strategy, as well as the specific answers the pupil provides. The administrator also has the chance to follow up on a pupil's response in order to clarify or comprehend it more completely. Most standardized, individually administered assessment devices require that the administrator have a great deal of training and experience. Some individually administered instruments, including the Stanford-Binet and the WISC, can only be given by persons who have been trained and certified to give the test.

While a classroom teacher's informal observation and interaction with pupils is less structured than individually administered paper-and-pencil tests, it is clear that teachers do focus upon and assess their pupils as individuals. When Ms. Lopez moved Jennifer to the high reading group, she did so on the basis of assessment evidence she had gathered about Jennifer's reading performance. When Ms. Lopez selected Martha, not Matt, to deliver a note, she did so because her individual assessment of Martha's personal qualities indicated that she was a responsible pupil who could be relied upon to carry out a nonsupervised task. Sending Ralph to the principal was based upon informal, unplanned observations of Ralph's behavior. When Ms. Lopez sat down with Tim's parents at a parent-teacher conference, much of the information she conveyed was based upon her assessment of Tim as an individual. Assigning grades to pupils is also an individualized assessment procedure.

Group Assessment

Administering group assessments saves time but provides less insight and information about individual pupils.

Group assessments, whether standardized or not, are more efficient to administer than individually administered ones. In the same amount of time needed to gather information from one student, group administered procedures gather information from a whole class. However, the cost of this efficiency is the loss of rapport, insight, and knowledge about each pupil that individually administered assessments provide. Virtually all group administered assessments rely on paper-and-pencil tests, since these permit many pupils to work simultaneously on a task. When the task to be assessed involves oral reading, giving a speech, assembling equipment, or some other performance, group administered procedures are not useful.

Informal group assessment occurs often in the classroom, primarily through teacher observation. Thus, when Ms. Lopez watched the class become silly and unruly during the lesson, she was performing group assessment. Similarly, when her pupils had difficulty answering her questions during the language lesson, she stopped what she was doing to review the previous day's lesson. This is another example of informal, group-based assessment.

In summary, assessments vary according to their purpose, the type of behavior they are intended to assess, the method by which information is collected, the degree to which the procedure is standardized, and whether they focus on individuals or groups. We can use these characteristics to describe different kinds of assessments. For example, a test such as the SAT or the ACT can be described as a standardized, group administered, paper-and-pencil, cognitive assessment. An assessment intended to determine how well a student can shoot free throws, use a hand saw, or assemble laboratory apparatus can be described as a standardized, individually administered, psychomotor performance assessment. Most teacher-constructed classroom tests are unstandardized, group administered, paper-and-pencil, cognitive assessments. Finally, a teacher's judgment about a pupil's ability to get along with his or her classmates in social situations would likely be based upon unstandardized, individual, affective, performance assessments.

CHARACTERISTICS OF GOOD ASSESSMENT: VALIDITY AND RELIABILITY

Assessment is the process of gathering, interpreting, and synthesizing information to aid decision making in the classroom. Whether assessment information helps teachers to make *good* decisions depends on whether the assessment information itself is good. We begin our examination into the characteristics of good assessment information with the following situation.

Whether assessment information helps produce good decisions depends on whether the assessment information is good.

Mr. Ferris has just finished a three-week math unit on computing long-division problems with remainders. During the unit he taught his pupils the computational steps involved in doing long-division problems and the concept of a remainder. He has given and reviewed both homework problems and examples from the text and has administered a few quizzes. Now, at the end of the unit, Mr. Ferris wants to gather assessment information to find out whether his pupils have learned to do computational problems involving long-division with remainders. He wants to gather this information to help him make a decision about how well his pupils have learned from his instruction so that he can assign a grade to each pupil.

To gather the information needed, Mr. Ferris decided to give a test containing items similar in content, format, and difficulty to those he has been teaching. From the millions of possible long-division with remainder items, Mr. Ferris selected 10 that were representative of his teaching. Note that if he had picked 10 items that covered different content or were much harder, easier, or presented in a different format than what he had taught in class, the results of the test would *not* have provided good decision-making information. To assess how well his students have learned from his instruction, his test items must closely match his instruction in content, format, and difficulty.

Mr. Ferris recognized this potential pitfall and avoided it by selecting 10 items of similar content, difficulty, and format to the items taught and practiced in his classroom. He wrote the items, assembled them into a test, administered the test during one class period, and scored the tests on a scale of 0 to 100. Mr. Ferris then had the assessment information he needed to make a decision about each pupil's grade.

Jill and Joe each scored 100 on the test and received an A grade for the unit. Stuart scored 30 and received a D grade. The grades were based upon Mr. Ferris's evaluation of their performance on the 10-item test. If one were to ask Mr. Ferris to interpret what Jill's and Joe's A grades meant, he would likely say that "Jill and Joe can do long-division with remainder items very well." He would also likely say that Stuart's D is "indicative of the fact that he cannot do such items well."

In making these statements, Mr. Ferris illustrates the relationship between assessment data and resulting teacher decisions. Consider carefully how Mr. Ferris described the performance of Jill, Joe, and Stuart. He said Jill and Joe "can do long-division with remainder items very well." He did not say "Jill and Joe can do the 10 items I included on my test very well." He judged and described their performance in *general* terms rather than in terms of his specific 10-item test. Similarly, Stuart was judged in general rather than test-specific terms.

The logic that Mr. Ferris and all teachers use in making such judgments is that if a pupil can do well on what was actually assessed, the pupil is likely to do well on similar items and performances that were not assessed. If a pupil does poorly on the assessed items, it is likely that the pupil also would do poorly on similar, unasked items. Hence, when asked to describe the performance of Jill and Joe, he indicated that they do very well on long-division with remainder problems in general.

The essence of classroom assessment is to look at some of a pupil's behavior and to use that information to make a generalization or prediction about the pupil's behavior in similar situations or on similar tasks.

Mr. Ferris's 10-item test illustrates a characteristic that is common to virtually all classroom assessment, regardless of whether it is formal or informal, paper-and-pencil or observational, standardized or unstandardized, or cognitive, affective, or psychomotor. The essence of classroom assessment is to look at *some* of a pupil's behavior and to use that information to make a generalization or prediction about the pupil's behavior in similar, unobserved situations. Mr. Ferris used performance on 10 test items to make a generalization about his pupils' likely performance on the millions of similar items that could have been, but were not, included on his test.

This process is not confined only to assessments of pupils' learning. Teachers often form lasting impressions of their pupils' personalities or motivation from a few brief observations made in the first week of school. They observe a small sample of the pupils' behavior and on the basis of this sample make general judgments such as "he is unmotivated," "she is a troublemaker," and "they are socially immature." These are informal generalizations about pupils that teachers routinely make based on only a small sample of the pupils' school behavior.

What if the behavior sample the teacher collects is irrelevant or incomplete? What if the items on Mr. Ferris's test were not typical of his classroom instruction? What if the pupil had an "off day" or the teacher's impatience did not permit a pupil to show his or her "true" performance? If these things happen, then the decision made about the pupil is likely to be wrong and probably unfair.

Validity

The single most important characteristic of good assessment information is its ability to help the teacher to make a correct decision (Messick, 1909). This characteristic is called **validity**. Without validity, the assessment data will not lead to correct decisions. When a teacher asks, as all teachers should, "Am I collecting the right kind of evidence for the decision I want to make," she is asking about the validity of her assessments. For any decision, some forms of evidence are more valid than others. For example, it was more valid for Mr. Ferris to determine his pupils' achievement by giving a test that contained items similar to those he had been teaching than it would have been for him to ask pupils to write an essay on their feelings about math. Similarly, it is more valid to determine pupils' motivation or ability by observing their classroom work over a period of time than to base judgments on the performance of their older siblings or the section of the city they come from. These latter indicators are likely to be less valid for decision making than more direct classroom observation.

We shall have more to say about validity throughout this text. At this point it is sufficient to say three things about the validity of assessment information. First, validity is concerned with whether the information being gathered is really relevant to the decision that needs to be made. Second, validity is the most important property assessment information can possess because without it, the assessment information is of no use. Third, concerns about validity pertain to all classroom assessment, not just to those involving formal, paper-and-pencil techniques. Each of the many decisions Ms. Lopez made during the school day was based upon some type of assessment information. It is appropriate, therefore, to ask about the validity of the assessment information behind each of Ms.

Validity is concerned with whether the information being gathered is relevant to the decision that needs to be made.

Invalid assessment information is of no use.

Validity (relevance to decision making) is just as applicable to informal teacher observations as it is to formally gathered paper-and-pencil information.

> **TABLE 1.3   KEY ASPECTS OF ASSESSMENT VALIDITY**
>
> 1. Validity is concerned with the general question, "To what extent will this assessment information help me make an appropriate decision?"
> 2. Validity refers to the decisions that are made from assessment information, not the assessment approach itself. It is not appropriate to say "This assessment information is valid" unless you also say what decisions or groups it is valid for. Assessment information valid for one decision or group of pupils is not necessarily valid for other decisions or groups.
> 3. Validity is a matter of degree; it does not exist on an all-or-nothing basis. Think of assessment validity in terms of categories: highly valid, moderately valid, and invalid.

Lopez's many daily decisions. Table 1.3 identifies key concerns in the validity of assessments.

Reliability

Reliability refers to the stability or consistency of assessment information, i.e., whether it is typical of a pupil's behavior.

A second important characteristic of good assessment information is its consistency, or **reliability**. Would the assessment results for this person or class be similar if they were gathered at some other time? If you weighed yourself on a scale, got off it, then weighed yourself again on the same scale, you would expect the two weights to be almost identical. If they weren't, you wouldn't trust the information provided by the scale. Similarly, if assessment information does not produce stable, consistent information, a teacher should exercise caution in using the information to make a decision about a pupil or the class.

Think of a friend whom you consider to be unreliable. Is she sometimes punctual and sometimes late? When she tells you something or promises to do something, can you rely on what she says? A person who is unreliable is inconsistent. It is the same with assessment information; unreliable or inconsistent information does not help teachers make decisions that they can rely on.

Recall that Ms. Lopez observed Rose's class interruptions and Joshua's inattentive behaviors over a period of time before deciding to take action. She did this to be sure that she was observing stable, consistent behavior on the part of Rose and Joshua. Did they behave the same way at different times and under different circumstances? By observing them over a period of time, Ms. Lopez could have faith in the reliability of her observations. Similarly, Mr. Ferris included 10 long-division with remainder questions on his test, not just one, so that he would obtain reliable information about his pupils' achievement. He can have more confidence about pupils' learning by assessing them on 10 items than on only 1 item.

Since any single assessment provides only a limited sample of a pupil's behavior, no single assessment procedure or instrument can be expected to provide perfect, error-free information. All assessment information contains some error or inconsistency due to factors such as ambiguous test items, interruptions during testing, differences in pupils' attention spans, clarity of directions, pupils' luck in guessing, mistakes in scoring (especially essay and observational assessments), and obtaining too small a sample of behavior to permit the pupil to show consistent, stable performance. These and other factors (Frisbie, 1988; Gronlund and Linn, 1990) conspire to introduce some amount of inconsistency into all assessment information. Table 1.4 reviews key aspects of the reliability of assessment information.

One of the purposes of this text is to suggest methods that can reduce the amount of unreliability in classroom assessment information. If a teacher cannot rely upon the stability and consistency of the information gathered during the assessment process, the teacher must be careful not to base important decisions on that information. Thus, along with validity, which asks, "Am I gathering assessment information that is relevant to the decision I wish to make?" the classroom teacher must also be concerned with reliability, which asks, "How consistent and stable is the information I have obtained?" Once again, validity is concerned with whether or not the targeted characteristic is being assessed appropriately, while reliability is concerned with the consistency of the assessment information.

Consider the following assertion regarding the relationship between validity and reliability. "Valid assessment must be reliable, but reliable

All assessment information contains some error or inconsistency; thus validity and reliability are both a matter of degree and do not exist on an all-or-nothing basis.

TABLE 1.4   KEY ASPECTS OF ASSESSMENT RELIABILITY

1. Reliability refers to the stability or consistency of assessment information and is concerned with the question, "How consistent or typical of the pupils' behavior is the assessment information I have gathered?"

2. Reliability is not concerned with the appropriateness of the assessment information collected, only with its consistency, stability, or typicality. Appropriateness of assessment information is a validity concern.

3. Reliability is a matter of degree; it does not exist on an all-or-nothing basis. It is expressed in terms of degree: high, moderate, or low reliability. Some types of assessment information are more reliable than others.

4. Reliability is a necessary, but not sufficient, condition for validity. An assessment that provides inconsistent, atypical results cannot be relied upon to provide information useful for decision making.

assessment need not be valid." The first half of the statement is fairly straightforward. One cannot make valid decisions if the assessment data on which the decisions are based is not consistent. So, in order to have a valid assessment, one must have reliable information.

As to the second part of the statement, imagine the following scenario. Suppose you ask a pupil in your class how many brothers and sisters he has. He tells you, and you ask him again. You repeat the question several times and each time the pupil indicates the same number of brothers and sisters. You have assessed with consistency and stability; the assessment information you have gathered is reliable. Suppose you then use this reliable information to make a decision about what reading group to place the pupil in—the more brothers and sisters, the higher the placement. Since the number of brothers and sisters has little relevance to a pupil's reading performance, a decision based on this information, no matter how reliable it is, would not be valid. In short, assessments can be reliable, but not necessarily valid. Succeeding chapters will explore the relationship between validity and reliability in greater detail and offer suggestions for improving the validity and reliability of classroom assessment.

ETHICAL ISSUES AND RESPONSIBILITIES

Teachers' assessments have important long- and short-term consequences for students; thus teachers have an ethical responsibility to make decisions using as valid and reliable information as possible.

Thus far we have considered many technical aspects of classroom assessment. However, assessment is more than just a technical activity; it is a human activity that influences and affects many people, including pupils, parents, teachers, coaches, college admission counselors, and employers. Think about the different kinds and purposes of assessment described in this chapter, and then think about all the ways people can be affected by them. This will give you a sense of the human side of assessment.

Teaching is a profession that has both a knowledge base and a moral base (Airasian, 1993; Scriven, 1988). Like other professionals who have knowledge their clients do not have and whose actions and judgments affect their clients in many ways, classroom teachers are responsible for conducting themselves in an ethical manner. This responsibility is particularly important in education because, unlike most other professions, pupils have no choice about whether they will or will not attend school. Also, compared to their teachers, pupils tend to be less experienced and more impressionable. Among the ethical standards that cut across all dimensions of teaching are the need to treat each pupil as an individual, to avoid physical or psychological abuse of pupils, to have respect for diversity, to be intellectually honest with pupils, to avoid favoritism and harassment, to provide a balanced perspective on issues raised in instruction, and to provide the best instruction possible for all pupils (Fenstermacher, 1990; Clark, 1990; Strike and Soltis, 1991).

In addition, there are ethical considerations specifically applicable to assessment. Classroom teachers are in a position to obtain a great deal of information about their pupils' academic, personal, social, and family backgrounds. But beyond having access to such information, teachers use it to make decisions which can have important short- and long-term consequences for their pupils. For example, college entrance and future employment opportunities, not to mention pupil self-esteem, often hang in the balance of teachers' assessment decisions. Consequently, responsibilities accompany both the collection and use of assessment information. Teachers should always strive to obtain valid and reliable information before making important decisions that can influence pupils. Moreover, once

---

TABLE 1.5   ETHICAL STANDARDS FOR TEACHERS' RELATIONS WITH PUPILS

Commitment to the Student
The educator strives to help each student realize his or her potential as a worthy and effective member of society. The educator therefore works to stimulate the spirit of inquiry, the acquisition of knowledge and understanding, and the thoughtful formulation of worthy goals.

In fulfillment of the obligation to the student, the educator:

1. Shall not unreasonably restrain the student from independent action in the pursuit of learning.
2. Shall not unreasonably deny the student access to varying points of view.
3. Shall not deliberately suppress or distort subject matter relevant to the student's progress.
4. Shall make reasonable effort to protect the student from conditions harmful to learning or to health and safety.
5. Shall not intentionally expose the student to embarrassment or disparagement.
6. Shall not on the basis of race, color, creed, sex, national origin, marital status, political or religious beliefs, family, social or cultural background, or sexual orientation, unfairly:
   a. Exclude any student from participation in any program
   b. Deny benefits to any student
   c. Grant any advantage to any student
7. Shall not use professional relationships with students for private advantage.
8. Shall not disclose information about students obtained in the course of professional service, unless disclosure serves a compelling professional purpose or is required by law.

SOURCE: From *NEA Handbook,* 1992–1993, copyright 1992, National Education Association of the United States. Reprinted with permission.

assessment information is collected, teachers have a responsibility to protect its privacy, recognize its decision-making limitations, and never use it to demean or ridicule a pupil.

Table 1.5 presents a list of ethical standards for teachers developed by the National Education Association. Note the range of ethical concerns and responsibilities that accompany teaching.

This chapter has suggested that classrooms are complex environments calling for teacher decision making in many areas. Within such an environment, teachers are not expected to be correct in every decision they make. That would be an unrealistic standard to hold anyone to, especially in fluid, decision-rich classroom settings where uncertainty abounds. However, teachers should be expected and morally bound to provide defensible assessment evidence to support classroom decisions and actions. This is the least that can be expected in an environment where teacher actions have such vital consequences for pupils.

CHAPTER SUMMARY

- ♦ Every day in every classroom, teachers make decisions about their pupils, their instruction, and their classroom's climate. Teachers collect and interpret various sources of evidence to help them evaluate and choose suitable courses of action.

- ♦ Assessment is the general process of collecting, synthesizing, and interpreting information to aid teachers in their decision making. Many forms of assessment evidence are used by teachers, including tests, observations, interviews, comments from prior teachers, and school record folders.

- ♦ There are many purposes for classroom assessment: diagnosis of pupil problems, judging pupils' academic performances, providing feedback to pupils, placing pupils, planning and conducting instruction, and establishing the classroom society.

- ♦ All the purposes of assessment can be divided into three general categories: sizing-up assessment, which occurs early in the school year and is used by teachers to get to know their pupils; instructional assessment, which includes both planning and delivering instruction to pupils; and official assessments such as grades, which teachers are expected to provide as part of their role in the school bureaucracy.

- ♦ Assessments can gather evidence from three behavior domains: cognitive, affective, and psychomotor. Observation and paper-and-pencil testing are the two most common ways assessment evidence is collected.

- ♦ Standardized assessments are intended to be administered, scored, and interpreted in the same way no matter when or where they are given. These conditions are necessary because a primary purpose of standardized assessments is to compare the performance of pupils across different classrooms.

- ♦ The goodness of assessments is determined by their validity and reliability. Validity, the most important characteristic of assessments, is concerned with the collection of information that is most relevant for making the desired decision. Reliability is concerned with the consistency or typicality of the assessment information collected.

◆ Although assessment is thought of as a technical activity, there are ethical concerns associated with the assessment process. Since teachers' decisions can influence pupils' self-perception and life chances, when assessing, teachers must be aware of their many ethical responsibilities.

QUESTIONS FOR DISCUSSION

1. In what ways do the three general types of classroom assessment described in this chapter influence and interact with each other? For example, how do sizing-up assessments influence instructional assessments?

2. What are some ways a teacher might determine the validity of the assessments he or she makes?

3. What factors influence the relative emphasis teachers place on cognitive, affective, and psychomotor behaviors in the classroom?

4. Do teachers' ethical responsibilities to their pupils change as pupils get older? How? Are there some ethical responsibilities that remain constant across age levels?

REFLECTION EXERCISE

This chapter described assessment as an aid to teacher decision making. Imagine that you are a teacher and have to size up a new group of pupils at the start of the school year, plan instruction for them, teach them your planned lesson, and assess their learning at the end of instruction. Reflect on what you would have to do to carry out each of these activities. List all the decisions you would have to make in order to carry out each activity successfully.

◆ Decisions related to sizing up pupils
◆ Decisions related to planning instruction for pupils
◆ Decisions related to teaching the plan to pupils
◆ Decision related to assessing pupil learning

ACTIVITY

Interview a teacher about classroom decision making. Ask the teacher how he or she sizes up students at the start of the school year: What characteristics are considered, on what basis are decisions about pupils made, etc.? Ask the teacher what are the two or three most important decisions made when planning instruction and the three most important made while teaching a lesson. Finally, ask what decisions are important when assessing pupils' learning.

Compare what the teacher said to your own answers in the preceding Reflection Exercise. How are they the same? How are they different? Why are they different?

REVIEW QUESTIONS

1. What are the three main types of classroom assessment? How do they differ in purpose, timing, and the types of information most likely to be used in carrying them out?
2. Explain the difference between higher-level and lower-level behaviors; cognitive and affective behaviors; standardized and nonstandardized assessments; supply and selection test items; and validity and reliability.
3. How would you explain the concept of validity to a fellow teacher? What examples would you use to make your point?
4. Why are validity and reliability important concerns in classroom assessments? Why is validity more important?
5. What are three ethical responsibilities a teacher has to her or his pupils? Give an example of how each responsibility might occur in a classroom.

REFERENCES

Airasian, P. W. (1989). Classroom assessment and educational improvement. In L. W. Anderson (Ed.), *The effective teacher* (pp. 333–342). New York: Random House.

_____ (1993). Critical pedagogy and the realities of teaching. In H. J. Perkinson, *Teachers without goals, students without purposes* (pp. 81–93). New York: McGraw-Hill.

Bloom, B. S., Englehart, M. D., Furst, E. J., Hill, W. H., and Krathwohl, D. R. (1956). *Taxonomy of educational objectives. Handbook 1. Cognitive domain.* New York: McKay.

Brophy, J. F., and Good, T. L. (1974). *Teacher-student relationships.* New York: Holt, Rinehart & Winston.

Clark, C. M. (1990). The teacher and the taught: Moral transactions in the classroom. In J. Goodlad, R. Soder, and K. Sirotnik (Eds.), *The moral dimensions of teaching* (pp. 251–265). San Francisco: Jossey-Bass.

Fenstermacher, G. D. (1990). Some moral considerations on teaching as a profession. In J. Goodlad, R. Soder, and K. Sirotnik (Eds.), *The moral dimensions of teaching* (pp. 130–151). San Francisco: Jossey-Bass.

Frisbie, D. A. (1988). Reliability of scores from teacher-made tests. *Educational Measurement: Issues and Practice, 7* (1), 25–35.

Gronlund, N. E., and Linn, R. (1990). *Measurement and evaluation in teaching.* New York: Macmillan.

Hannah, L. S., and Michaels, J. U. (1977). *A comprehensive framework for instructional objectives: A guide to systematic planning and evaluation.* Reading, MA: Addison-Wesley.

Harrow, A. J. (1972). *A taxonomy of the psychomotor domain.* New York: McKay.

Jackson, P. W. (1990). *Life in classrooms.* New York: Teachers College Press.

Krathwohl, D. R., Bloom, B. S., and Masia, B. B. (1964). *Taxonomy of educational objectives. Handbook II: Affective domain.* New York: McKay.

Messick, S. (1989). Validity. In R. L. Linn (Ed.), *Educational measurement, third edition* (pp. 13–103). New York: American Council on Education/Macmillan.

Quellmalz, E. S. (1985). Developing reasoning skills. In J. R. Baron and R. Sternberg (Eds.), *Teaching thinking skills: Theory and practice* (pp. 86–105). New York: Freeman.

Rist, R. (1970). Student social class and teacher expectations: The self-fulfilling prophesy in ghetto education. *Harvard Educational Review, 40,* 411–451.

Scriven, M. (1988). Duty-based teacher evaluation. *Journal of Personnel Evaluation in Education, 1*(4), 319–334.

Strike, K., and Soltis, J. (1991). *The ethics of teaching.* New York: Teachers College Press.

Terman, L. M., and Merrill, M. A. (1973). *Stanford-Binet intelligence scale: Manual for the third revision (Form L-M).* Iowa City, IA: Riverside.

Wechsler, D. (1974). *Manual for the Wechsler Intelligence Scale for Children—revised.* New York: Psychological Corp.

CHAPTER 2

ASSESSMENT IN PLANNING AND DELIVERING INSTRUCTION

THE INSTRUCTIONAL PROCESS
Purpose of Planning Instruction

LEARNING ABOUT PUPILS: SIZING-UP ASSESSMENT
Pupil Characteristics
Sources of Information
Forming Descriptions of Pupils
Features of Sizing-up Assessments
Quality of Sizing-up Assessments
Improving Sizing-up Assessments

CHARACTERISTICS CONSIDERED IN PLANNING INSTRUCTION
Pupil Characteristics
Teacher Characteristics
Instructional Resources

LESSON PLANS

EDUCATIONAL OBJECTIVES
Stating Educational Objectives
Questions about Educational Objectives

TEXTBOOK OBJECTIVES AND LESSON PLANS

IMPROVING PLANNING ASSESSMENTS

ASSESSMENT DURING INSTRUCTION
Teachers' Tasks during Instruction
Teachers' Thinking during Instruction
Assessment Indicators

THE QUALITY OF INSTRUCTIONAL ASSESSMENTS
Problems That Affect Validity
Problems That Affect Reliability

IMPROVING ASSESSMENTS DURING INSTRUCTION

CHAPTER SUMMARY

Education is the process of helping to change students' knowledge and behavior in desired ways.

The purpose of schools is to educate pupils, but what does it mean "to educate"? Under what circumstances can a teacher claim credit for helping to educate a pupil? To **educate** means to help pupils change their behavior, to help them learn things they did not previously know. When teachers take pupils who could not read, identify parts of speech in a sentence, use the scientific method, or write a cohesive paragraph, and help them to do these things, then they have educated the pupils.

Most experts describe education as a process intended to help change the behavior of pupils in desired ways (Popham, 1988; Tyler, 1949). This view leads to a fundamental question all teachers have to ask themselves: "What do I want my pupils to know or be able to do following instruction that they did not know or do at the start of instruction?" Education is the process of fostering these desired changes.

It is important to point out, however, that this view of education is not the only possible one. Thoughtful critics (Eisner, 1979; Perkinson, 1993) suggest that education conceived solely as a process of planned pupil behavior change can lead to a preoccupation with narrow outcomes and afford the pupil virtually no role in the creation of his or her educational program. Critics recognize the importance of a teacher's ability to artistically build upon a pupil's prior experience and to seek multiple, not necessarily predefined, outcomes from instruction. Despite the merits of alternative views, for most people, education is conceived, practiced, and assessed as if its primary function were to help change the behavior of learners in desired ways.

A curriculum describes the knowledge, skills, performances, and attitudes pupils are expected to learn in school, while instruction refers to the methods of teaching the curriculum.

A **curriculum** describes the skills, performances, knowledge, and attitudes pupils are expected to learn in school. The curriculum contains statements of desired pupil learnings and descriptions of the methods and materials that will be used to help pupils attain them. The methods and processes actually used to change pupils' behavior are called **instruction.** Lectures, discussions, worksheets, cooperative projects, and homework are all instructional techniques; they are all methods used to help pupils learn.

Achievement refers to school-based learning, while ability and aptitude refer to broader learning acquired mostly through nonschool sources such as parents and peer groups.

Pupils undergo many changes during their school years and many sources besides school instruction contribute to these changes: maturation, peer groups, family, reading, and TV, among others. The term **achievement** is used to describe school-based learning, while terms like **ability** and **aptitude** are terms used to describe broader learning that stems from sources like parents, peer groups, and various nonschool activities. Since the focus of schooling is to help pupils attain particular behaviors, skills, and processes, almost all of the formal tests that pupils take in school are intended to assess their achievement. The Friday spelling test, the unit test on chemical equations, the math test on the Pythagorean Theorem, the delivery of an oral speech, the autobiographical book report, and midterm and final examinations all should seek to assess pupil achievement, that is, how well pupils have mastered the things that were taught during school instruction.

To summarize, we have seen that the purpose of schools is to educate and that the mainstream view of education is to help change the behavior of pupils in desired ways. The school curriculum identifies these planned behavior changes and the general guidelines for bringing them about. Instruction includes the methods that are used to enact the desired pupil changes. Pupil achievements are those changes that are brought about as a result of school-based instruction.

THE INSTRUCTIONAL PROCESS

The instructional process is comprised of three steps (Furst, 1958; Popham, 1988; Tyler, 1949). The first step involves planning instruction, which includes identifying desired pupil behavior changes, selecting materials, and organizing learning experiences into a coherent, reinforcing sequence. The second step involves delivering the planned instruction to pupils. The third step involves determining whether the desired pupil changes have occurred, that is, whether or not pupils have achieved the planned curriculum goals.

The instructional process involves three interdependent steps: planning, delivering, and assessing.

Figure 2.1 shows these three steps and the relationships among them. Notice that the diagram is presented as a triangle, rather than as a straight line. This indicates that the three steps are interrelated in a more complicated way than a simple one-two-three sequence. For example, in planning instruction (step 1), one has to consider the characteristics of pupils and the resources and materials available to help attain desired changes (step 2). Similarly, the information gained at the time of assessment (step 3) can be useful in assessing the appropriateness of the learning experiences provided pupils (step 2) and the suitability of intended pupil achievements (step 1). Thus, the three steps are interdependent pieces in the instructional process.

All three steps in the instructional process involve teacher decision making and assessment. Obviously step 3, assessing pupil learning, involves

All three steps in the instructional process involve assessment and teacher decision making.

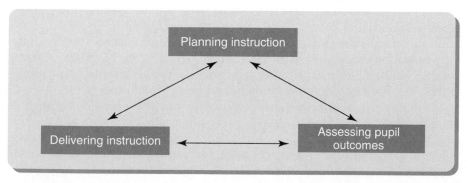

FIGURE 2.1
Steps in the Instructional Process

the collection and synthesis of information about how well pupils are learning or have learned. But the other two steps in the instructional process are also dependent upon a teacher's assessment activities. For example, a teacher's planning decisions will incorporate information about pupil readiness, appropriate methods, available instructional resources and materials, and school district policy. Similarly, during instruction the teacher is constantly "reading" the class to obtain information to help make decisions about lesson pace, reinforcement, interest, and comprehension. Thus, the entire instructional process, not just the formal assessment step, depends upon decisions that rely upon assessment evidence of various kinds.

Teachers define their own success and rewards in terms of their students' learning.

The processes of planning and providing instruction are important activities for classroom teachers. Not only do they occupy a substantial amount of their time, but teachers define their teaching rewards in terms of their pupils' instructional successes. Teachers are rewarded when they feel that their instruction has "reached" their pupils (Feiman-Nemser and Floden, 1986). Since the classroom is where pride in teaching is forged, it is not surprising to find that teachers guard their classroom instructional time jealously. They want few interruptions to distract them from their teaching responsibilities and rewards.

Purpose of Planning Instruction

Teachers plan in order to fit the curriculum to the unique characteristics of their particular class.

Teachers plan in order to modify the curriculum to fit the unique characteristics of their particular class. When teachers plan, they decide what pupils should learn from instruction, the topics to be covered, whether to add or delete textbook sections, the time to be allocated to instruction, the specific activities pupils will be exposed to, the sequence and pace in which these activities will be presented, the homework that will be assigned, and the techniques to be used to assess pupil learning. All of these planning activities and the assessments upon which they are based help teachers feel comfortable about instruction by providing them with a sense of command and personal ownership over the teaching act.

Most teachers feel that unit or chapter plans are their most important ones, followed by weekly and daily plans.

According to teachers, their most important plans are unit or chapter plans, followed by weekly and daily lesson plans (Clark and Peterson, 1986). Unit or chapter plans provide an overview of a sufficiently large block of material to permit development of weekly and daily plans. Planning only daily lessons would not provide the generalization and continuity needed for successful instruction. Thus, teachers tend to plan in manageable chunks like units or chapters and use the cohesiveness of these chunks to provide a structure for daily and weekly planning.

Planning is important because classrooms are complex environments (Airasian, 1989; Lieberman, 1982). The uncertainties, complexity, and strains of the classroom require some order and control, especially when teachers carry out formal instruction. In such an environment, some form of planning and organization is needed to impose structure.

Planning in advance of teaching helps teachers in three ways (Clark and Yinger, 1979b; Freiberg and Driscoll, 1992). First, it helps reduce teachers' uncertainty and anxiety about instruction by providing them with a sense of purpose and subject matter focus. Second, it affords teachers an opportunity to review and become familiar with the subject matter and activities before actually teaching. Third, it includes ways to get instruction started, activities to be pursued, and a framework to use during the actual delivery of instruction.

Planning helps teachers bring needed structure into the complex and fast-paced classroom environment.

LEARNING ABOUT PUPILS: SIZING-UP ASSESSMENT

A classroom is more than a group of pupils who happen to be in the same place at the same time. It is a complex environment, a society, in which people communicate with each other, pursue common goals, and follow rules of order. It is also an instructional setting in which teaching and learning are expected to take place. And finally, it is a place where one member, the teacher, has responsibility for other members, the pupils, thus making it a moral environment.

Further, although all classrooms are simultaneously social, academic, and moral environments, the specific features of particular classrooms differ greatly from one another. For example, the academic and socioeconomic backgrounds of pupils, as well as their mix of personalities, learning styles, and interests, differ from classroom to classroom. Even from one year to the next, a teacher cannot count on having similar groups of pupils. Because of these differences, planning and delivering instruction are context-bound activities; that is, the ways that teachers plan and teach are dependent upon the characteristics of their pupils and the nature of their resources (Shavelson and Stern, 1981; Freiberg and Driscoll, 1992). Try to imagine planning a lesson for a group of pupils you know nothing about or with no knowledge of what instructional resources are available. Such a lesson is almost inevitably doomed to failure.

In planning and delivering instruction, teachers have a great deal of control over certain classroom features, but very little control over others. In planning and delivering instruction, teachers must arrange the factors they do control (classroom rules and routines, methods of instruction, and grading practices) to compensate for the factors they do not.

Teaching is a context-bound activity involving many things teachers cannot control, such as the characteristics of their students and the resources available to them.

Table 2.1 contains descriptions of two teachers' classrooms. Imagine that these classrooms are at the same grade level and that the teachers are each planning a lesson on the same topic. Notice that all of the characteristics listed are ones the teachers normally would have little control over; they would be the "givens" that each teacher had to work with. Which characteristics are most important and how might they influence the way these two teachers planned instruction? Which would be most advanta-

TABLE 2.1　COMPARISON OF TWO CLASSROOM CONTEXTS

Classroom A	Classroom B
22 pupils	34 pupils
Range of pupil abilities	Mainly low-ability pupils
Strong pupil self-control	Poor pupil self-control
Good prerequisite skills	Range of prerequisite skills
Intense parental interest	Moderate parental interest
Ten-year-old textbooks	New textbooks
Mandated district curriculum	Teacher-selected instructional topics
Poor school library	Excellent school library
Small classroom size	Large classroom size
Individual pupil desks	Pupils sit at four-person tables
Little colleague support	Strong colleague support

geous to a teacher and which most disadvantageous? Would the teachers construct identical lessons? Answering these questions should give you some sense of how instructional planning is always dependent on classroom context.

Pupil Characteristics

In order to teach well, teachers must know and accommodate the needs and characteristics of their pupils. But how do teachers do this? What assessment information do they rely upon? What are some of the ways teachers commonly go about getting to know or "sizing-up" their pupils so that they can interact with them, plan for them, instruct them, and help them function as an organized classroom society? These are important questions to ask, not just in relation to planning and delivering instruction, but also in relation to the social interactions that characterize all classrooms.

The teacher's main task in the first few days of school is to get to know each pupil and the group as a whole and to organize them into a classroom society that is characterized by communication, order, and learning. Thus, an important and often overlooked type of assessment that all teachers must accomplish takes place at the start of the school year and lays the foundation for classroom activities and interactions for the rest of the school year. During these initial school days, the teacher must collect a broad range of information about pupils and use this information to form an initial set of perceptions and expectations about them. These perceptions and expectations will influence the way the teacher plans for, interacts with, and manages pupils and instruction.

At the beginning of each year teachers must get to know their pupils so that they can organize them into a classroom learning community.

While the information teachers seek about their pupils differs by grade level, all teachers need to size up their pupils to some extent. How do you think sizing-up assessment differs for elementary and high school teachers? Which pupil characteristics do you think both would be concerned with and which do you think would be specific to each level?

Sources of Information

The information teachers use to size up their pupils comes from a variety of sources: the school grapevine, comments of other teachers, school records, performance of siblings, classroom observations, pupil comments, and formal assessments. For example, sit and listen in the teachers' room. Hear Ms. Robinson or Mr. Rutherford complain about Jim or Jane's continual inattentiveness or defiant behavior in class. Listen to Mr. Hobbs describe Marion's cooperation and insight. Hear Ms. Jeffry complain about Mike's interfering and demanding parents. One does not have to know Jim, Jane, Marion, or Mike personally to begin forming impressions of them as persons and pupils. Many pupils' reputations precede them into the classroom and teachers who may never have set eyes upon them may already have heard a great deal about their strengths and weaknesses. Listen to several teachers who were asked what information they collected to help them "size up" their pupils at the start of the school year.

Teachers use a variety of information to size up their students including personal observations, school records, comments from other teachers, and formal assessments.

School records are kept in the office and are available on all pupils. I could look at these before the school year started to get information about my pupils' abilities, prior school performance, home situation, and learning problems.

Sometimes when I compare my class list with another teacher's, the other teacher may comment on a pupil, the sibling of the pupil, or the parents of the pupil. Susie's brother was a nice, quiet boy. Sam's sister was defiant and disruptive in class. Andy is the last of the eight Rooney children, thank goodness. Be careful, Mrs. Roberts is overly protective of Peter and very concerned about grades.

By the end of the first week of school I will know whether each child is going to work, care about school, get along with the other pupils, be responsible enough to relay messages for me, and their personality in class. I know these things by observing the children in class. Whether a student volunteers an answer or comments willingly or if he needs to be called on to give an answer tells me about the pupil's type of personality. I watch how they get along with each other. The look of interest on their faces tells me about how hard they will work.

During the first few days, teachers have their antennae up, constantly searching the environment for information about their students. Sometimes their search leads them to expected places: school record folders, prior teachers' perceptions, diagnostic or readiness tests, and the way pupils interact with them and their peers. The search also leads to some unexpected places that would, on the surface, seem to have little to do with the main task of the school: the way pupils dress, their posture and body language, pupil discussions in the hallways and cafeterias, and who they "hang around" with. By the end of the first or second week of school teachers have sized up their pupils and classes and can provide fairly detailed descriptions of pupil characteristics.

Teachers rely heavily on informal observations when initially sizing up their students.

Two characteristics of this early sizing-up information deserve attention. First, most of it comes from informal observations. Teachers do not rely heavily on tests or formal assessments to determine pupil characteristics. If they seek such information, and many do not, they often go to the school record folders where only past performance is recorded. Second, because this initial information is obtained largely by means of informal observations, teachers are exposed to only a small sample of each pupil's behavior. Since teachers can observe any given pupil only part of the time, it is inevitable that their informal observations will be incomplete and limited to what the pupils happened to be doing when the teacher glanced their way.

Forming Descriptions of Pupils

Teachers synthesize their sizing-up assessments into general descriptions.

> John (a first grader) is such a pretty boy with big old brown eyes, and he smiles all the time, even his eyes smile. He wants to please, is well behaved. Really joins in with any activity that is going on, and his work has been nice. I'm expecting him to be one of the better boys. (Willis, 1972)

> Joslyn (a fifth grader) walks into class each day with a worried and tired look on her face. Praising her work, or even the smallest positive action will crack a smile on her cheeks, though the impact is brief. She is inattentive, even during the exercises we do step by step as a class together. She is shy, but sometimes will ask for help, but before she gives herself a chance, she will put her head down on her desk and close her eyes. I don't know why she lacks motivation so severely. Possibly it's a chemical imbalance or maybe problems at home. She will probably be this way all year.

> David (an eighth grader) is a smooth talker, a Cassanova. He is a nice dresser, a nice kid with a head on his shoulders. Unfortunately David is very unmotivated, most likely because of his background. He's street smart, loves attention, and has a good sense of humor. He is able to "dish it out" but can also take it. David is loud in class but not to the point of disruption; he knows where to draw the limit. If only he had some determination, the kid could go a long way.

These are rich and detailed descriptions of pupils. Each includes many different pupil characteristics, relies heavily on informal information, and conveys a perception about many dimensions of pupil behavior and background. Many make a prediction about how the pupil will perform during the school year. That teachers size up pupils is not in itself remarkable; people in any social situation size each other up. What is important, however, is the speed at which teachers form impressions about almost all the pupils in the class.

Sizing-up assessments produce a set of perceptions and expectations that influence the manner in which the teacher plans for, instructs, and interacts with the pupils throughout the school year (Anderson and Evertson, 1978; Brophy and Good, 1974). This is, after all, the purpose of sizing-up assessment: to help the teacher get to know the pupils so he or she can organize them into a classroom society and know how to interact with, motivate, and teach them.

To get a sense of the use and importance of sizing-up assessment, imagine that it is the middle of January and you have been called in to substitute for the regular sixth-grade teacher at the Memorial Middle School. You have detailed plans for the subject matter to be covered during the day. Just after the beginning bell rings, a boy in the back of the room raises his hand and asks to go to his locker to get a book he has forgotten. Should you let him go? Can he be trusted to return after getting the book or will he wander the corridors for an hour? What is the classroom teacher's policy on forgotten books? A few minutes later two girls get up and start to leave the room. "We always go to the library to see Ms. Flanders for extra help at this time on Wednesday. We'll be back in about an hour." Do they? Will they? Shortly thereafter, a boy and a girl start arguing over the last copy of a reference book. The argument grows louder and begins to disturb the class. How should you react? What strategy will pacify this particular boy and girl? The classroom teacher knows the answers to all these questions because she or he is a founding member of the classroom society, the person who has sized up the pupils' characteristics and established the routines. You are an outsider, a stranger to this society and thus do not know its workings or personalities. Sizing-up assessments provide the teacher with the kinds of practical, nitty-gritty knowledge needed to make a classroom function (Feiman-Nemser and Floden, 1986; Bullough, Knowles, and Crow, 1992; Solas, 1992). Table 2.2 reviews the main characteristics of sizing-up assessment.

Sizing-up assessments provide teachers with the kinds of practical, nitty-gritty information needed in order to make a classroom function effectively.

Sizing-up assessments are simply a special case of our natural tendency to observe and assess people on the basis of what we see and hear about them in everyday interactions (Downey, 1977); they help bring order into social situations. They allow us to "know" or "label" others so that we no longer have to interact with them as if they were strangers. They provide a frame of reference within which social interaction and meaningful instruction can take place.

Features of Sizing-Up Assessments

Because sizing-up assessments are the basis for many important judgments throughout the school year, teachers have an ethical responsibility

TABLE 2.2   CHARACTERISTICS OF SIZING-UP ASSESSMENT

1. **It is done at the start of the school year.** Most teachers can describe the personal, social, and academic characteristics of each pupil and the class as a whole after the first two weeks of school.

2. **It is pupil-centered.** Pupils and their characteristics are the focus of assessment.

3. **Informal observation is used.** Much of the information about pupil behavior and performance is collected through spontaneous, informal observations.

4. **Observations are synthesized into perceptions.** Teachers put together their observations in idiosyncratic ways to form a generalized perception of pupils.

5. **Teacher impressions are rarely written down.** Unlike test scores or grades, which are written down in rank books or report cards, the perceptions formed from sizing-up assessments are unwritten and selectively communicated.

6. **Observations are broad and diverse.** Teachers attend to a broad range of cognitive, affective, and psychomotor characteristics when they size up their pupils.

7. **Early impressions tend to become permanent.** Teachers are very confident about the accuracy of the sizing-up assessments they do in the first days of school. Initial perceptions are very stable from the first week of school to the end of the school year.

Because initial sizing-up assessments have important consequences for pupils, teachers have an ethical responsibility to make them as valid and reliable as possible.

to make them as valid and reliable as possible. However, an assessment process that is based upon quickly obtained, often incomplete evidence has the potential to produce incorrect, invalid decisions about pupils. Consider some features of sizing-up assessments.

First, teachers' initial impressions of their pupils tend to remain stable over time. Once a teacher forms an impression of a pupil that impression is likely to stick, and teachers will act to maintain their pupil impressions and labels, even in the face of contradictory evidence (Airasian, Kellaghan, and Madaus, 1977; Airasian, Kellaghan, Madaus, and Pedulla, 1977; Brophy and Good, 1974; Peterson and Barger, 1984). In general, classroom teachers are fairly accurate in their beginning-of-the-year predictions of pupils' academic performance as measured by test scores (Evertson, Brophy, and Good, 1972; Jackson and Lahaderne, 1967; Kellaghan, Madaus, and Airasian, 1982). However, even the most accurate teacher is not correct about every pupil. Teachers' accuracy when assessing pupils' affective behaviors such as motivation, interest, self-concept, and social adjustment is less well examined, with the few studies to date producing mixed and inconclusive results (Hawkes, 1971; Jenkins, 1972). Overall, these studies indicate that teachers' affective perceptions are less accurate than their cognitive and academic perceptions.

Second, sizing-up assessments not only influence the way teachers perceive, treat, and make decisions about pupils during the school year, they often, usually unintentionally, are transmitted to pupils. Offhand comments tell individuals and the class a great deal about the teacher's perceptions: "Oh Robert, can't you even remember what we just talked about"; "All right Sarah, will you tell the rest of the class the answer it can't seem to understand"; "Didn't Ruby read that paragraph with a lot of expression." Sometimes perceptions are conveyed indirectly as when a teacher waits patiently for one pupil to think through a problem but allows another only a few seconds; expresses encouragement and assurance to one but says "at least try" to another; encourages one to "think" but another to "take a guess." Tone of voice, physical proximity, gestures, seating arrangements, and other signals all tell pupils how they are perceived in the classroom.

Teachers often communicate their sizing-up assessments to pupils in unintended ways, and students may live up or down to these teacher perceptions.

Teachers' perceptions and expectations may even create a **self-fulfilling prophesy,** in which a teacher's expectation for a pupil leads the teacher to interact with that pupil in a particular manner. The pupil, in turn, observes the way the teacher interacts with him and begins to behave in the way or function at the level the teacher expects, whether or not the original expectation was correct. Needless to say, it is the teacher's ethical responsibility to avoid this situation by making their sizing-up assessments as fair and accurate as possible for all pupils. This is especially so since the sizing-up process happens so quickly, is often done unconsciously, and leaves no permanent record outside the teacher's head.

To summarize, we have seen that sizing-up assessments are largely based upon information that is gathered in the first few days of school, that teachers form these assessments quickly, and that they remain fairly stable throughout the school year. Sizing-up assessments determine perceptions and expectations, which in turn influence teachers' interactions with pupils. Because sizing-up assessments can be so influential in setting expectations, influencing pupil-teacher interactions, and affecting pupils' performance and self-perception, it is important to examine more closely the dangers inherent in that process, and the strategies teachers can use to improve their initial pupil assessments.

Quality of Sizing-Up Assessments

As stated in Chapter 1, the two main criteria of good assessments are validity and reliability. Validity is concerned with the collection of *appropriate* evidence, that is, evidence that is related to the pupil characteristic under consideration: "Does the evidence I have gathered tell me about the characteristic I wish to judge?" Reliability pertains to collecting *enough* evidence to be certain that the pupil's *typical* performance is being observed: "Is the evidence gathered indicative of the pupil's typical or normal performance?" Validity and reliability work hand in hand to ensure that the perceptions formed from sizing-up assessment are appropriate and trustworthy, leading to good decisions about pupils.

Threats to Validity

Observer prejudgment can stem from prior knowledge, first impressions, or personal prejudices and often interferes with fair and valid assessments.

There are two main problems that occur during sizing-up assessment that diminish the validity of the information gathered: observer prejudgment and logical error. **Observer prejudgment** occurs when a teacher's prior knowledge, first impressions, or personal prejudices and beliefs interfere with the ability to make a fair and valid assessment of a pupil (Nisbett and Ross, 1980). All of us have personal prejudices or beliefs; we prefer some things to other things and some kinds of people to other kinds. We have beliefs, interests, ideas, and expectations that differentiate us from others. However, when these likes, dislikes, beliefs, and prejudices interfere with our ability to make fair pupil assessments, there is a real problem.

Prejudging students results from three main sources. The first is *prior information* that a teacher has obtained before meeting the pupil. Information passed through the school grapevine or the performance of prior siblings often influence and prejudice a teacher's perceptions, even before the pupil enters the teacher's classroom. The second is *initial impressions,* which tend to influence subsequent impressions. If the teacher judges a pupil on how she is dressed on the first day of school or how he behaved in study hall last year, the teacher may unconsciously let this impression dictate subsequent observations and interpretations.

Teachers should be careful not to interpret cultural differences as cultural deficits.

The third is teachers' *personal theories and beliefs* about particular kinds of pupils (Gordon, 1987), which can lead to stereotyped perceptions. When teachers think: "This pupil is from Oldtown, and kids from Oldtown are poor learners and discipline problems," "Girls do poorly in math," "Everyone knows that members of that group have no interest in school," or "He's just another dumb jock," they are expressing their personal theories or stereotypes of what certain people are like and how they behave. Being labeled with such stereotypes without a fair chance to show one's true characteristics can injure pupils and inhibit their learning. This is especially so with regard to teachers' gender, racial, cultural, handicapping, and social-class prejudices and stereotypes. Teachers often interpret what are really cultural *differences* as if they were cultural *deficits* when they judge pupils who are different from themselves. The dangers of prejudgment are real and consequential. Teachers must strive to judge each individual pupil on the basis of how he or she actually performs and behaves in class. Each pupil is an individual entitled to be judged on his or her own merits. This is a teacher's ethical responsibility.

Many teachers recognize that prejudgments and prejudices can invalidate the sizing-up assessments that they make, as the following statements indicate.

I don't like to hear anything about a student's behavior from past instructors. Every teacher is different, just like every student is different. A student may have a negative experience with one teacher, but a positive experience with another teacher. I prefer to make my own decision about every child.

I remember the time I stereotyped three of my female students as "valley girls"—not too bright and mainly superficial—on the first day of class. This assessment came about due to their physical appearances and their shallow contributions in discussion. Yet when it came time for formal assessment, these three individuals ranked the highest in the class.

Logical errors occur when teachers select the wrong indicators to assess pupil characteristics, thereby making their judgments invalid. It is tempting to read a great deal into a single pupil observation, especially at the start of the year when teachers want to quickly characterize each pupil in order to know and organize their classes. It would be convenient, for example, to read a whole series of inferences about motivation, attention span, interest in the subject, self-concept, and leadership from a pupil's eager hand raising. Maybe all the interpretations would prove to be correct, but it is dangerous not to recognize the difference between what is directly observed and interpretations made from the observation. When observation of one characteristic (hand raising) is used to make inferences about other unobserved characteristics (motivation, interest), the potential for logical errors and invalid assessment is great.

The labels teachers use to describe their pupils represent their interpretations of observed behaviors. Teachers do not directly observe characteristics such as "motivation," "intelligence," "leadership," "self-confidence," "aggressiveness," "anxiety," "shyness," "intolerance," and the like. Rather, teachers observe a pupil's behaving in some way, interpret what the behavior signifies, and give the behavior a name. In most cases, it is the name given to the behavior that attaches to the pupil, not the specific behavior that prompted the name. Teachers remember that a pupil is a bully, self-confident, aggressive, aloof, motivated, or shy, but they rarely remember the specific observations that led them to label the pupil in that way. Because teachers' labels "stick" to pupils, it is important to be sure that the observations that lead to a label are valid indicators of that label.

Teachers should be careful not to injure students by mislabeling them based on observations that don't justify the label.

Threats to Reliability

While validity is concerned with collecting information that is relevant to some targeted pupil characteristics, reliability is concerned with collecting enough information to be sure that the behaviors observed represent typical pupil behavior. Whether formal or informal, teachers' assessments are based upon samples of their pupils' behavior that are used to form perceptions about pupils' general behavior patterns. Thus, an important issue in teacher assessment is how well the observed samples represent pupils'

Teachers should be careful not to form a permanent perception of pupils based on one or two observations that may not be typical behavior.

general behavior patterns. Reliable information captures consistent and stable pupil characteristics.

The nature of sizing-up assessment creates special reliability problems. The spontaneity of informal classroom observations limits what teachers are able to see and what pupils are willing to show. Also, the time available to observe pupils often is brief, since attention must be distributed among many pupils and classroom activities, especially at the beginning of the school year. In short, the samples of behavior that are observed under these circumstances may not be reliable indicators of a pupil's typical behavior. Many teachers recognize this problem.

> First impressions are so important. They can either make or break a child. It all depends on how much opportunity a particular teacher gives to a student to prove himself or herself before passing a judgment.

> The first three days are very difficult. The students will not even present their "normal" classroom behaviors to you in the first three days. They are somewhat intimidated and uncomfortable; they don't know you. Even kids who are badly behaved in the first three days, they're just feeling you out, they're testing, trying to see how far they can get.

> Carol breaks up with her boyfriend a week before the beginning of school, leaving her depressed and unmotivated. Does her English teacher know the reason for Carol's behavior? Is her assessment of Carol after one day of school correct?

The implication of these comments is that teachers must be sure they observe sufficient samples of pupils' behavior before they solidify their initial perceptions and use them for decision making. There are times, such as at the start of the school year, when pupils' behavior may not be indicative of their typical behavior. What is typical behavior cannot be determined by observing a pupil just once, especially at a time when the pupil may feel uncomfortable in new surroundings. Table 2.3 summarizes the threats to validity and reliability that we have been discussing.

Improving Sizing-Up Assessments

Following are some strategies that teachers can use to improve their sizing-up assessments. While teachers will never be correct in all their sizing-up assessments, it is their ethical responsibility to do everything possible to minimize errors and to revise judgments when initial impressions prove to be wrong.

1. *Be aware of sizing-up assessment and of its effects on pupils.* Sizing-up assessment is such a natural behavior that teachers are often unaware that they are doing it and hence do not recognize the dangers of forming incorrect impressions of pupils. As a first step, it is important that teachers be aware of this type of assessment and be sensitive to the consequences

LEARNING ABOUT PUPILS: SIZING-UP ASSESSMENT

TABLE 2.3 THREATS TO THE VALIDITY AND RELIABILITY OF
SIZING-UP ASSESSMENTS

Validity Threats
I. Observer prejudgments: Prevents teachers from making an objective
    assessment of the pupils:
    A. Prior information from school grapevine, siblings, or nonclassroom
        experiences
    B. First impressions that influence subsequent impressions
    C. Personal theories or attitudes that influence subsequent observation
        (e.g., girls can't do math or athletes have no interest in serious
        academic pursuits)
II. Logical errors: Teachers judge pupils based on the wrong characteristics
    (e.g., observe attention and judge learning; observe clothes and judge
    ability)

Reliability Threats
Inadequate behavior sampling: Too few observations prevent learning about
pupils' typical behavior and characteristics:
I. Basing decisions about a pupil on a single piece of information
II. Observing behaviors in one setting (e.g., the playground) and assuming
    behavior will be the same in another setting (e.g., the classroom)

---

of making incorrect judgments based on incomplete or prejudiced observations.

2. *Treat initial impressions as hypotheses to be confirmed or corrected by subsequent observations and information.* First impressions should be considered tentative hypotheses that need to be confirmed or disproved by subsequent observation and information. Refrain from judging and labeling pupils on the basis of hearsay or a single brief observation. Gather your own evidence about pupils and confirm first impressions with subsequent observations and information. Do not be afraid to change an incorrect first impression.

Teachers should treat initial impressions as hypotheses to be confirmed or corrected by later information.

3. *Use direct indicators to gather information about pupil characteristics.* To size up pupils, teachers must interpret the pupil observations they have made. Some observations require less interpretation than others. For example, actually listening to a pupil read aloud provides more direct evidence about a pupil's oral reading than the reading grades a pupil got from his or her prior teacher. The closer the observed behavior is to the pupil trait a teacher wishes to describe, the more valid the resulting information.

In sizing-up assessments, teacher-pupil encounters are often brief, and the tendency is for the teacher to focus on superficial, indirect characteris-

When making assessments, teachers should try to use information that requires a minimum of interpretation.

tics such as dress, facial expression, helpfulness, or general appearance. Teachers then read into these superficial observations complex traits and personality factors like motivation, self-concept, trustworthiness, self-control, and interest (Nisbett and Ross, 1980). Such indirect generalizations are likely to be invalid. The moral then is to focus evidence gathering on direct behaviors and indicators.

Because informal observations involve spontaneous behavior that may not be repeated, teachers should supplement their informal observations with more structured activities.

4. ***Supplement informal observations with more formal, structured activities.*** There is no rule requiring that only informal observations be used to size up pupils. In fact, complete reliance on informal observations means that the teacher does not have control over many of the behaviors that occur, especially in the first few days of school. Good teachers recognize this limitation and supplement their informal sizing-up observations with more structured activities such as the following.

- Administer textbook review or diagnostic pretests to assess pupils' entering levels

- Require pupils to keep a journal during the first week of school or write an essay on "What I Did Last Summer" to assess pupils' experiences, writing skills, and thought processes

- Carry out group discussions or group projects to assess how pupils interact and work in groups

- Let pupils read aloud to determine reading facility

- Play classroom games based on spelling words, math facts, geographical knowledge, or current events to assess general knowledge, interest, and competitiveness

- Use games related to listening skills to assess pupils' abilities to follow directions and process auditory information

- Employ more formal observational instruments (Guerin and Maier, 1983; Cartwright and Cartwright, 1984)

Formal assessments that require students to perform the same behavior permit comparisons among pupils.

Some school systems collect samples of pupils' work into what are called "portfolios." These portfolios often accompany the pupils as they progress from grade to grade and provide a new teacher with concrete examples of a pupil's work. Note that having actual samples of a pupil's work from previous years is quite different from the hearsay evidence teachers accumulate through the school grapevine. Portfolios and other formal methods of assessing pupil performance will be described more fully in Chapter 4. Formal assessments provide information about pupil interests, styles, and academic performance that is not always obtainable from informal observations. Also, they require all pupils to perform the same behavior and thereby permit comparisons among pupils on desired characteristics.

5. *Observe long enough to be certain that you have perceived the pupil's typical behavior.* Reliable information is that which represents the *typical* behavior of a pupil. To obtain reliable data, the teacher must look for *patterns* of behavior, not single, one-time behaviors. The greater the consequences that an assessment is likely to have for pupils, the more the teacher should strive to gather reliable information. A good rule of thumb to follow is to "see it at least twice," to make sure the behavior being observed is typical.

Reliable assessments usually require multiple observations in order to identify typical student behavior.

6. *Determine whether different kinds of information confirm each other.* Teachers can have more confidence in their pupil perceptions if they are based upon two or more kinds of supporting evidence. For example, are test scores supported by classroom performance? Are classroom observations of a pupil's needs consistent with those identified by last year's teacher and the pupil's parents? Do classroom behavior patterns persist in the lunchroom and on the playground?

Whenever possible, teachers should base their decisions on different kinds of information that support each other.

These questions suggest the use of multiple sources of information to corroborate the teacher's perception of a pupil. However, note that it is better if the present teacher forms her own impressions of the pupil *before* obtaining corroborative information from other sources. By doing this, the teacher's perceptions will not be influenced or prejudiced by the perceptions of others. Table 2.4 summarizes the strategies for improving the validity and reliability of sizing-up assessments.

TABLE 2.4   STRATEGIES TO IMPROVE SIZING-UP ASSESSMENT

1. Recognize that sizing-up assessment is going on; without this awareness, it is difficult to improve the process.
2. Let first impressions represent initial hypotheses to be confirmed or rejected by additional information; see behaviors at least twice before judging pupils.
3. Observe important pupil behaviors directly rather than inferring them from ancillary behaviors and characteristics.
4. Supplement informal observation with more formal, structured assessments such as pretests and games.
5. Pick one pupil characteristic per day and structure classroom activities to permit pupils to demonstrate that characteristic.
6. Determine whether different types and sources of information (e.g., informal observation, formal observation, tests, or other teachers' comments) provide similar information about pupil characteristics.

CHARACTERISTICS CONSIDERED IN PLANNING INSTRUCTION

Having sized up pupils, the teacher is in a better position to plan meaningful and appropriate lessons. The following sections describe the many factors teachers must consider when planning instruction.

Pupil Characteristics

An initial and extremely important consideration is the present status and needs of the pupils. What are they developmentally ready to learn? What topics have they mastered thus far in the subject area? How complex are the instructional materials they can handle? How well do they work in groups? Are they independent learners? Do they have special needs? The answers to such questions provide needed perspective and valuable insights about what to teach and how to teach it.

Instructional planning tends to be more complex in elementary schools because students tend to be more differentiated and teachers must plan in many subject areas.

Instructional planning in elementary schools is generally more complex than in high schools because the pupil characteristics that need to be considered are more numerous and differentiated in the elementary grades. For example, in addition to content, the teacher must take into account pupil readiness, attention span, learning styles, and how a lesson will fit with other lessons of the day. Moreover, the elementary teacher often works with differentiated pupil groupings, whose instructional materials vary with the level of each group. Plans for each group differ according to the ability, needs, and socialization levels in the group. Further, most elementary school teachers are responsible for planning instruction in all subjects, not just one or two as is typical at the high school level.

It is obvious that pupil characteristics such as ability, readiness, independence, and self-control should be taken into account in planning instructional activities. Not to do so would be irrational. However, it is very important to recognize that much of this information comes to teachers from the initial, sizing-up assessments that were made early in the school year. Consequently, it is crucial that teachers strive to make their initial sizing-up assessments as valid and reliable as possible.

Teacher Characteristics

Most teachers do not take themselves into account when planning instruction. In particular, teachers' knowledge limitations, personalities, and physical limitations are important factors in planning and delivering instruction.

It is impossible for teachers to have equal knowledge of all the topics they teach, nor can they be expected to keep abreast of all advances in subject matter knowledge or pedagogy. Consequently, the topics teachers choose to cover, the accuracy and up-to-dateness of their topical coverage, and their teaching methods all are influenced by their knowledge limitations. Moreover, teachers' personalities often lead them to favor certain instructional techniques. While individual preferences are to be expected among teachers, it is important to understand that when carried to the extreme, such preferences can result in an overly narrow repertoire of teaching methods. Finally, since teaching can be a rigorous, fatiguing activity, teachers should consider their own physical limitations when planning instruction. This caution is especially appropriate for beginning teachers, whose enthusiasm and lack of experience often lead them to overestimate what they can physically accomplish in the classroom. A common complaint heard from college students experiencing their first full-time classroom practicum is how mentally and physically draining a day in the classroom can be.

Instructional Resources

The instructional resources available to a teacher influence not only the nature of instruction but also the learning outcomes that can be sought. The word "resources" is used here in its broadest sense to include available supplies, equipment, space, aids or volunteers, texts, and time. Each of these resources influences the nature of instruction and, therefore, the pupil achievements that can be pursued.

When planning instruction, teachers should take their own characteristics and knowledge into account along with their pupils' characteristics and the time and resources available.

A biology teacher may wish her class to learn about the internal organs of a frog by having each pupil perform a dissection. However, if the school has no biology laboratory and no dissecting equipment, the teacher must forgo this outcome. The availability of classroom aids or volunteers who read to pupils, work with small groups, or serve as "microscope moms" during a unit on the microscope, can free the classroom teacher to plan and pursue enrichment activities that might not have been possible otherwise. Resources of all kinds are important to consider when planning instruction.

Time is another important, though often overlooked, resource that greatly influences planning. Implicitly, each teacher's decisions about what content to stress or omit is based upon the instructional time available. While teachers make decisions about the allocation of instructional time on a daily basis, it is in the last few weeks of the school year that these decisions become most apparent: "We must cover subtraction of fractions before the end of the year, but we can omit rate, time, and distance word problems"; "If I don't finish parts of speech this year, next year's teacher will be upset, so I'll take some time from the poetry unit." Time is a limited resource and thus has important consequences for planning instruction.

A final resource that greatly influences what is planned, taught, and learned in classrooms is the textbook. More than any other resource, the textbook determines instructional plans. A number of studies have shown that a large part of student's learning time (up to 85 percent) and a large part of the teacher's instructional time, are focused on textbook use (Eisner, 1979; Farr and Tulley, 1985; Stodolsky, 1988; Woodward and Elliott, 1990).

The teacher's editions of most textbooks are supplemented with many resources to help teachers plan, deliver, and assess instruction. However, teachers should not abdicate their planning, teaching, and assessment decision-making responsibilities to the textbook. To do so reduces the classroom teacher from a professional decision maker to a mindless technician carrying out the instructional program of others. It is incumbent upon all teachers to assess the status and needs of *their* pupils, the curriculum requirements of *their* state or community, and the resources available to *their* classrooms when planning instruction for *their* pupils. In the end, decisions about what to emphasize rest with the individual classroom teacher, who knows her pupils better than anyone else and who is in the best position to plan and carry out instruction that is suited to their needs.

To slavishly follow the lessons in a textbook is to abdicate instructional decision making.

LESSON PLANS

Once information about pupil, teacher, and instructional resources are collected, the task of the teacher is to synthesize this information into a set of instructional plans. When planning, teachers try to visualize their teaching, mentally rehearsing the learning activities they contemplate using in the classroom. Doing this provides a sense of direction for pupils and teachers, as well as a mental dress rehearsal of the lesson.

There are many different instructional models that teachers can and do use when planning instruction (Eby, 1992). Models such as Madeline Hunter's Lesson Design Cycle Model (1982), the Instructional Event Model of Gagne, Briggs, and Wagner (1988), Cooperative Learning Models (Johnson and Johnson, 1984), and Management by Objectives (Brandt, 1992) or Outcomes-Based Education (*Educational Leadership,* 1994), among others, describe steps or activities that should take place when a lesson is taught. While the specific steps and activities contained in instructional models differ somewhat, they all include four basic elements: educational objectives, needed materials, teaching/learning strategies, and assessment procedures. Table 2.5 describes what is usually included in each element of a lesson plan.

Most experienced teachers' lesson plans are less detailed than the general planning model shown in Table 2.5. Typically, experienced teachers' plans consist mainly of a list of activities to be performed during instruction, a list that directs the teacher and/or pupil to "do this," "say this,"

> ### TABLE 2.5   COMPONENTS OF A LESSON PLAN
>
> **Educational objectives.** Description of the things pupils are to learn from instruction; what pupils should be able to do after instruction (e.g., the pupils can write a summary of a story; the pupils can differentiate adverbs from adjectives in a given passage)
>
> **Materials.** Description of the resources, materials, and apparatus needed to carry out the lesson (e.g., overhead projector, clay, map of United States, Bunsen burners; video on the Civil Rights Movement, etc.)
>
> **Teaching activities and strategies.** Description of the things that will take place during instruction; often includes factors such as determining pupil readiness, identifying how the lesson will start, reviewing prior lessons, providing advanced organizers, specific instructional techniques to be used (e.g., discussion, lecture, silent reading, demonstration, seatwork, game, cooperative activities, etc.), sequence of techniques, providing pupils practice, and ending the lesson
>
> **Assessment.** Description of how pupil learning from the lesson will be assessed (e.g., homework assignment, oral questions, writing an essay, etc.)

"write this," "ask this," or "show this" (Clark and Yinger, 1979a; Doyle, 1986). In planning, one advantage experienced teachers have over beginning teachers is a "mental notepad" (Leinhardt, 1989) filled with past experiences that can be called up from memory by a brief list of phrases and activities. When these teachers prepare lesson plans, they typically think mainly about what they and the students will be doing during instruction. While such plans describe both pupil and teacher activities, they rarely indicate what pupils are to learn from the activities (educational objectives) or how teachers will determine the success of their instruction (assessment). This is unfortunate, since it focuses planning on activities, which are merely the means to an end. To help keep the real purpose of instruction in mind, it is recommended that all teachers include in their lesson plans statements of **educational objectives,** which specify the pupil accomplishments that are to result from instruction.

EDUCATIONAL OBJECTIVES

Educational objectives are statements that describe what pupils are expected to learn from instruction. Other names for educational objectives are "instructional objectives," "learning objectives," "performance objectives," "behavioral objectives," "curriculum objectives," "achievement tar-

The use of educational objectives helps teachers focus not just on what students are to learn but on the instructional activities used to promote that learning.

gets" and "pupil outcomes." Whatever their label, educational objectives should be included in lesson plans and should represent important targets that pupils are ready to master. Objectives are logically and closely tied to assessment, since one critical role of assessment is to determine how well pupils have learned the intended educational objectives.

Stating Educational Objectives

There are many ways to state educational objectives, but not all of them convey clearly what pupils are to learn from instruction. Examine the sample objectives in Table 2.6 and consider their usefulness for guiding instruction. Remember, the intent of an educational objective is to clearly identify an expected pupil learning outcome in order to (1) communicate to others the purpose of instruction, (2) help teachers select appropriate instructional methods and materials, and (3) help plan assessments that tell whether or not pupils have learned what was taught.

Objectives 1, 2, and 3 all have the same deficiency. Each describes a body of content that will be covered in instruction, but each omits information about what the pupils will be expected to do with that content. Should they be expected to identify causes of the war, match generals to battles, cite strengths and weaknesses of the two sides? And what should a pupil be able to do after being taught about the laws of motion: write them from memory, use them to solve problems, or relate them to planetary motion? Without information about expected pupil behaviors related to a content topic, it is hard to select appropriate instruction materials, activities, and assessment techniques.

Objectives 4, 5, and 6—"analyze," "understand," and "appreciate"—provide no reference to content matter. When one sees these statements, the first question that occurs is, "Analyze, understand, and appreciate what?" Just as a content description by itself lacks clarity because it does not

---

TABLE 2.6   SAMPLE STATEMENTS OF EDUCATIONAL OBJECTIVES

1. The Civil War
2. American government
3. The laws of motion
4. Analyze
5. Understand
6. Appreciate
7. Worthy use of leisure time
8. Pursue lifelong learning
9. Become a good citizen

include a desired pupil behavior, so too does a behavior by itself lack clarity if there is no reference to a targeted body of content.

There is an additional problem in objectives 4, 5, and 6. Words like *analyze, understand,* and *appreciate* are themselves unspecific. They can be interpreted in many different ways and hence do not clearly convey what pupils are to learn. For example, one teacher might interpret "understanding" the basic features of a society as pupils' ability to explain the features in their own words, while another teacher might expect pupils to give real-life examples of the features studied. A third teacher might want pupils to distinguish between correct and incorrect applications of features. Although sharing a common educational objective, each teacher would be completely wrong about the others' intents, plans, instruction, and assessment. Such misunderstandings can be avoided by teachers describing educational objectives in terms of the actual behaviors pupils are expected to perform after instruction: *explain* features in their own words, *give real-life examples* of the features, or *distinguish correct from incorrect* applications of the features, rather than by describing them in nonspecific terms like *understand.*

Well-written educational objectives should clearly specify what students are to learn and how they are to demonstrate that learning.

In stating educational objectives, it is better to describe the specific behavior the pupil will perform than to use more general, ambiguous terms that are open to many different interpretations. Thus, it is better to say "*explains* the importance of conserving natural resources" than to say "realizes the importance of conserving natural resources"; better to say "*translates* Spanish sentences into English" than to say "understands Spanish sentences"; better to say "can *differentiate* subjects and predicates" than to say "knows about subjects and predicates"; better to say "*states* three differences between good and bad art" than to say "appreciates art." In each example, the first statement describes a pupil behavior that can be observed, instructed, and assessed, while the second uses less clear, unobservable, and ambiguous terms.

Objectives 7, 8, and 9 are too general and complicated to be achieved by pupils in a single subject area or grade level. These outcomes not only take years to develop, their generality provides the classroom teacher with little guidance regarding the activities and materials that could be used to attain them. Broad objectives such as these must be narrowed by the classroom teacher before they can be used to instruct and assess pupils. In summary, the basic requirements for well-stated educational objectives are that they: (1) describe a *pupil* behavior that should result from instruction; (2) state the behavior in *terms that can be observed* and assessed; and (3) *indicate the content* on which the behavior will be performed. A simple model for preparing educational objectives is: The pupils can *(observable behavior) (content).* Here are examples of appropriately stated educational objectives.

The pupils can list three causes of the Civil War.

The pupils can solve word problems requiring the sum of two numbers.

The pupils can write a correctly formatted and punctuated business letter.

The pupils can translate a French paragraph into English.

The pupils can count to 20 aloud.

The pupils can list three differences in the climates of Canada and Mexico.

The pupils can write balanced chemical equations.

The pupils can state the main idea of a short story.

The pupils can explain the water cycle in their own words.

Notice how these objectives focus the description of the changes instruction is to help bring about in pupils and thus help the teacher select suitable instructional activities, materials, and assessments.

Other information can be added to elaborate educational objectives (Slavin, 1994). For example, some teachers wish to include information in their objectives about the conditions of pupil performance and about how well the pupil must perform the objective in order to master it. Such extended educational objectives would be written as follows:

Extended objectives provide additional details about the conditions under which pupils must demonstrate their learning and the level of performance they must show.

♦ Given 10 word problems requiring the sum of two numbers, the pupils can solve at least 8 correctly.

♦ Given a diagram of the water cycle, the pupils can explain in their own words what the water cycle is with fewer than 2 errors.

♦ Given a French paragraph of less than 20 lines and a dictionary, the pupils can translate the paragraph into English in five minutes with fewer than 6 errors.

Extended objectives provide more details about the conditions under which the behavior must be performed and the level of performance the pupil must show. Extended objectives take more time to prepare than their simpler counterparts and are sometimes difficult to state prior to the start of instruction. Consequently, the simpler model suffices in most instructional situations.

Questions about Educational Objectives

Educational objectives are the starting point in the instructional process because they identify desired pupil outcomes.

Educational objectives are the starting point in the instructional process because they identify the desired outcomes or targets of instruction in terms of pupil behaviors. Because objectives are important, a few common issues and questions about educational objectives require attention.

1. *Is it necessary to write down one's educational objectives?* Beginning teachers and students in a teaching practicum usually are required to write lesson objectives. Even if you are an experienced teacher, writing down your objectives is useful in reminding you to focus on what pupils are expected to get out of instruction, not just on your teaching activities. Even if you have been teaching for many years, annual assessment of existing educational objectives is an important part of any teacher's classroom assessment responsibilities, because each year pupils and curriculum change.

2. *What are higher-level educational objectives?* Cognitive behaviors can be divided into lower-level ones such as memorizing and remembering, and higher-level ones requiring more complex thinking behaviors. Higher-level behaviors, or higher-order thinking skills (HOTS), include activities such as analyzing information, applying facts and rules to solve new problems, comparing and contrasting objects or ideas, and synthesizing disparate pieces of information into a single, organized idea. In the following examples, the lower-level objective calls only for memorization, while the higher-level objective calls for a more complex behavior.

Lower level: The pupil can write a definition of each vocabulary word.

Higher level: The pupil can write sentences using each vocabulary word correctly.

Lower level: The pupil can match quotes from a short story to the characters who said them.

Higher level: The pupil can contrast the motives of the protagonist and the antagonist in a short story.

Lower level: The pupil can write the formula for the Pythagorean Theorem.

Higher level: The pupil can use the Pythagorean Theorem to solve word problems involving the length of ladders needed by the fire department.

All teachers should be aware of the difference between lower- and higher-level thinking skills and should strive to incorporate some higher-level objectives in their plans and instruction.

3. *How many objectives should I state in a subject area?* The answer to this question depends in part upon the time frame being considered: the longer the period of instruction being considered, the more objectives one can expect pupils to attain. Thus, one might have sixty, seventy, or more objectives for an entire year of instruction in a subject area, but many fewer for a textbook chapter, and one or two for a single lesson. The number also depends upon the complexity of the objectives. Higher-level

Higher-level objectives include cognitive activities such as analysis, application, synthesis, and evaluation. These take longer to teach and evaluate than lower-level objectives involving rote memorization.

objectives usually take longer to teach, so fewer of them can be taught in a given instructional period; it takes longer to teach pupils to interpret graphs than to memorize a formula. Teachers who have hundreds of objectives for the year's instruction either are expecting too much of themselves and their pupils or are stating their objectives too narrowly. On the other hand, teachers who have only five or ten objectives for the school year are either underestimating their pupils or stating their objectives much too broadly.

4. *Are there any cautions I should keep in mind regarding educational objectives?* Educational objectives are stated before instruction actually begins and are meant to guide both instruction and assessment. However, they are not meant to be followed slavishly when circumstances suggest the need for instructional adjustments. Because objectives are written *before* instruction starts and because it is difficult to anticipate the flow of classroom activities during instruction, teachers must exercise discretion regarding how closely they will follow the objectives they stated prior to the start of actual instruction.

Because educational objectives are written before instruction begins, teachers must be ready to deviate from them when necessary.

TEXTBOOK OBJECTIVES AND LESSON PLANS

Modern textbooks and their accompanying teacher aids provide a great deal of information to help teachers plan, deliver, and assess their instruction. The richest, and most-used, source of information is the teacher's edition of the textbook. Figure 2.2 shows the range of resources found in most teacher's editions of textbooks. While not every textbook or instructional package provides every one of the resources listed in Figure 2.2, most provide a majority of them. More instructional aids are generally found in elementary school texts and instructional packages than in high school ones, but this disparity is diminishing.

Figure 2.3 presents two pages from a teacher's edition of a fifth-grade mathematics textbook. The top-middle section of the figure shows what the pupil's textbook looks like for a particular lesson. The rest of the figure shows the resources provided the teacher to carry out instruction. The lesson objective is in the upper-left corner. Beneath the objective are the lesson theme, new vocabulary, materials needed, an introduction to the lesson, and a series of specific teaching suggestions and activities. The middle-bottom section shows four different worksheets that come with the text that can be used for practice, reteaching, enrichment, or as an extra activity. The top-right of the figure lists assignments for three math groups of different levels, and a variety of lesson follow-ups. Each lesson of the text is presented in essentially the same format. The arrangement of the teacher's edition shown in Figure 2.3 is similar to ones used in most ele-

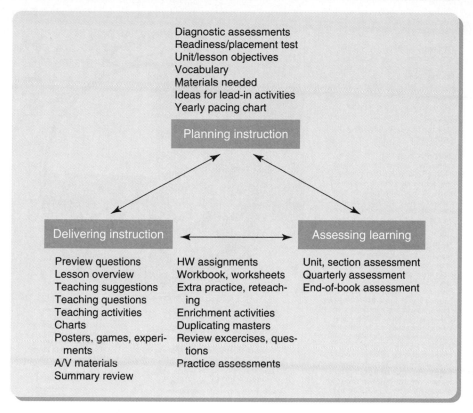

Diagnostic assessments
Readiness/placement test
Unit/lesson objectives
Vocabulary
Materials needed
Ideas for lead-in activities
Yearly pacing chart

Planning instruction

Delivering instruction

Preview questions	HW assignments
Lesson overview	Workbook, worksheets
Teaching suggestions	Extra practice, reteach-
Teaching questions	ing
Teaching activities	Enrichment activities
Charts	Duplicating masters
Posters, games, experi-	Review excercises, ques-
ments	tions
A/V materials	Practice assessments
Summary review	

Assessing learning

Unit, section assessment
Quarterly assessment
End-of-book assessment

FIGURE 2.2
*Instructional
Resources in
Teacher's Editions of
Textbooks*

mentary texts. High school teacher's editions have similar information but may be arranged so that objectives, teaching suggestions, homework, and the like are presented in the beginning. Examine some teacher's editions of textbooks to get a sense of how much support textbooks' authors provide for you in planning instruction in subjects you will teach. Especially read the introductory sections of the teacher's edition which describe all the resources and materials provided to help teachers plan, instruct, and assess.

The objectives, teaching strategies, worksheets, assessment tools, and other resources that accompany textbooks and instructional packages can be very useful to the classroom teacher, and a teacher might be tempted to rely exclusively upon them. To do so, however, is to abdicate one's instructional and assessment decision-making responsibilities. Textbook authors cannot possibly tailor objectives, plans, and assessments to every user. They cannot take the status, needs, and readiness of all classes into account, so they offer resources that they think *most* teachers would agree with and accept. It is the responsibility of all classroom teachers to assess a textbook's suitability for their own particular situation. Blindly following what is in the textbook undermines the classroom teacher's responsibility

*It is the teacher's
responsibility to adapt
textbook materials to the
specific needs of his or
her students.*

Objective 82 (Target Objective)
Write a fraction for part of a whole.

Lesson Theme
Home Activities: Cooking

Vocabulary
Denominator, fraction, numerator

Materials
• Fraction models (Punchouts)
• Index cards

Introduction
Discuss with students the meaning of the word *fraction.* Point out that fractions are numbers that name parts of a whole. Time and money are the main contexts in which students hear or read about fractions. Tell them that phrases like "half an hour" and "quarter of a dollar" involve fractions.

Using the Pages
Teach   In Example A, ask students what units they would use to give the times spent eating and for a day. They should realize that the units must be the same. For easier computation, encourage them to use whole hours when finding the fractions. If students change a week and a year to hours and find the fractions based on total times for a week or a year, they may wish to use a calculator for their computation. Have them compare the fractions for a day, a week, and a year. [They are the same.] For instance, if students use 24 hours to name one day, they must also use hours to name the portion of the day spent snacking. In Example B, help students to see that in order for the pieces to all be fourths, they must be of equal size. Ask if four copies of any of the pieces would equal the whole. [No, so the pieces are not fourths.] After working through Example C, point out that the line in a fraction stands for division. In Example D, point out that 4/4 = one whole and 0/4 = zero. Use division to verify this. [4 ÷ 4 = 1; 0 ÷ 4 = 0]

Try   *Using Concrete Materials*   When discussing Exercise b, have students use punchout fraction models to draw diagrams to illustrate 3/3, 4/4, 5/5, 6/6, and so on. Ask what conclusion they can draw from their diagrams. [All fractions with the same numerator and denominator are equal to 1.] In a discussion of Exercise c, students should conclude that any fraction with zero as the numerator and a nonzero denominator is equal to zero. Have them use their models to illustrate Exercises a and d.
(Continued on page 213.)

212   Chapter 8

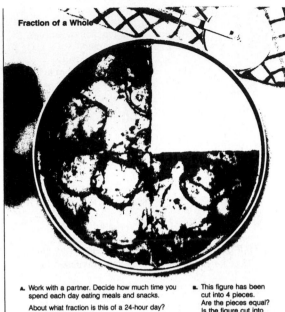

Fraction of a Whole

A. Work with a partner. Decide how much time you spend each day eating meals and snacks.

About what fraction is this of a 24-hour day? of a week? of a year?

How much time do you spend each day doing something other than eating meals and snacks?

About what fraction is this of a 24-hour day? of a week? of a year?

Explain your thinking to your partner.
See Using the Pages.

212

B. This figure has been cut into 4 pieces. Are the pieces equal? Is the figure cut into fourths? Discuss why or why not with your partner.
No; no

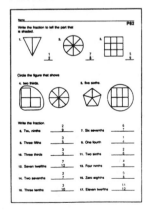

Practice 82

Reteaching 82

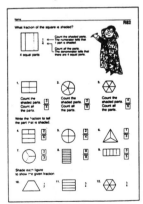

FIGURE 2.3
Example of Teacher's Edition Pages
SOURCE: *From Teacher's Edition, Invitation to Mathematics:* 5, 1988. Glenview, IL: Scott, Foresman and Company, pp. 212–213.

c. The pizza on page 212 was divided into 4 equal pieces. 3 of the 4 pieces are shown.

Number of pieces shown → **3** ← *Numerator*
Number of equal pieces → **4** ← *Denominator*
in whole pizza

three fourths

$\frac{3}{4}$ of the pizza is shown.

A number like $\frac{3}{4}$ is a *fraction*.

d. How many of the 4 pieces are gone? Write a fraction for the number of pieces that are gone. Write a word name for the fraction. 1; $\frac{1}{4}$; **one fourth**

All of the pizza had peppers. How many fourths of the pizza had peppers? Give a fraction and a whole number for this amount. 4; $\frac{4}{4}$; 1

None of the pizza had onions. How many fourths of the pizza had onions? Give a fraction and a whole number for this amount. 0; $\frac{0}{4}$; 0

Try Write the fraction.

a. Five sixths $\frac{5}{6}$ **b.** Three thirds $\frac{3}{3}$ **c.** Zero eighths $\frac{0}{8}$ **d.** One half $\frac{1}{2}$

Practice Write the fraction to tell the part that is shaded.

1. $\frac{2}{3}$ **2.** $\frac{3}{5}$ **3.** $\frac{5}{8}$ **4.** $\frac{6}{12}$

Tell whether the first or second figure shows

5. two sixths. **Second**   **6.** three fourths. **First**   **7.** seven tenths. **First**

Write the fraction.

8. One third $\frac{1}{3}$ **9.** Zero fifths $\frac{0}{5}$ **10.** Five ninths $\frac{5}{9}$ **11.** Four fifths $\frac{4}{5}$

12. Seven eighths $\frac{7}{8}$ **13.** Six sixths $\frac{6}{6}$ **14.** Three fourths $\frac{3}{4}$ **15.** Nine twelfths $\frac{9}{12}$

16. Write two tenths as a fraction and as a decimal. $\frac{2}{10}$; 0.2

17. Draw a picture to show two tenths. **Pictures may vary.**

Apply Tell what fraction of the

18. cup is filled.
$\frac{1}{3}$

19. cup is empty.
$\frac{3}{4}$

More Practice Set 82, page 396 **213**

Enrichment 82

Additional Resource 82

Math Poster GG *Fraction of a Whole* From left to right, the fraction of each window that is covered is 6/12, 10/12, 8/12, and 9/12. See *Answer Key* for teaching suggestions.

Assignment Guide

basic   1–19
average   1–19
enriched 1–19

More Practice Set 82, page 396

(Continued from page 212.)
Practice *Error Analysis* In each of Exercises 1–4, watch for students who do not count the total number of parts in the figure to find the denominator. Remind these students that the denominator represents the total number of equal parts of the whole and does not change when different numbers of parts are shaded. (See **Reteaching 82**.) In Exercise 16, students should discover that decimals may be written as fractions with denominators that are multiples of 10.

Apply *Problem Solving* In Problem 19, make sure students are aware that they are to give a fraction for the part of the cup that is *not* filled.

Follow-Up

Reteaching Use index cards to make fraction flashcards. Divide each card into a number of equal parts, shading some of the parts. Have students give the fraction that names the shaded region. You may want to write the correct fraction on the back of each card.

Enrichment *Draw a picture* Give students a worksheet with four squares of the same size. Ask them to show 1/4 of each square in different ways. For example:

Computer Assisted Instruction
Mathematics Courseware Series
• Fraction 1, Activity 1

Daily Maintenance
Choosing a computation method
Have students choose whether to do each exercise mentally or with paper and pencil. Then have pairs of students compare to see if they made the same choices.
1. 7 × 0.006   [0.042]
2. 0.125 × 0.4   [0.05]
3. 23 × 0.001   [0.023]
4. 0.06 × 0.003   [0.00018]
5. 3.06 × 0.4   [1.224]
6. 0.059 × 0.8   [0.0472]

FIGURE 2.3
(Cont.)

to determine outcomes, instructional activities, and assessment strategies that are well matched to the needs of pupils. Table 2.7 provides specific questions that should be asked when reviewing the appropriateness of textbook objectives and lesson plans.

Three general questions are important to ask. First, "Do the objectives and lesson plans contain a clear description of a behavior the pupils will learn and the instructional activities that foster learning?" Second, "Are the objectives and plans appropriate for the particular pupils in my class?" Every teacher must answer this question for himself or herself. Third, "Does the textbook include all the important outcomes that pupils should attain?" Relatively few textbook objectives call for higher-level thinking, so if teachers wish to include or emphasize higher-level objectives in their instruction, they may be forced to supplement textbook objectives with some of their own to broaden pupil learning. Table 2.8 lists the advantages and disadvantages of textbook objectives and lessons.

Since most textbooks focus on lower-level objectives, teachers may be forced to supply their own higher-level objectives.

TABLE 2.7   BASIC FACTORS TO CONSIDER WHEN EXAMINING TEXTBOOK OBJECTIVES AND LESSON PLANS

Textbook Objectives

1. **Clarity.** Are objectives clearly stated, especially the behavior pupils are to perform after instruction?
2. **Comprehensiveness.** Do the objectives include most learner outcomes for this topic?
3. **Level.** Do the objectives include both higher- and lower-level thinking behaviors?
4. **Prerequisites.** Do pupils have the prerequisite skills needed to master the objectives?
5. **Time.** Can pupils reasonably be expected to master the objectives in the time available for instruction?

Textbook Lesson Plans

1. **Pertinence.** Do plans help foster the stated objectives?
2. **Level.** Do plans include activities for fostering both higher- and lower-level objectives?
3. **Realism.** Are plans realistic given pupil ability, learning style, reading level, attention span, and so on?
4. **Resources.** Are the resources and materials needed to implement plans and activities available?
5. **Follow-up.** Are follow-up materials (e.g., worksheets, enrichment exercises, and reviews) related to the objectives and do they reinforce lesson plans and activities?

TABLE 2.8   ADVANTAGES AND DISADVANTAGES OF TEXTBOOK OBJECTIVES AND LESSON PLANS

Advantages	Disadvantages
Convenient, readily available objectives and plans	Designed for teachers and pupils in general, not necessarily for a given teacher or class
Can save valuable time in planning	
Provides an integrated set of objectives, plans, activities, and assessments	Heavy emphasis on lower-level objectives and activities
Contains many ancillary materials for planning, instructing, and assessing	Lesson activities tend to be didactic and teacher led
	If accepted uncritically, can lead to inappropriate instruction for pupils

---

IMPROVING PLANNING ASSESSMENTS

In planning instruction, there are a few common guidelines that teachers can follow to strengthen the effectiveness of their plans.

1. *Perform complete sizing-up assessments of pupils' needs and characteristics.* Since the purpose of instruction is to help pupils to do things they were unable to do before instruction, planning responsive lessons requires that the needs and characteristics of pupils be taken into consideration. Knowledge of pupils' readiness, abilities, and attention span stemming from sizing-up assessments help the classroom teacher to correctly plan such things as how long to make lessons, whether they should involve whole class or small group activities, and whether they should be teacher led or pupil directed. The more valid and reliable pupil and class sizing-up assessments are, the more appropriate lesson plans are likely to be.

In planning instruction, good sizing-up assessments provide an important starting point.

2. *Use sizing-up assessment information when planning.* A teacher may have done a very adequate job of sizing up pupils, but if the teacher does not use that information when planning lessons, the information is useless. Planning involves fitting instruction to pupil needs and characteristics, and it is the teacher's responsibility to use sizing-up assessment information when doing this.

3. *Do not rely entirely and uncritically on textbooks and their accompanying aids when planning.* As we have seen, teachers' guides can provide much of the information needed to plan instruction, but usually not all. It is important to match the suitability of textbook plans and assessments with pupil characteristics and needs. Teachers' guides should be assessed, adapted, and supplemented to provide the best possible instruction to each teacher's class.

Good lesson plans should include a mix of higher- and lower-level objectives.

4. *Include a combination of lower-level and higher-level objectives.* The instructional activities offered in most teachers' guides are heavily weighted towards whole-class practices such as recitation, teacher presentation, and seatwork. Such practices normally emphasize lower-level objectives. It is important, therefore, that lesson plans and activities (whether textbook or teacher made) include *both* lower- and higher-level objectives.

5. *Include a wide range of instructional activities and strategies.* Teachers who use the same strategy (e.g., lecture, seatwork, or boardwork) every day with little change or variety create two problems. First, they risk boring pupils and reducing their motivation to attend to the repetitive activity. Second, by limiting their teaching repertoire to a single or very few strategies, they may not be reaching pupils whose learning styles are best suited to some other method (e.g., small-group instruction or hands-on materials). It is important to include varied teaching strategies and activities in one's plans.

6. *Create a match between educational objectives and teaching strategies and activities.* Educational objectives describe the desired results of instruction. Teaching strategies and activities represent the means which are used to achieve those results. In order to reach the desired ends, the means must be relevant and appropriate. Without pupil ends clearly in mind, it is difficult to judge the adequacy of an instructional plan or the activities that are part of that plan. Table 2.9 shows the relationship between statements of means (teaching activities) and ends (objectives).

Effective instruction is keyed to lesson objectives.

7. *Recognize one's own knowledge and pedagogical limitations.* Teachers assess many things when planning instruction, but one often neglected

---

TABLE 2.9   EXAMPLES OF INSTRUCTIONAL MEANS AND ENDS

Means. Read a short story silently.
End. The pupils can summarize a short story in their own words.
Means. Show a film on the computer.
End. The pupils can differentiate between computer hardware and software.
Means. Do seatwork on pp. 47-8 in math book.
End. The pupils can calculate the areas of squares and triangles.
Means. Discuss the organization of the periodic table.
End. The pupils can place an element in its periodic group when given a description of the element's properties.

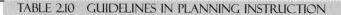

TABLE 2.10   GUIDELINES IN PLANNING INSTRUCTION

◆ Perform complete sizing-up assessments of pupils' needs and characteristics.
◆ Use sizing-up assessments when planning.
◆ Do not rely entirely and uncritically on textbooks and their accompanying aids when planning.
◆ Include a combination of lower- and higher-level objectives.
◆ Include a range of instructional activities and strategies.
◆ Create a match between educational objectives and teaching strategies and activities.
◆ Recognize one's own knowledge and pedagogical limitations and preferences.
◆ Include assessment strategies in instructional plans.

area is self-assessment. Content knowledge limitations may lead a teacher to omit an important topic, to teach it in a perfunctory, superficial manner, or to provide pupils with incorrect information. Likewise, preferences for one or two teaching methods may deprive pupils of exposure to other methods or activities that would enhance their learning. When a teacher's knowledge limitations and pedagogical preferences outweigh pupil considerations in determining what is or is not done in classrooms, serious questions can be raised about the adequacy of the teacher's instructional plans.

8. *Include assessment strategies in instructional plans.* The object of planning and conducting instruction is to help pupils learn new content and behaviors. Consequently, all lesson plans should include some formal measure or measures to determine whether pupils have learned the desired objectives and to identify areas of misunderstanding or confusion. While informal assessments about pupil enthusiasm and participation can be useful, they are not substitutes for more formal assessments such as follow-up seatwork, homework, quizzes, or oral questioning. Table 2.10 summarizes the guidelines to follow in planning lessons.

ASSESSMENT DURING INSTRUCTION

The assessment activities that teachers carry out when planning instruction are very different from those carried out when delivering it. The most obvious difference between the two is the time at which assessment occurs. Planning assessments take place before or after instruction, while instructional assessments take place during instruction. Planning assessments are focused upon identifying appropriate objectives, content topics, and activities to carry out, while assessments during instruction are focused upon making instantaneous decisions about what to do, say, or ask next to keep instruction flowing smoothly. During instruction, lesson plans are put to the ultimate test.

Instructional assessment refers to those assessments made during instruction that indicate how well the lesson is going.

Although discussed separately in this chapter, it is important to understand that planning and delivering instruction are integrally related. The instructional process constantly cycles from planning to delivering instruction to revised planning to delivering more instruction and so on. There is a logical, ongoing, and natural link between the two processes.

Teachers' Tasks during Instruction

Once instruction begins, teachers have a twofold task to accomplish (Doyle, 1986). First, they must deliver the instruction that they have planned. Second, they must constantly assess the progress and success of their instruction so that it can be modified if necessary. For many reasons, things do not always go as planned in classrooms. Interruptions, misjudgments about pupil readiness and attention, shifts in pupil interest, and various spontaneous events all operate to alter planned instruction. As a result, the teacher must constantly be aware, sensing the class' mood, and making decisions about what to do next. Thus, once the teacher initiates instruction, he or she engages in an ongoing process of assessing its progress and deciding about the pupils' reactions to it.

Doing this, of course, is a complicated task, since instruction, assessment and decision making are taking place almost simultaneously. For example, during class discussion,

> a teacher must listen to student answers, watch other students for signs of comprehension or confusion, formulate the next question, and scan the class for possible misbehavior. At the same time, the teacher must attend to the pace of the discussion, the sequence of selecting students to answer, the relevance and quality of the answers, and the logical development of the content. When the class is divided into small groups, the number of simultaneous events increases, and the teacher must monitor and regulate several different activities at once (Doyle, 1986, p. 384).

Certainly, many teacher decisions are required during instruction, and these decisions, in turn, are informed by assessments that teachers make as part of the instructional process.

Figure 2.4 illustrates this process. Once **teaching** begins, the teacher constantly **assesses** its progress by observing pupil reactions and asking

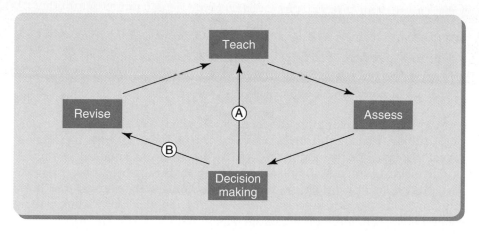

FIGURE 2.4
Steps in Instructional Assessment

them questions. On the basis of these reactions and responses, the teacher makes a **decision** about how instruction is going. If the teacher decides that the lesson is progressing satisfactorily, the teacher continues teaching as planned (path A). If the teacher senses a problem such as lack of pupil understanding or interest, the teacher **revises** the planned instructional activity to alleviate the problem and initiates another teaching activity or strategy (path B). This cycle is repeated many times in the course of a single lesson.

Teachers' Thinking during Instruction

A few research studies provide fairly consistent evidence about what teachers think about when they are teaching (cf. Clark and Peterson, 1986; Bullough, Knowles, and Crow, 1992). A large proportion of teachers' instructional thoughts concern the adequacy of their instruction and how it could be changed for a pupil or the class. Teachers described much of their thinking in such terms as these:

I was thinking about the fact that they needed another example of this concept.

I was trying to get him to see the relationship between the Treaty of Versailles and Hitler's rise to power without actually telling him.

I was thinking about a worksheet that would reinforce the idea.

I decided that it was necessary to review yesterday's lesson.

The largest proportion of teachers' thoughts were concerned with the *effect* of instruction on pupils, on how they were attending to and profiting from the instruction. This form of teacher thinking is closest to the concept of "reading one's audience" and was expressed through thoughts such as:

Teachers tend to look more for signs of student engagement than of student learning.

I realized that they didn't understand the concept at all.

I thought, at least everyone is concentrating on the topic.

I figured I'd better call on Larry, just to make sure he was with us.

I asked Mike to explain it because I thought he would know it and could explain it in a way many pupils could understand.

Note that when planning, the focus is upon pupil characteristics, readiness, subject matter objectives, and learning activities. Once instruction actually begins, the focus shifts to more action-oriented concerns, with the principal focus on how pupils are reacting to the instructional process. This shift is logical, of course, the result of being caught up in the "here and now" of a complex process. During instruction, teachers collect assessment data to help monitor factors such as

- Interest level of individual pupils and the class as a whole
- Apparent or potential behavior problems
- Appropriateness of the instructional technique or activity being used
- Most appropriate pupil to call on next
- Adequacy of a pupil's answer
- Pace of instruction
- Usefulness and consequences of pupils' questions
- Smoothness of transitions from one concept to another and from one activity to another
- Usefulness of examples used to explain concepts
- Degree of comprehension on the part of individual pupils and the class as a whole
- Desirability of starting or ending a particular activity

Information about these factors leads to decisions about instructional activities. For example, depending upon the appropriateness of the answer one pupil gives, the teacher may try to (1) draw out a better answer from the pupil, (2) seek another pupil to provide a more complete answer, or (3) ask the next logical question in the content sequence. In short, the need to respond to a variety of immediate classroom needs allows teachers little time to reflect on what they are doing or the motives for their actions. Nonetheless, when asked (Lortie, 1975), teachers said that they have a good sense of their instructional success, which implies that they do assess many environmental cues.

Assessment Indicators

Given the pace and complexity of instructional activities and the need to keep instruction flowing smoothly, it is no surprise that teachers rely much more heavily upon informal than formal assessment evidence to monitor instruction. Teachers usually rely upon behavioral cues like student attention or facial expressions rather than more formal paper-and-pencil assessments because the latter usually break the flow of the lesson and pupil involvement. To determine what types of indicators teachers use to monitor and judge the success of their instruction, we asked teachers how they knew when their instruction was successful.

> It is easy to tell when things are not running as planned. Children get impatient, facial expressions become contorted, their body language, voice level, and eyes tell the story of their reaction to instruction.

> If my class is daydreaming, looking blankly out the window and unresponsive that tells me something. At times like these I have to decide what to do, since I don't want the pupils to think that by acting disinterested they always can make me change my plans.

> Some examples of a good lesson are when the pupils are eager to be called on, raise their hands, give enthusiastic answers, look straight at me, scream out answers, show excitement in their eyes. During a bad lesson, the kids have their heads on the desk, look around the room, play with little objects at their desks, talk to their neighbor, or go to the bathroom in droves.

To summarize, the direction, flow, and pace of instruction will be dictated by the "chemistry" of the classroom at any given time. The assessment task of the teacher during instruction is to monitor the progress and success of the lesson. In most classrooms, this monitoring boils down to assessing the appropriateness of the instructional procedures and the pupils' reaction to them. Decisions that teachers make during the instructional process are prompted by (1) unusual pupil behavior that requires a response or action on the teacher's part and (2) typical issues that arise during instruction, such as responding to a pupil's question, deciding who to call on next, and deciding whether to move on to the next topic. The assessment information that teachers gather when they monitor their instruction comes mostly from informal observations of the pupils. These cues plus the teacher's knowledge of the class support the quick decisions that teachers make during classroom instruction.

The assessment information that teachers gather during instruction comes mostly from informal observation of their pupils.

THE QUALITY OF INSTRUCTIONAL ASSESSMENTS

Because there is little time for a teacher to reflect on what is observed or to collect additional information during instruction, teachers must make decisions and act on the basis of incomplete and uncertain evidence. Even so, good teachers are quite successful in overcoming these difficulties and carry out informative instructional assessment. In spite of the success of some teachers, however, it would be naive and inappropriate to overlook validity and reliability problems associated with instructional assessment.

Problems That Affect Validity

Validity relates to collecting evidence that will help the teacher correctly interpret observed pupil behavior and make decisions about the attention, comprehension, and learning of the pupils as well as the pace and suitability of the instructional activities. We have seen that teachers assess these areas mainly from the physical and verbal reactions of their pupils. The validity question in this process is, "Do pupils' physical and verbal reactions provide the information teachers need to make appropriate decisions about the success of instruction?" Two potential problems threaten the validity of such assessment evidence: (1) the lack of objectivity by teachers when they observe and judge the instructional process and (2) the incompleteness of the evidence used to make decisions about instruction and pupil learning.

Objectivity of the Teacher/Observer

Because teachers want to feel good about their instruction, there is the danger that they will look only for positive student reactions.

Being participants in the instructional process makes it difficult for teachers to be dispassionate, detached observers who can make unbiased judgments about their own instruction. Because teachers have a clear stake in the success of instruction and derive their primary rewards from it, they have a strong personal and professional investment in the instructional process. Every time a teacher makes a favorable judgment about instruction or pupil learning, the teacher is also rewarding himself or herself. Because teachers rely primarily upon their own observations to assess their instruction, one can ask whether teachers see only what they want to see, that is, only those things that will give them reinforcement. If so, the evidence they use to assess their instruction may be invalid.

Teachers sometimes ask easy, low-level questions in order to get correct answers that make them feel good about their instruction.

Evidence of teachers' invalid assessment of their instruction is not hard to find. For example, the types of questions teachers ask can influence their sense of effectiveness. Simple, factual questions are likely to produce more correct pupil responses than open-ended, complex questions. Concentration on lower-level, rote skills and information, rather than on higher-level skills and processes, typically ensures more pupil participation and mastery. A statement such as "This topic is too hard for my pupils, so I'll skip over it" may be a realistic appraisal of pupil readiness or it may simply be a way for teachers to avoid instructional disappointments. In short, the desire to achieve teaching satisfaction may bias the teacher's observations and produce invalid conclusions about the success of instruction, with harmful consequences for pupils.

Incompleteness of Instructional Indicators

The primary indicators that teachers use to monitor instruction are those that are most readily available, most quickly surveyed, and least intrusive: pupil reactions such as facial expressions, posture, participation, questions, and attending behavior. Using such indicators, teachers "read" the class to judge the success of their instruction. But the real criterion of teachers' instructional success is *pupil achievement*. Although the *process* of instruction (its flow, pace, and student reactions) is important and should be assessed, it does not provide any direct measures of learning itself. It deals only with intermediate events that lead to another end, pupil learning.

Being attentive and involved in instruction does not necessarily mean that learning is taking place. Thus, valid assessment of instruction should include appropriate information about *both* pupil involvement and pupil learning. If it does not, if it focuses only on the intermediate activities occurring during instruction, judgments about the ultimate goal, how well pupils are learning, may be invalid.

Instructional assessment should focus on student learning as well as student involvement.

Problems That Affect Reliability

Reliability is concerned with the stability or consistency of the assessment data that are collected. If the message a teacher gets from her observations changes each time new evidence is gathered, then the teacher cannot rely upon that evidence to help in decision making. Since teachers obtain most of their information about the success of instruction by observing their pupils, the broader the group of pupils observed, the more reliable the information will be.

Often, because of seating arrangements or an unconscious preference for certain pupils (Adams and Biddle, 1970; Rist, 1970), teachers tend to use an overly narrow sample of pupils when assessing the success of instruction. This, of course, reduces the reliability of their assessment. It must be understood, however, that problems of narrow sampling during instruction result as much from the rapidity of classroom events as from the teacher's inattention to particular class members. Table 2.11 summarizes validity and reliability problems in instructional assessment.

Instructional assessment that involves feedback from a broad range of students is more reliable than assessments based on the reactions of one or two students.

TABLE 2.11 VALIDITY AND RELIABILITY PROBLEMS IN INSTRUCTIONAL ASSESSMENT

Validity Problems
1. Lack of objectivity by classroom teacher-observer
2. Concentrating instruction on objectives and assessments that will provide the teacher maximum reinforcement but which narrow instruction for pupils
3. Focusing on instructional process indicators (e.g., facial expressions, posture, or participation) without also considering instructional outcome indicators (e.g., pupil learning)

Reliability Problems
1. Fast pace of classroom activities and decision making inhibit the opportunity to collect corroborative evidence
2. Focusing on a limited number of pupils to obtain information about the process of instruction and pupil learning

IMPROVING ASSESSMENTS DURING INSTRUCTION

In basketball we talk often about a player who has a shooting "touch." Beyond the mechanics of knowing how to shoot a basketball, the player has an intangible ability to put the ball into the basket with unusual success. Likewise, we have discussed an actor's ability to "read" the audience and react to it. This activity also goes beyond the technical aspects of acting; it involves a special sensitivity to the audience. Just as the basketball player has "touch" and the actor can "read" an audience, so too does successful instructional assessment depend upon a teacher's "feel" for the instructional process. This "feel" is dependent in large measure upon the teacher's sizing up and practical knowledge of the pupils' characteristics and typical behavior.

Good teachers can sense the success or failure of their instruction just as a skillful actor can sense the reaction of an audience.

Assessments made during instruction depend in some measure on an intangible, unarticulated process. To try to describe the instructional assessment process by spelling out a detailed list of rules and procedures would be to corrupt the natural flow of classroom events and likely destroy the process altogether. Teachers will always have to rely in part upon their "feel" for the classroom situation when gathering assessment information and making decisions during instruction. This fact, however, does not mean that the process cannot be made more valid and reliable. Keeping the following recommendations in mind during instruction should improve the validity and reliability of the assessment process.

1. *Include a broad sample of pupils when assessing instruction.* As stated earlier, teachers evaluate themselves largely in terms of pupil involvement and attention during instruction. Consequently, they may observe or call only on those higher-achieving pupils whose behaviors or answers are likely to reinforce their perception of instructional success. Likewise they may be tempted to focus on lower-level instructional activities that are more easily attained by their pupils. To avoid these pitfalls, an effort must be made to sample a wide range of pupils in the class. Unless the teacher attends to a wide range of pupils, evidence about the progress and success of instruction may be invalid and unreliable.

Teachers should supplement their informal assessments of instruction with formal feedback such as homework, worksheets, and lesson reviews.

2. *Supplement informal assessment information with more formal information about pupil learning.* In order to get a more complete and reliable picture of instructional success, teachers should supplement their informal observations with more formal types of evidence taken from sources such as homework papers, chapter and lesson review exercises, and worksheets. Each of these is a valuable source of assessment information that can tell the teacher something about how well pupils have mastered the lesson objectives.

3. *Use appropriate questioning techniques and strategies to assess pupil learning.* To gather needed information about pupil learning during

instruction, teachers rely heavily on oral questions. Oral questions are the major instructional assessment technique for most classroom teachers, with some teachers asking as many as 300 to 400 questions per day (Gall, 1984; Morgan and Saxton, 1991).

Oral questioning is the most common form of instructional assessment.

Purposes of Questioning

During instruction, teachers ask questions for many reasons (Morgan and Saxton, 1991).

1. *To promote attention.* Questioning is a way to keep pupils' attention during a lesson, a way to engage them actively in the process of learning.

2. *To promote deeper processing.* Questioning lets pupils verbalize their thoughts and ideas, thereby promoting the thinking and reasoning that lead to deeper processing of information.

3. *To promote peer teaching and learning.* Questioning allows pupils to hear their peers' interpretations and explanations of ideas, processes, and issues. Often, other pupils explain things in ways that are more in tune with the minds of their peers.

4. *To provide reinforcement.* Questioning is used by teachers to reinforce important points and ideas. The questions teachers ask cue pupils regarding what and how they should be learning.

Teachers ask questions in order to reinforce important points, to diagnose problems, to keep student attention, and to promote deeper processing of the information.

5. *To provide pace and control.* Questions that require brief, correct responses keep pupils engaged in learning and require them to pay continuous attention. Questions that are more general and openended slow the pace of instruction so pupils can reflect upon and frame their answers and explanations.

6. *To provide diagnostic information.* Questioning provides the teacher with information about pupil and class learning. Teachers' questions can supplement their informal observations of pupil learning in the least disruptive way. Also, for group or cooperative learning activities, questioning of group members after completion of their task is a useful way to assess the success of the group.

Types of Questions

Not all teacher questions are alike. There are higher- and lower-level questions and convergent and divergent questions. Convergent questions have a single correct answer: "What is the capital of Brazil?" "Who is credited with the discovery of radium?" "How many corners does a cube have?" Divergent questions may have many appropriate answers: "What are the benefits of a good education?" "Describe some differences between the American and French systems of government." "What kinds of jobs do people in your neighborhood have?" Both types are important to use during instruction.

Convergent questions are those that have a single correct answer, whereas divergent questions may have several appropriate answers.

Lower-level, factual questions generally begin with words such as who, what, *and* when, *whereas higher-level questions begin with action words such as* explain, predict, distinguish, *and* solve.

Questions also can be categorized in terms of whether they require higher or lower levels of pupil thinking. Lower-level, factual questions generally begin with words such as *who, when, what,* and *how many.* Examples of such questions are: "When did the U.S. Civil War take place?" "What is the definition of *taxonomy*?" "Where is the city of Beijing located?" Such information is important because solving more complex, higher-level problems generally depends upon retrieving and manipulating basic facts.

Most teachers also want their pupils to apply, analyze, and synthesize factual knowledge in order to solve new problems. Higher-level questions typically start with words such as *explain, predict, relate, distinguish, solve, contrast, judge,* and *produce.* Examples of such questions are: "Explain in your own words what the main idea of the story was." "Predict what will happen to the price of oil if the supply increases but the demand remains the same." "Distinguish between statements that are facts and statements that are opinions in the passage we have just read." Questions such as these set tasks that require pupils to think and to go beyond factual recall of dates, names, and places. Note, however, that if the answers to these questions had been specifically taught to pupils during instruction, they would not be higher-level questions, since pupils could answer them from memory, rather than having to construct an answer for themselves.

Table 2.12 provides examples of questions at different levels of Bloom's Taxonomy. While the taxonomy provides a useful model, it is less important to ask questions at specific taxonomic levels than it is to focus generally on asking a range of questions that stimulate both memory and reflection.

Questioning Strategies

The following strategies can be used to increase the effectiveness of oral questioning.

1. *Ask questions that are related to your educational objectives.* Teachers' questions communicate what topics are important and in what ways these topics should be learned, so there should be consistency among objectives, instruction, and questioning. It is especially useful to prepare a few higher-level questions before instruction begins and to incorporate them into the lesson plan.

2. *Avoid global, overly general questions.* Do not ask, "Does everyone understand this?" because many pupils will be too embarrassed to admit they don't and others will think they understand what's been taught when in reality they don't. Ask questions that probe pupils' comprehension of what's being taught. Similarly, avoid questions that can be answered with a simple "yes" or "no" unless the pupils are also expected to explain their answers.

Teachers should be aware of their questioning patterns to avoid distributing questions unfairly among different groups of students.

3. *Be aware of patterns in the way questions are distributed among pupils and try to involve the entire class in the questioning process.* Some

TABLE 2.12 EXAMPLES OF QUESTIONS FOR THE LEVELS OF BLOOM'S COGNITIVE TAXONOMY

Knowledge (remembering)	What is the definition of a noun?
	How many planets are in our solar system?
	In what year did the Boston Tea Party occur?
Comprehension (understanding)	Summarize the story in your own words.
	Explain what $E = MC^2$ means.
	Paraphrase the author's intent.
Application (using information to solve new problems)	What is a real-world example of that principle?
	Predict what would happen if the steps in the process were reversed.
	How could the Pythagorean theorem be used to measure the height of a tree?
Analysis (reasoning, breaking apart)	Which of these statements are facts, and which are opinions?
	How did the main character change after her scary nightmare?
	Explain the unstated assumption that underlies this argument.
Synthesis (constructing, integrating)	What do all these pictures have in common?
	Describe a generalization that follows from these data.
	State a conclusion supported by these facts.
Evaluation (judging)	What was the most important moment in the story and why?
	Describe your opinion of the school policy for grades and extracurricular participation.

teachers call on high-achieving pupils more frequently than low achievers, on girls more than boys, or on those in the front rows more than those in the back. Other teachers do the opposite. Be sensitive to such questioning patterns and strive to give all pupils an equal opportunity to respond.

4. *Allow sufficient "wait time" after asking a question*. This permits pupils to think about and frame a response. Pupils need time to process their thoughts, especially when the question is a higher-level one. Remember, silence after a question is good because it means the pupils are thinking. Three to five seconds is a suitable "wait time" that permits most pupils, even the slower ones, to think about an answer to the question. Giving pupils time to think also leads to improved answers.

5. *State questions clearly and directly in order to avoid confusion*. Avoid vague questions or prompts like "What about the story?" or "Talk to me about this experiment." If pupils are to think in desired ways, the teacher must be able to state questions in ways that focus and produce that type of thinking. Clarity focuses thinking and improves the quality of answers. Again, preparing key questions before teaching a lesson is a useful practice.

6. *Probe pupil responses with follow-up questions*. Ask "Why?" "Explain how you arrived at that conclusion." and "Can you give me another example?" Such probes indicate to pupils that the "whys" or logic behind a response is as important as the response itself and will encourage them to articulate their reasoning.

7. *Allow private questioning time for pupils who are shy and difficult to engage in the questioning process*. If possible, allow private questioning time for these pupils, perhaps during seatwork or study time. Then, as they become more confident in their private responses, gradually work them into public discussions, first with small groups and then with the whole class.

8. *Remember that oral questioning is a social process involving interaction between teacher and pupils that occurs in a public setting*. Consequently, all pupils should be treated with encouragement and respect. Incorrect, incomplete, or even unreasonable answers should not evoke demeaning, sarcastic, or angry teacher responses. Be honest with pupils; don't lie to or try to bluff them when they pose a question that you can't answer. Find the answer and report it to pupils the next day.

CHAPTER SUMMARY

♦ Education is the process of helping pupils acquire new skills and behaviors. A curriculum is the statement of the things pupils are expected to learn in school or in a course. Instruction includes the methods used to help pupils acquire the desired skills and behaviors. Changes in pupil behavior brought about through formal instruction are called achievements.

♦ The instructional process is comprised of three steps: identifying desirable objectives for pupils to learn, selecting materials and providing instruction to help pupils learn, and assessing whether pupils have learned. Each step requires teacher decision making and assessment.

♦ Planning instruction involves understanding and modifying the curriculum and instruction to fit the needs and characteristics of pupils. Planning helps teachers reduce anxiety and uncertainty about their instruction, review and become familiar with subject matter before teaching, and select ways to get the lessons started.

♦ Planning is dependent upon the context in which instruction takes place and must take into account both classroom characteristics teachers control and those they do not.

♦ In order to organize the classroom and plan appropriate instruction, teachers must carry out good sizing-up assessments to learn their pupils' characteristics. From a variety of mainly informal sources, teachers construct rich descriptions of pupils, early in the school year.

♦ Sizing-up assessments are a natural part of social interaction. However, they do lead teachers to form and often communicate expectations to pupils. Moreover, teachers' first impressions of pupils tend to remain stable, although they are not always accurate. As a consequence, teachers must consider carefully when sizing up and labeling pupils at the start of the school year.

♦ Two main problems affect the validity of sizing-up assessments. Observer pre-judgments occur when a teacher's prior knowledge, first impression, or personal beliefs interfere with the ability to make a fair and objective assessment of a pupil. Logical error occurs when teachers use the wrong kind of information to judge pupil characteristics, as, for example, when they judge interest by where a pupil sits in a class.

♦ Reliability is a special problem in sizing-up assessment because the process takes place so quickly and is based upon many fleeting observations, which make it difficult to assess pupils' typical or consistent performance.

♦ Six suggestions for improving sizing-up assessments are: (1) be aware that you are sizing up pupils and its potential effects on them; (2) treat initial impressions as hypotheses to be confirmed or corrected by subsequent observation and information; (3) use direct, low-inference indicators to gather information about pupil characteristics; (4) supplement informal observations with more formal, structured activities; (5) observe long enough to be fairly certain that you have perceived the pupil's typical behavior; and (6) determine whether different kinds of information confirm each other.

♦ Most instructional models identify four basic elements that teachers should include in their lesson plans: educational objectives, materials needed, teaching strategies and activities, and assessment procedures. Lesson plans should be written down in advance of instruction.

♦ Educational objectives describe the behaviors pupils are expected to perform after instruction is completed and, therefore, help in selecting appropriate methods and resources, communicating the purposes of instruction to others, and planning appropriate pupil assessment.

♦ Well-stated educational objectives describe an observable pupil behavior and the content matter on which the behavior will be performed.

♦ Higher-level educational objectives are ones that require pupils to do more than just memorize facts and rules. Higher-level objectives involve behaviors that require application, analysis, synthesis, or evaluation of content and ideas.

♦ Planning instruction is greatly aided by modern textbooks and their accompanying aids and resources. Teachers must remember that every class is different and that they must assess the textbook and its resources in light of their own classes' unique needs, readiness, and learning styles.

♦ Planning lessons can be improved by knowing and considering pupils' learning needs and characteristics; critically examining the textbook and its accompanying aids for appropriateness; emphasizing both lower- and higher-level educational objectives; using a range of instructional strategies and activities; recognizing the relationship between objectives and teaching activities; understanding one's own content and teaching strategy weaknesses; and including assessment activities in plans.

♦ During instruction, teachers must accomplish two tasks simultaneously: they must deliver instruction to pupils and they must constantly assess the progress and success of that instruction.

♦ Assessments during instruction are more spontaneous and informal than assessments during planning, focusing on indicators such as pupil body language, participation, facial expressions, and questions.

♦ Because of its informal, spontaneous nature, assessment during instruction must overcome validity problems such as the lack of teacher objectivity regarding the success of instruction and the tendency to judge instructional success by facial expressions and participation, not by actual pupil achievement.

♦ Reliability problems during instructional assessment center on the difficulty of observing pupils in detail given the fast pace of instruction and the fact that teachers often observe or call on only some pupils in the class.

♦ Questioning is the most useful strategy a teacher can use to assess the progress of instruction. It gives information to the teacher about pupil learning, lets pupils articulate their own thoughts, reinforces important concepts and behaviors, and influences the pace of instruction.

♦ Good questioning technique includes: asking both higher- and lower-level questions; keeping questions related to the objectives of instruction; involving the whole class in the process; allowing sufficient "wait time" for pupils to think about their responses; probing responses with follow-up questions that have the pupils defend or explain why they chose their answer; and never demeaning or embarrassing a pupil for a wrong or unreasonable answer.

QUESTIONS FOR DISCUSSION

1. How does the fact that a classroom is a social setting influence things that go on in classrooms such as planning, teaching, grading, managing, and interacting with pupils?

2. What are the advantages and disadvantages of examining a pupil's school (cumulative) record folder before the start of class? Under what circumstances would you examine a pupil's record folder?

3. How much must teachers really know about a pupil's home and family background? What home and background information is absolutely essential for teachers to know? Why? What information does a teacher have no right to know about a pupil's home or background?

4. What pupil characteristics are most important to take into account when planning instruction? How realistic is it to expect a teacher to plan instruction that takes into account all the important needs of her pupils?

5. How might the fact that a teacher is the planner and deliverer of instruction *and* the assessor of its success negatively influence the ways the teacher plans and delivers instruction?

6. In what ways can the teacher's edition of a textbook both enhance and detract from good instruction?

REFLECTION EXERCISE

♦ List as many factors as you can (at least 20) that can affect a pupil's learning and behavior in school.

♦ Put an X beside the three factors you think are the most important for pupil learning.

♦ Put a Y beside all the factors you think a teacher would know about from sizing-up assessment.

♦ Put a Z beside all the factors the teacher has very little control over.

♦ Review your responses and pick the three factors a teacher is likely to know about and should be able to influence in the classroom.

ACTIVITIES

1. Using the model shown in Table 2.5, develop a lesson plan for a topic you would like to teach to a class. Your plan should address the following areas:
    ♦ Objectives (at least three, one a higher-level objective)
    ♦ Materials needed
    ♦ Lesson activities (e.g., capturing student interest, advanced organizer, sequence of activities, opportunity for pupil practice, ending activity and summary)
    ♦ Assessment of learning

2. Select a recent (1990 or later) teacher's edition of a textbook in a subject matter and grade level you are interested in teaching. Select a chapter or unit in the teacher's edition. Using the criteria shown in Table 2.7, write a two-page critique of the chapter or unit you have selected. What are its strong and weak points? Are the various parts of the lesson integrated and reinforcing?

3. Using the content in the chapter or unit selected in the above activity, write one question that assesses each of the six levels of the taxonomy. See Table 2.12.

REVIEW QUESTIONS

1. What factors make a classroom a social setting or society? How do these factors influence teachers' assessment responsibilities?

2. What are the main problems of validity and reliability in sizing-up assessment and assessments for planning and delivering instruction?

3. Explain the differences among education, achievement, instruction, and curriculum.

4. How does sizing-up assessment contribute to planning and delivering good instruction to pupils? In what ways does sizing-up assessment influence classroom decisions?

5. What are the advantages and disadvantages of teacher's editions of classroom textbooks? What cautions should teachers exercise when using them?

6. What strategies of oral questioning can a teacher use to make assessment during instruction more valid and reliable?

7. How does the assessment process differ for planning instruction and delivering instruction?

8. How do decisions about educational objectives influence decisions about instruction and assessment?

REFERENCES

Adams, R., and Biddle, B. (1970). *Realities of teaching: Explorations with video tape.* New York: Holt, Rinehart and Winston.

Airasian, P. W. (1989). Classroom assessment and educational improvement. In L. W. Anderson (Ed.), *The effective teacher* (pp. 333–342). New York: Random House.

Airasian, P. W., Kellaghan, T., and Madaus, G. F. (1977). The stability of teachers' perceptions of pupil characteristics. *Irish Journal of Education,* 11(1 & 2), 78–84.

Airasian, P. W., Kellaghan, T., Madaus, G. F., and Pedulla, J. (1977). Proportion and direction of teacher rating changes of pupil progress attributable to standardized test information. *Journal of Educational Psychology,* 69(6), 702–709.

Anderson, L. M., and Evertson, C. M. (1978). *Classroom organization at the beginning of school: Two case studies.* Paper presented to the American Association of Colleges for Teacher Education, Chicago, IL.

Bloom, B. S., Englehart, M. D., Furst, E. J., Hill, W. H., and Krathwohl, D. R. (1956). *Taxonomy of educational objectives. Handbook 1. Cognitive domain.* New York: McKay.

Brandt, R. (1992). On outcomes-based education: A conversation with Bill Spady. *Educational Leadership,* 50(4) 66–70.

Brophy, J. F., and Good, T. L. (1974). *Teacher-student relationships.* New York: Holt, Rinehart & Winston.

Bullough, R. V., Knowles, J. G., and Crow, N. A. (1992). *Emerging as a teacher.* New York: Routledge.

Cartwright, C. A., and Cartwright, G. P. (1984). *Developing observation skills.* New York: McGraw-Hill.

Clark, C. M., and Peterson, P. L. (1986). Teachers' thought processes. In M. C. Wittrock (Ed.), *Handbook of research on teaching* (pp. 255–296). New York: Macmillan.

Clark, C. M., and Yinger, R. J. (1979a). Teachers' thinking. In P. L. Peterson and H. J. Walberg (Ed.), *Research on teaching* (pp. 231–263). Berkeley, CA: McCutchan.

Clark, C. M., and Yinger, R. J. (1979b). Three studies of teacher planning. (Research Series No. 55). East Lansing: Michigan State University.

Downey, M. (1977). *Interpersonal judgments in education.* London: Harper & Row.

Doyle, W. (1986). Classroom organization and management. In M. C. Wittrock (Ed.), *Handbook of research on teaching* (pp. 392–431). New York: Macmillan.

Eby, J. W. (1992). *Reflective planning, teaching, and evaluation for the elementary school.* New York: Merrill.

Educational Leadership (1994). The challenge of outcome-based education. 51(6).

Eisner, E. W. (1979). *The educational imagination.* New York: Macmillan.

Evertson, C., Brophy, J., and Good, T. (1972). *Communication of teacher expectations: First grade* (91). Research and Development Center for Teacher Education, University of Texas at Austin.

Farr, R., and Tulley, M. A. (1985). Do adoption committees perpetuate mediocre textbooks? *Phi Delta Kappan,* 66, 467–471.

Feiman-Nemser, S., and Floden, R. E. (1986). The cultures of teaching. In M. C. Wittrock (Ed.), *Handbook of research on teaching* (pp. 505–526). New York: Macmillan.

Freiberg, H. J., and Driscoll, A. (1992). *Universal teaching strategies.* Boston: Allyn & Bacon.

Furst, E. J. (1958). *Constructing achievement tests.* New York: McKay.

Gagne, R. M., Briggs, L. J., and Wagner, W. W. (1988). *Principles of instruction.* New York: Holt, Rinehart, and Winston.

Gall, M. (1984). Synthesis of research on teacher's thinking. *Educational Leadership,* 42, 40–47.

Gordon, M. (1987). *Nursing diagnosis: Process and application.* New York: McGraw-Hill.

Guerin, G. R., and Maier, A. S. (1983). *Informal assessment in education.* Palo Alto, CA: Mayfield.

Hawkes, T. H. (1971). Teacher expectations and friendship patterns in the elementary classroom. In M. L. Silberman (Ed.), *The experience of schooling* (pp. 308–315). New York: Holt, Rinehart & Winston.

Hunter, M. (1982). *Mastery teaching.* El Segundo, CA: TIP.

Jackson, P., and Lahaderne, H. (1967). Inequalities of teacher-pupil contacts. *Psychology in the Schools,* 4, 204–211.

Jenkins, B. (1972). *Teachers' views of particular students and their behavior in the classroom.* Unpublished doctoral dissertation, University of Chicago.

Johnson, D., and Johnson, R. (1984). *Circles of learning.* Alexandria, VA: Association for Supervision and Curriculum Development.

Kellaghan, T., Madaus, G. F., and Airasian, P. W. (1982). *The effects of standardized testing.* Boston: Kluwer-Nijhoff.

Leinhardt, G. (1989). Math lessons: A contrast of novice and expert competence. *Journal for Research in Mathematics Education,* 20, 52–75.

Lieberman, A. (1982). Practice makes policy: The tensions of school improvement. In A. Lieberman and M. W. McLaughlin (Ed.), *Policy making in education. The eighty-first yearbook of the National Society for the Study of Education. Part I* (pp. 249–269). Chicago: University of Chicago Press.

Lortie, D. C. (1975). *Schoolteacher.* Chicago: University of Chicago Press.

Morgan, N., and Saxton, J. (1991). *Teaching, questioning, and learning.* New York: Routledge.

Nisbett, R. E., and Ross, L. (1980). *Human inference: Strategies and shortcomings of social judgment.* Englewood Cliffs, NJ: Prentice-Hall.

Perkinson, H. (1993). *Teachers without goals, students without purposes.* New York: McGraw-Hill.

Peterson, P. L., and Barger, S. A. (1984). Attribution theory and teacher expectancy. In J. B. Dusek (Ed.), *Teacher expectancies* (pp. 159–184). Hillsdale, NJ: Lawrence Erlbaum.

Popham, W. J. (1988). *Educational evaluation.* Englewood Cliffs, NJ: Prentice-Hall.

Rist, R. (1970). Student social class and teacher expectations: The self-fulfilling prophesy in ghetto education. *Harvard Educational Review,* 40, 411–451.

Shavelson, R. J., and Stern, P. (1981). Research on teachers' pedagogical thoughts, judgments, decisions, and behavior. *Review of Educational Research,* 51, 455–498.

Slavin, Robert E. (1994). *Educational psychology. Theory and practice.* Boston: Allyn and Bacon.

Solas, J. (1992). Investigating teacher and student thinking about the process of teaching and learning using autobiography and repertory grid. *Review of Educational Research,* 62(2) 205–225.

Stodolsky, S. S. (1988). *The subject matters.* Chicago: University of Chicago Press.

Tyler, R. W. (1949). *Basic principles of curriculum and instruction.* Chicago: University of Chicago Press.

Willis, S. (1972). *Formation of teachers' expectations of students' academic performance.* Unpublished doctoral dissertation, The University of Texas at Austin.

Woodward, A., and Elliott, D. L. (1990). Textbooks: Consensus and controversy. In D. L. Elliott and A. Woodward (Eds.), *Textbooks and schooling in the United States. The eighty-ninth yearbook of the National Society for the Study of Education, Part I* (pp. 146–161). Chicago: University of Chicago Press.

CHAPTER 3

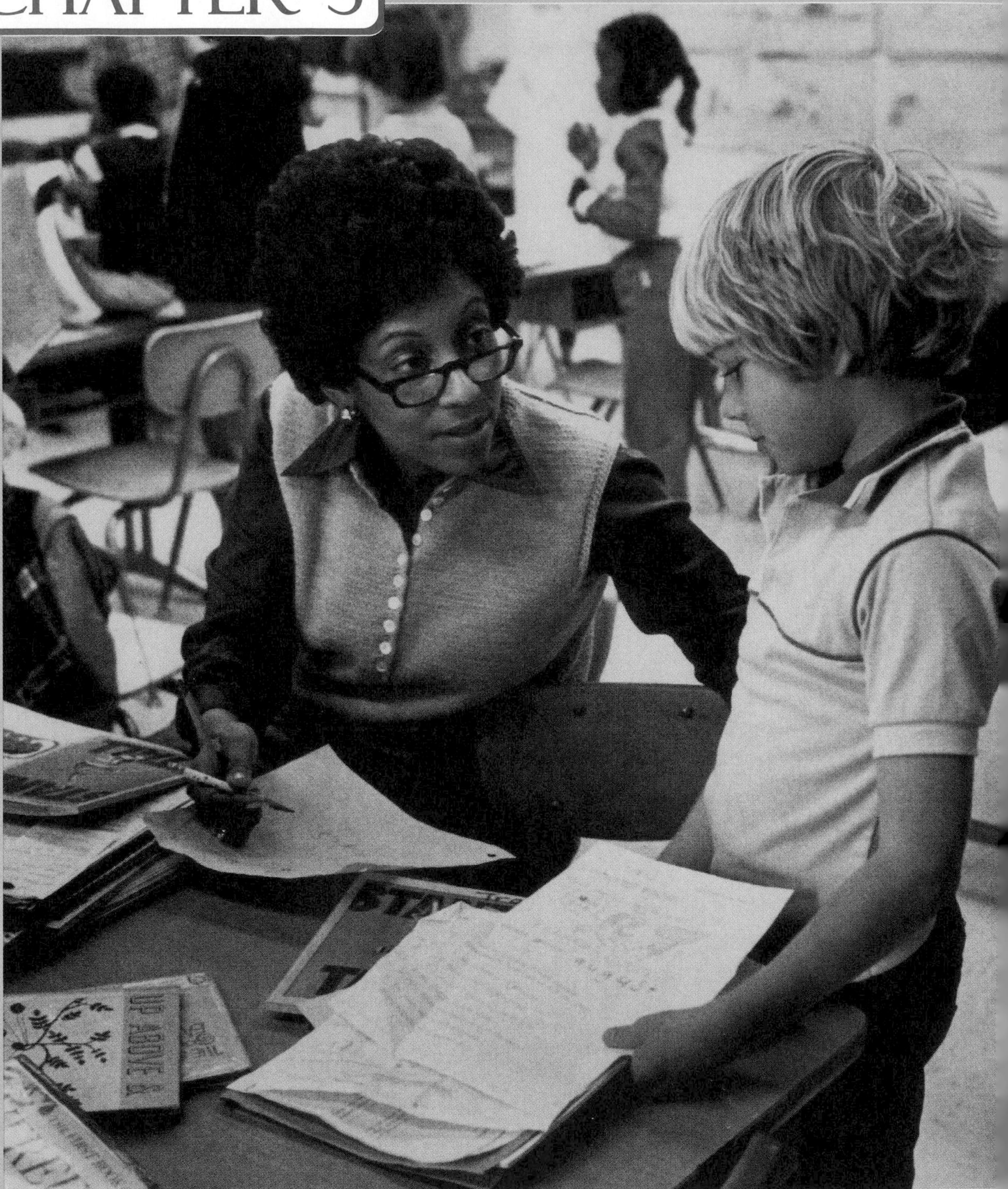

FORMAL ASSESSMENT: TEACHER-MADE TESTS

THE LOGIC OF
FORMAL ASSESSMENT

PREPARING FOR ASSESSMENT
An Example

PREPARING PUPILS FOR FORMAL
ACHIEVEMENT TESTING
Issues of Test Preparation
Provide Good Instruction
Review before Testing
Familiarity with Question Formats
Scheduling the Test
Giving Pupils Information
   about the Test

PAPER-AND-PENCIL
TEST QUESTIONS
Types of Test Items
Higher-Level Test Items

GENERAL GUIDELINES FOR
WRITING AND CRITIQUING
TEST ITEMS
Cover Important Objectives
Write Clearly and Simply: Six Rules
Review Items before Testing

ASSEMBLING THE TEST

ADMINISTERING THE TEST
Physical Setting
Psychological Setting
Cheating

SCORING TESTS
Scoring Selection Items
Scoring Short-Answer
   and Completion Items
Scoring Essay Items

DISCUSS TEST RESULTS
WITH PUPILS

CHAPTER SUMMARY

T hus far we have seen that assessment plays an important role in classrooms and that teachers use assessment to help them:

♦ Get to know pupils early in the school year
♦ Establish the classroom as a learning community with rules and order
♦ Select appropriate educational objectives for pupils
♦ Develop lesson plans
♦ Select and critique instructional materials and activities
♦ Monitor the instructional process and pupil learning during instruction

Much of the evidence that supports these decisions comes from informal observations and perceptions. Rarely written down, they are used mainly to guide teachers' moment-to-moment decisions about solving pupil problems, controlling the class, conducting a lesson, and judging pupils' reactions to instruction. Such assessments are used primarily to "form" or alter ongoing classroom processes and are called **formative assessments** because they provide information when it is still possible to influence the everyday processes which are at the heart of teaching.

Formative assessments are those used to alter or improve instruction while it is still going on.

Although critical to teachers' decision making, informal assessments should be supplemented by more formal kinds of evidence. Such formal assessments usually come at the end of instruction when it is difficult to alter or rectify what has already occurred. Called **summative assessments** (Crooks, 1988; Scriven, 1967), they are used to evaluate the outcomes of instruction and are exemplified by end-of-chapter tests, projects, term papers, and final examinations. Table 3.1 contrasts formative and summative assessments.

Summative assessments are those used to evaluate the outcomes of instruction and take the form of tests, projects, term papers, and final exams.

Summative assessments represent a third type of classroom assessment called **official assessment** (Airasian, 1989). Official assessments are more formal and systematic than either sizing-up or instructional assessments. They help teachers to make decisions that the school bureaucracy requires of them: testing, grading, and grouping pupils; recommending whether pupils should be promoted or placed in an honors section; and referring pupils to special education services if they have special needs. These decisions are official assessments.

Official assessments are those needed by the school bureaucracy for purposes such as pupil testing, grading, and placement.

Unlike sizing-up and instructional assessments, official assessments are usually made public in report cards, record folders, and reading- or track-group designations. Further, most official assessments inform decisions about individual pupils rather than groups or classes; we grade, promote, honor, and place individuals, not groups. Because they are public, have important consequences for pupils, and often must be defended, official assessments are usually based upon formal evidence like tests, projects, or reports.

TABLE 3.1 CHARACTERISTICS OF FORMATIVE AND SUMMATIVE ASSESSMENTS

	Formative	Summative
Purpose	To monitor and guide a process while it is still in progress	To judge the success of a process at its completion
Time of assessment	During the process	At the end of the process
Type of assessment technique	Informal observation, quizzes, homework, pupil questions, worksheets	Formal tests, projects, and term papers
Use of assessment information	Improve and change a process while it is still going on	Judge the overall success of a process; grade, place, promote

Teachers have mixed emotions about official assessments like tests, as the following comments show.

I hate giving them. I find the testing situation to be one where tests become public expressions of what I already knew about the kid and what the kid already knew about the subject matter. In other words, I knew who would get A's and who would get F's because I taught the class.

Each test gives me some feedback on what I'm doing right and what I'm not, as well as what the class is learning best. I like to give a large number of tests to get this feedback.

My tests are helpful in that they offer concrete evidence to show parents if the student is deficient in an area. I'll tell a parent that Johnny can't add and they'll sometime respond 'I know he can add when he wants to.' Then I show them a classroom test which shows Johnny's deficiency. One drawback to the tests, especially in the early grades, is that a child sometimes will become upset during testing.

Although teachers differ in their views of official assessment, it is clear that no matter how teachers feel about them, they use them at least some of the time in their classrooms.

Despite their sometimes lukewarm endorsement by teachers, it is a grave mistake to underestimate the importance of official assessments. Pupils, their parents, and the public at large consider them to be very important and take them quite seriously (Airasian, 1988). The grading, placement, promotion, and other decisions that result from official assessments influence pupils' lives both in and out of school. They are the public record of a pupil's school accomplishments and are often the sole information a parent has of how a child is doing in school. Thus,

Official assessments can have important consequences for students and should be taken quite seriously by teachers.

although official assessment occurs infrequently compared to other assessments, its perceived importance makes it a central part of any classroom's activities.

THE LOGIC OF FORMAL ASSESSMENT

Good teaching refers to what teachers do during instruction, while effective teaching refers to the outcomes of instruction.

There is an important difference between good teaching and effective teaching (Berliner, 1987). Good teaching refers to the *process* of instruction, while effective teaching refers to the *outcomes* of instruction. A good teacher is one who, among other things, provides a review at the start of a new lesson, maintains an appropriate level of lesson difficulty, engages pupils in the learning process, emphasizes important points during instruction, gives pupils practice doing what they are expected to learn, and maintains an orderly classroom.

Effective teaching goes one step beyond good teaching to focus on whether pupils have actually learned from instruction. An effective teacher is one whose pupils learn what they have been taught. Clearly there is a relationship between good and effective teaching: the better the teaching, the more likely that it will be effective. Teachers who misjudge the level of their pupils' ability, fail to review or point out important concepts to pupils, and permit disciplinary problems to distract from instruction have a poorer chance of fostering learning than do good teachers.

Sizing-up and instructional assessment focus attention primarily on the instructional process, while official assessment focuses attention primarily on pupil achievement at the completion of that process. In short, official assessments seek to obtain evidence about teaching effectiveness. This is another way of saying that official assessment must be matched to the objectives, activities, and instruction provided, since it is impossible to assess pupils' achievement if the things assessed do not match the things pupils were taught.

The primary aim of assessing achievement is to provide pupils an opportunity to demonstrate what they have learned from the instruction provided.

Bear in mind that the primary aim in assessing pupil achievement is to *provide pupils a fair opportunity to demonstrate what they have learned from the instruction provided.* It is not to trick pupils into doing poorly, entertain them, or ensure that most of them get A grades. It is not to determine how much total knowledge pupils have accumulated as a result of all their learning experiences, both in and out of school. It is simply to let pupils show what they have and have not learned from the things they have been taught in a particular classroom. Let's now examine some of the considerations that all teachers must confront when they set out to formally assess their pupils' achievement.

PREPARING FOR ASSESSMENT

At the time of formal achievement testing, usually at the completion of instruction on a unit or chapter, the teacher must decide the following:

1. What should be tested?
2. What type of assessment should be given?
3. How long should the assessment take?
4. Should a teacher-made or textbook assessment be used?

An Example

Mr. Wysocki is a seventh-grade English teacher who is teaching his class about descriptive paragraphs. Based upon his sizing-up assessments, the pupils' previous English curriculum, the textbook, and other instructional resources available to him, Mr. Wysocki decided that the unit would focus upon the following educational objectives:

◆ The pupil can explain in his or her own words the three stages of the writing process (i.e., prewriting, writing, and editing).
◆ The pupil can select the topic sentence in a given descriptive paragraph.
◆ The pupil can write a topic sentence for a given descriptive topic.
◆ The pupil can construct a descriptive paragraph with a topic sentence, descriptive detail, and a concluding statement.

Once his objectives were identified, Mr. Wysocki developed lesson plans for them. In selecting activities, he considered the ability levels of his pupils, their attention spans, the suggestions made in the textbook, and the additional resources that were available to supplement and reinforce the textbook. With the objectives and the planned activities identified, Mr. Wysocki commenced instruction.

First, he introduced pupils to the three steps in the writing process: (1) prewriting—identifying one's intended audience, purpose, and initial ideas; (2) writing; and (3) editing what one has written. Next, he gave pupils topics and had them describe how they would go through the three steps. He had them give reasons why each step was necessary for good writing. He then introduced them to the concept of a paragraph and they read descriptive paragraphs to find a common structure. He noted that a paragraph is made up of a topic sentence, detail sentences, and a concluding sentence. Then he had the pupils identify the topic sentences in several paragraphs. Later, he had them write their own topic sentences.

Instruction seemed to go along fairly well except that pupils had a hard time finding the common structure in paragraphs, so Mr. Wysocki had to give additional explanation to the class. Also, even after instruction, his end-of-lesson assessments indicated that many pupils had the mistaken idea that the topic sentence always came first in a paragraph, so he devised a worksheet in which many of the topic sentences were not at the start of the paragraph.

Finally, Mr. Wysocki had pupils write descriptive paragraphs. First he had them all write on the same topics so pupils could compare topic sentences and the amount of detail in each other's paragraphs. He thought this strategy might be useful because pupils could learn from one another's efforts. Homework assignments were returned to pupils with suggestions for improvement and pupils were required to edit and rewrite their paragraphs. Later, pupils were allowed to construct descriptive paragraphs on topics of their choice.

Not all teachers would have instructed their pupils in this fashion; different teachers have different pupils, resources, and styles. But Mr. Wysocki did what he judged was best for his particular class. He instituted instructional procedures that gave pupils practice on the behaviors they were expected to learn, provided feedback on pupil performance during instruction, and revised his plans based upon his observations during instruction. We would say that he demonstrated the characteristics of a good teacher.

Mr. Wysocki felt that he had a fair sense of how well the class had mastered the objectives. Although he knew something about the achievement of each pupil, he wasn't sure about everyone's achievement of all four objectives. He felt a formal, end-of-unit assessment would provide information about each pupil's mastery of all he had taught. Then he would not have to rely upon incomplete, informal perceptions when grading his pupils. However, in order to develop the assessment, he had to make some decisions about the nature of the test he would administer.

A fair and valid test covers information and skills similar to those covered during instruction.

1. *What should I test?* The first important decision when preparing to assess pupil achievement is to identify the information, behaviors, and skills that will be tested. A valid achievement test is one that provides pupils a fair opportunity to show what they have learned from instruction. Therefore, in deciding what to test, it was necessary for Mr. Wysocki to focus attention upon both his objectives and the actual instruction that took place. Usually the two are very similar, but sometimes it is necessary to add or omit an objective once teaching begins. In the final analysis, the things that were actually presented during instruction are most important to assess.

Thus, Mr. Wysocki knew that he had to gather information about how well pupils could explain in their own words the three stages of the writing process, select the topic sentence in a paragraph, write a suitable topic sentence themselves, and compose a descriptive paragraph with a topic sentence, descriptive detail, and summarizing statement. But what about other important skills such as taking notes on a topic or knowing the difference between a descriptive and an expository paragraph? These are useful skills. Shouldn't they also be on Mr. Wysocki's test?

The answer to these questions is NO! There will always be more objectives to teach than there is time to teach them. There will always be useful topics and skills that have to be omitted from tests because they could not be taught. This is why thoughtfully planning instruction in terms of pupil needs and resources is so important. Including untaught skills on an achievement test diminishes its validity, making it less than a true and fair assessment of what pupils have learned from classroom instruction.

By confining his test questions to what he actually taught, Mr. Wysocki can say to himself, "I decided what the important objectives were for pupils, I provided instruction on those objectives, I gave pupils practice performing the objectives, and I gave a test that asked pupils to do things similar to those I taught. The results of the test should fairly reflect how much the pupils have achieved in this unit and permit me to grade fairly."

2. What type of assessment should be given? The key to gathering appropriate information about learning is found in the objectives and the instruction provided. Table 3.2 contains a grid that shows Mr. Wysocki's objectives and some techniques he could use to gather evidence about pupil learning. Each objective contains a target behavior that pupils were taught and should be expected to perform after instruction. The behaviors in three of the objectives, "explain in his or her own words," "write," and "construct," call for open-ended essay or short-answer questions. These are known as **supply questions** because they call for the pupil to produce (supply) his or her own answer or product. The remaining objective calls for **selection questions** in which the pupil chooses (selects) the topic sentence in a paragraph. A multiple-choice-type question could be used to assess learning of this objective, since such items require the pupil

The type of assessment procedure chosen depends on the nature of the objective being assessed.

TABLE 3.2   OBJECTIVES AND TESTING METHODS GRID FOR MR. WYSOCKI'S UNIT TEST

Objectives	Multiple Choice	Short Answer	Essay	Oral Presentation
Explain in own words the three stages of writing.		X		
Select correct topic sentence.	X			
Write own topic sentence.		X		
Construct own descriptive paragraph.			X	

to select a correct answer from those provided. Thus, the nature of the behavior contained in an objective should determine the format used to gather information. The X's in Table 3.2 show how each objective's behavior is matched to the appropriate type of question. A grid such as this can be useful to a teacher when planning a test.

Many teachers feel that only essay tests are good. Others use multiple-choice items as much as possible, and still others believe that tests should contain a variety of question types. If one talks to teachers about the kinds of questions they use in their tests, one gets responses similar to the following:

> I always give the kids essay tests because that's the only way I can see how well they think.

> Multiple-choice items are easy and fast to score, so I use them most of the time to test pupils' achievement. Besides, most standardized tests like the SAT are made up of multiple-choice questions, so my tests give the pupils practice with this kind of item.

> I make sure that every test I make up has some multiple-choice questions, some fill-in questions, and at least one essay question. I believe that variety in the kinds of questions keeps students interested and give all students a chance to show what they know in the way that's best for them.

Each of these teachers states a reason for following a particular classroom testing strategy. The reasons are neither wrong nor inappropriate, but they are secondary to the main purpose of achievement testing, which is to permit pupils to show how well they have learned the *behaviors they were taught*. Thus, no single assessment procedure is applicable all the time. What makes a particular procedure useful or not useful depends on whether it matches the objectives and instruction provided.

3. *How long should the test take?* Since time for testing is limited, choices must be made in deciding the length of a test. Usually, practical matters such as the age of the pupils or the length of a class period are most influential. Since the stamina and attention span of young pupils is less than that of older ones, a useful strategy to follow with elementary school pupils is to test them fairly often using short tests that assess only a few objectives. Because of their typical attention spans, fifteen- to thirty-minute tests, depending on the grade and group, are suggested for elementary pupils.

Factors such as the age of the students, the subject being tested, and the length of the class period all relate to the length of a test.

Curricula for some school subjects such as history, social studies, and English are composed of relatively discrete, self-contained units. In other subjects such as mathematics, foreign language, and science, knowledge must be built up in a hierarchical sequence. Whereas topics in history may stand on their own, topics in mathematics or Spanish usually cannot be understood unless prior math and Spanish lessons are mastered. Consequently, when teaching in a hierarchical subject area, it is useful to give more frequent tests to keep pupils on task in their studying and to make sure they grasp the early ideas which provide the foundation for subsequent, more complex ideas.

Testing in middle, junior, and high schools is usually restricted by the length of the class period. Most teachers at these levels plan their tests to last almost one complete class period. Mr. Wysocki's class periods are fifty minutes long. He wanted a test that would take about forty minutes for most pupils to complete. A forty-minute test would allow time for distribution and collection of the tests, as well as a few minutes for those pupils who always want "one more minute" before handing in their test.

In deciding how many questions to ask for each objective, Mr. Wysocki tried to balance two factors: (1) the instructional time spent on each objective and (2) its importance. Usually there are some objectives that are more important than others. These objectives tend to be the more general ones, which call for the integration of several narrower objectives. Thus, even though a great deal of instructional time was spent on writing topic sentences, Mr. Wysocki values this skill less for it own sake than for its contribution to the more general objective of constructing a descriptive paragraph. Thus, the number of test questions dealing with writing topic sentences probably won't be proportional to the instructional time he spent on it. It is not necessary to include an equal number of questions for each objective, but all four objectives should be assessed by some items. On the basis of these factors and the instruction he had provided, Mr. Wysocki felt that a test with the following format would be fair to pupils and would provide a valid and reliable assessment of their learning.

The number of test questions per objective depends on the instructional time spent on each objective and its importance.

- The pupils can *explain* in their own words the three stages of the writing process (e.g., prewriting, writing, and editing). Use a short-answer question.
- The pupils can *select* the topic sentence in a given descriptive paragraph. Use three multiple-choice items, each consisting of a paragraph and a list of possible topic sentences from which the pupil has to select the correct one.
- The pupils can *write* a topic sentence for a given descriptive topic. Use three short-answer questions which give the pupils a topic area and require them to write a topic sentence for each area.
- The pupils can *construct* a descriptive paragraph using a topic sentence, descriptive detail, and a concluding statement. Use an essay question in which each pupil writes a descriptive paragraph on a topic of his or her choice. The paragraph cannot be on a topic the pupil used previously during instruction and practice.

4. *Should a teacher-made or a textbook test be used?* Teachers are inevitably confronted with the question of whether to use the textbook test or to construct their own. The very availability of textbook tests is seductive and causes many teachers to think, "After all, the test comes

with the textbook, seems to measure what is in the chapter I'm teaching, looks attractive, and is readily available, so why shouldn't I use it?" Mr. Wysocki asked himself the same question.

Notice that the decision about using a textbook test or constructing one's own cannot be answered until *after* the teacher has reflected on what was taught and identified the topics and behaviors to be tested. One cannot judge the usefulness of any achievement test without reference to the planned objectives and actual instruction.

Textbook tests furnish a ready-made instrument for assessing the objectives stressed in the textbook and can save classroom teachers much time. Test formats vary across textbook publishers in terms of length, format, and question type. Look through the teacher's edition of some textbooks to see the range of textbook tests available in subject areas you might teach.

Before using such tests, teachers should consider the conditions under which they can use a textbook or teacher-made test with confidence. The basic concern is whether the items on the test match the instruction provided pupils. Table 3.3 identifies important points to consider when deciding about using textbook tests.

Regardless of whether a teacher is constructing his or her own test or judging the adequacy of a textbook test, the teacher must consider the same basic validity issue: Do the items on the test match the instruction provided pupils? The more a teacher alters and reshapes the textbook cur-

---

TABLE 3.3   KEY POINTS TO CONSIDER IN JUDGING TEXTBOOK TESTS

1. The decision to use a textbook test must come *after* a teacher identifies the objectives that he or she taught and now wants to assess.

2. Textbook tests are designed for the typical classroom, but since few classrooms are typical, most teachers deviate somewhat from the text in order to accommodate their pupils' needs.

3. The more classroom instruction deviates from the textbook objectives and lesson plans, the less valid the textbook tests are likely to be.

4. The main consideration in judging the adequacy of a textbook test is the match between its test questions and what pupils were taught in their classes:

    a. Are questions similar to the teacher's objectives and instructional emphases?
    b. Do questions require pupils to perform the behaviors they were taught?
    c. Do questions cover all or most of the important objectives taught?
    d. Is the language level and terminology appropriate for pupils?
    e. Does the number of items for each objective provide a sufficient sample of pupil performance?

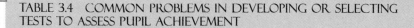

> **TABLE 3.4   COMMON PROBLEMS IN DEVELOPING OR SELECTING TESTS TO ASSESS PUPIL ACHIEVEMENT**
>
> 1. Failure to consider objectives and instructional emphases when planning a test
> 2. Failure to assess all of the important objectives and instructional topics
> 3. Failure to select item types that permit pupils to demonstrate the desired behavior
> 4. Adopting a test without reviewing it for its relevance to the instruction provided
> 5. Including topics or objectives not taught to pupils
> 6. Including too few items to assess the consistency of pupil performance
> 7. Using tests to punish pupils for inattentiveness or acting out

riculum, the less valid its accompanying tests become. As one teacher put it, "The textbook tests look good and can be time savers, but they often don't test exactly what I've been doing in the classroom. Every time I change what I do from what the test suggests I do, and every time I leave out a lesson or section of the text from my instruction, I have to look at the text test carefully to make sure it's fair for my pupils." In the end, Mr. Wysocki decided to construct his own achievement test.

The main consideration in judging the adequacy of a textbook test is the match between its questions and what pupils were actually taught in class.

To summarize, both textbook and teacher-made tests should (1) assess those pupil behaviors that constitute the objectives and instruction and (2) include sufficient questions to measure all or most of those objectives. That way, the test will provide a valid sample of pupil learning. Table 3.4 provides a summary of common problems teachers encounter in judging achievement tests.

PREPARING PUPILS FOR FORMAL ACHIEVEMENT TESTING

Mr. Wysocki's actions point out that fair and valid assessment includes a number of steps: determining appropriate educational objectives, providing good instruction on the objectives, and determining how the objectives are best assessed. With these decisions made, Mr. Wysocki could then determine whether a textbook or a teacher-made test was most appropriate. After these initial decisions, other decisions arise, including issues related to preparing pupils for testing, constructing clear and valid test questions, scoring the test, and assigning grades to pupils.

Fair and valid assessment involves preparing appropriate objectives, providing good instruction on these objectives, and determining how these objectives are best assessed.

Issues of Test Preparation

Tests are intended to gather valid and reliable samples of student behavior that can be used to generalize about student learning.

We use tests and other assessments to help make decisions about pupils' learning in some area. Performance on the test or assessment is meant to represent pupils' mastery of a broader body of taught knowledge and skills than just the specific examples used in class. Thus, tests gather *samples* of a pupil's behavior and use that information to generalize about how the pupil is likely to perform if confronted with similar tasks or items. For example, the performance of a pupil who scores 90 percent on a test of poetry analysis, chemical equation balancing, or capitalization rules is interpreted as indicating that the pupil has mastered about 90 percent of the general content domain he was taught and tested on. The specific tasks or test items are selected to represent a larger group of similar tasks or items.

Throughout this chapter, two points have been stressed. First, assessment of pupil achievement should provide a fair and representative indication of how well pupils have learned what they were taught. Second, in order to do this, test questions must ask pupils to perform behaviors similar to those they were taught during instruction. The important word here is *similar.*

Achievement tests should give information about how well a student can answer questions similar, but not identical, to those that were taught in class.

There is an important ethical difference between teaching to the test and teaching the test itself. Teaching to the test involves teaching pupils the general skills, knowledge, and behaviors that they need to answer the questions on the test. This is an appropriate and desirable practice. It is what good teaching and testing are all about. But teaching the test itself, that is, teaching pupils the answers to the specific questions that will appear on the test, is neither appropriate nor ethical. It produces a distorted, invalid picture of pupil achievement. Such a test will give information about how well pupils can remember the specific items they were taught, but it will not tell how well they can do on questions that are similar, but not identical, to the ones they have been taught. Teachers have an educational and ethical responsibility not to corrupt the meaning of pupils' achievement test performance by literally teaching them the test (Canner, et al., 1991).

Provide Good Instruction

Good instruction is the most important preparation for formal achievement testing.

The single most important thing a teacher can do to prepare pupils for formal classroom achievement tests is to provide them with good instruction. A primary ethical responsibility of teaching is to provide the best instruction possible, without corrupting the achievement test in the ways described above. In the absence of good instruction, little else is important.

Review before Testing

While teaching a unit or chapter, many objectives are introduced, some early and others at the end of instruction. Because the topics most remembered tend to be the ones most recently taught, it is good practice to provide pupils a review prior to formal testing. The review can take many forms: a question-and-answer session, a written or oral summary of main ideas, or administration of a review test. The review serves to: remind pupils of objectives taught early in the unit, provide one last chance to practice important behaviors and skills, and afford an opportunity to ask questions about things that are unclear. Often, the review exercise itself provokes questions that help pupils grasp partially understood ideas.

Many teachers fail to conduct a review because they feel it might "tip pupils off" to the kinds of things that will be on the test. This is faulty reasoning. The purpose of a review is to indicate to pupils that "These are examples of the ideas, behaviors, and skills that I expect you to have learned. See how well you have learned them. Practice them before the test that counts towards your grade. If you have questions or difficulties, we'll go over them before the test. After that, you're on your own." A pertinent review prior to the test will help pupils do their best.

Test reviews often provoke questions that help students grasp partially understood ideas.

Notice that the review exercises or questions should be *similar,* but not identical, to the exercises or questions that will make up the final test. If they are the actual test questions, then a valid assessment of pupil learning cannot be obtained, because the test will have been reduced to a short-term memory exercise rather than a measure of long-term mastery of general learning objectives. Most textbooks contain chapter or unit reviews that can be used prior to testing.

Familiarity with Question Formats

If the classroom test contains questions that use an unfamiliar format, pupils should be given practice with that format prior to testing. The need for such practice is especially important in the elementary grades where pupils first encounter matching, multiple-choice, true-false, short-answer, and essay questions. To do their best and to provide a valid indication of their learning, pupils must know how to respond to each type of question. Clearly, an opportune place to teach these things is during the review exercises prior to the chapter or unit test.

If students aren't familiar with the types of questions used on a test, the test can't produce a valid assessment of what they have learned.

In addition to familiarizing pupils with new types of questions and new response formats, there is a general set of test-taking guidelines that can help pupils do their best on tests (Annis, 1983; Ebel and Frisbie, 1991). Thus, it is helpful for pupils to know that when taking a test they should:

- Read and follow the test directions.
- Find out how questions will be scored. Will all questions count equally; will points be taken off for spelling, grammar, neatness?
- Pace themselves so that they can complete all the questions.
- Plan and organize essay questions before responding.
- When using a separate answer sheet, check often to make certain that they are marking their responses in the correct place.
- Be in good physical and mental condition at the time of testing by avoiding late-night cram sessions.

Another set of skills, called **testwiseness skills,** helps pupils identify errors on the part of question writers that provide clues to correct answers (Hills, 1981; Millman and Pauk, 1965; Sarnacki, 1979). For example, when responding to multiple-choice questions, the testwise pupil knows that

To be "testwise" is to be able to identify unintended clues to the correct answers.

- If the words *some, often,* or similar vague words are in one of the options, it is likely to be the correct option.
- The option that is longest or most precisely stated is likely to be the correct one.
- Any choice that has grammatical or spelling errors is not likely to be the correct one.
- Choices that do not attach smoothly to the stem of the question are not likely to be correct.

There are many other testwise strategies that pupils use to overcome a lack of content knowledge. More detailed descriptions of these can be found in the references. As regards one's own classroom tests, it is best to make pupils aware of such general test-taking skills and then concentrate on writing fair, appropriate test questions that do not contain errors that can be "psyched out."

Scheduling the Test

It has already been recommended that teachers not administer an achievement test immediately after completing instruction, in order to provide pupils the opportunity to review, study, and reflect on the instruction before being tested. But there are other considerations about the times when pupils are most likely to show their best performance. For example, if a teacher were to test pupils the day of the school's championship football game, the period after an assembly or lunch, or on the first day after a long school vacation, the likelihood is that pupils would give a subpar test performance. Likewise, should a teacher schedule a test on a day that he will be away so that the substitute teacher will have something to keep the pupils busy? The answer is no, because the substitute may not be able to answer pupils' questions about either the test or the meaning of particular questions. Further, if it is an elementary classroom, the presence of a stranger in the classroom may make the pupils uncomfortable and unable to do their best. While no teacher has complete control over scheduling tests, it is useful to bear in mind that there are some times when pupils are better able to perform on tests than others.

Giving Pupils Information about the Test

Usually a chapter or unit review alerts pupils to the fact that a formal assessment for grading purposes is coming. It is a good idea, however, to inform pupils about the test by telling them when it will be given, what will be on it, what kinds of questions it will contain, how many questions will there be, how much it counts, and how long it will be. The answers to these questions undoubtedly influence your own test preparation. By providing this information, the teacher helps reduce some of the anxiety that inevitably accompanies the announcement of a test.

Of course, unless a teacher has thought about the nature of the test to be given, it is impossible to provide the pretest information pupils need to prepare for the test. The specifics of test content, types of questions, and test length need to be considered well before the test is given. Hastily planned tests too often focus mainly on memorization skills and fail to cover a representative sample of the instruction provided pupils. Thus, in order to inform pupils about test characteristics, a teacher should not put off planning the test until the last minute.

Hastily planned tests too often focus on memory items and fail to cover a representative sample of the instruction provided.

PAPER-AND-PENCIL TEST QUESTIONS

Thus far we have seen that a good assessment plan takes many things into consideration: identifying important educational objectives, selecting question formats that match these objectives, deciding whether to construct one's own test or use one from the textbook, and providing good instruction, review, and information about the test. The success of these important preparatory steps can be undone, however, if the actual test questions are faulty or confusing. Poorly constructed or unclear questions do not give pupils a fair chance to show what they have learned and, consequently, do not provide a valid foundation for decision making.

Tests are comprised of a series of short communications called questions or **items.** Each question must be brief and set a clear problem for the pupil.

Types of Test Items

There are two basic types of paper-and-pencil test questions: **selection items** and **supply items.** As their names suggest, selection items are those in which a pupil selects the correct answer from among a number of options presented, while supply items are those in which the pupil supplies or constructs his or her own answer. Within the general category of selection items are true-false, matching, and multiple choice. Supply items consist of short-answer or completion (also called fill-in-the-blank) items and essay questions.

Multiple Choice

Multiple-choice items consist of a **stem,** which presents the problem or question to the pupil, and a set of **options,** or choices, from which the pupil selects an answer. The multiple-choice format is widely used in achievement tests of all types, primarily to assess learning outcomes at the recall and comprehension levels. However, with suitable introductory material, it can also be used to assess higher-level thinking involving application, analysis, and synthesis. Item 3 below is an example of a multiple-choice item that assesses higher-level thinking. The main limitations of the multiple-choice format are that it does not allow pupils to construct, organize, and present their own answers and it is susceptible to guessing. Here are examples of multiple-choice items.

1. You use me to cover rips and tears. I am made of cloth. What am I?
   A. perch　　B. scratch　　C. patch　　D. knot

2. The basic purpose of the Marshall Plan was to
   A. provide military defense for Western Europe
   B. develop industry in African nations
   C. help American farmers during the Great Depression
   D. rebuild business and industry in Western Europe

3. Read the following passage:
   (1) For what men say is that, if I am really just and am not also thought just, profit there is none, but the pain and the loss on the
   (3) other hand is unmistakable. But if, though unjust, I acquire the reputation of justice, a heavenly life is promised to me. Since then
   (5) appearance tyrannizes over truth and is lord of happiness, to appearance I must devote myself. I will describe around me a
   (7) picture and shadow of virtue to be the vestibule and exterior of my house; behind I will trail the subtle and crafty fox.

   Which one of the following states the major premise of the passage?
   A. For what men say (line 1)
   B. if I am really just (line 1)
   C. profit there is none, but the pain and the loss (line 2)
   D. appearance tyrannizes over truth and is the lord of happiness (line 5)
   E. a picture and shadow of virtue to be the vestibule and exterior of my house (lines 7-8)

True-False

The true-false format requires pupils to classify a statement into one of two response categories: true-false, yes-no, correct-incorrect, or fact-opinion. True-false items are used mainly to assess recall and comprehension behaviors, although they also can be used to assess higher-level ones (Frisbie, 1992). The main limitation of true-false questions is their susceptibility to guessing. The following are typical true-false items:

1. The chemical symbol for calcium is Cl.   T   F

2. In the equation $E = mc^2$, when the value of m increases, the value of E also increases.   T   F

3. Read the statement. Circle T if it is true and F if it is false. If the statement is false, rewrite it to make it true by changing only the underlined part of the statement.

   The level of the cognitive taxonomy that describes recall and memory behaviors is called the synthesis level.   T   F

The main limitation of multiple-choice and true-false questions is their susceptibility to guessing.

Although primarily used to assess recall and comprehension, both multiple-choice and true-false items can be used to assess higher-level thinking.

Matching

Matching items consist of a column of **premises,** a column of **responses,** and directions for matching the two. The matching exercise is similar to a set of multiple-choice items, except that in a matching question, the same set of options or responses is used for all the premises. Its main disadvantage is that it is limited to assessing mainly lower-level behaviors. Below is an example of a matching exercise:

Matching items consist of a column of premises, a column of responses, and directions for matching the two. They assess mainly lower-level thinking.

On the line to the left of each invention in Column A, write the letter of the person in Column B who invented it. Each name in Column B may be used only once or not at all.

Column A
_____ 1. Telephone
_____ 2. Cotton gin
_____ 3. Assembly line
_____ 4. Vaccine for polio

Column B
A. Eli Whitney
B. Henry Ford
C. Jonas Salk
D. Henry McCormick
E. Alexander Graham Bell

Short Answer

Short-answer and completion items are very similar. Each presents the pupil with a question to answer. The short-answer format presents the problem with a direct question (e.g., What is the name of the first president of the United States?), while the completion format presents the problem as an incomplete sentence (e.g., The name of the first president of the United States is _____.). In each case, the pupil must supply his or her own answer. Typically, the pupil is asked to reply with a word, phrase, number, or sentence, rather than with a more extended response. Short-

Short-answer items use a direct question to present a problem; completion items use an incomplete sentence. Both tend to assess mainly factual knowledge and comprehension.

answer questions are fairly easy to construct and diminish the likelihood of pupils' guessing answers. However, they tend to assess mainly factual knowledge or comprehension.

1. Scientists who specialize in the study of plants are called _____.

Next to each state write the name of its capital city.

2. Michigan   _____

3. Massachusetts   _____

4. South Carolina   _____

5. In a single sentence, state one way that inflation lowers consumers' purchasing power.

Essay

Essay questions are most useful for assessing higher-level thinking skills but are time-consuming to answer and score and favor the student with writing ability.

Essay questions give pupils the greatest opportunity to construct their own responses. They are most useful for assessing higher-level thinking processes like analyzing, synthesizing, and evaluating. The essay question is also the main way teachers assess pupils' ability to organize, express, and defend ideas. The main limitations of essays are that they are time-consuming to answer and score, permit testing only a limited amount of pupils' learning, and place a premium on writing ability.

1. What is the value of studying science? Give your answer in complete, correct sentences. Write at least five sentences.

2. "In order for revolutionary governments to build and maintain their power, they must control the educational system." Discuss this statement using your knowledge of the American, French, and Russian Revolutions. Do you agree with the statement as it applies to the revolutionary governments in these three countries? Include specific examples to support your conclusion. Your answer will be judged on the basis of the similarities and differences you identify in the three revolutions and the extent to which your conclusion is supported by specific examples. You will have forty minutes to complete your essay.

Supply questions are most useful for assessing students' ability to organize and present their thoughts, defend positions, and integrate ideas.

Table 3.5 provides a comparison of selection and supply questions across a number of characteristics. It shows that supply questions are much more useful than selection questions in assessing pupils' ability to organize thoughts, present logical arguments, defend positions, and integrate ideas. Selection questions, on the other hand, are more useful when assessing application and problem-solving skills. Given these differences, it is not surprising that knowing the kind of item that will be on a test can influence the way pupils prepare for the test. In general, supply items encourage global, integrative study, while selection items encourage a more detailed, specific focus.

TABLE 3.5 COMPARISON OF SELECTION AND SUPPLY TEST ITEMS

	Selection	Supply
Types of items	Multiple choice, true-false, matching, interpretive exercise	Short answer, essay, completion
Behaviors assessed	Memory, recall, and comprehension; thinking and reasoning behaviors like application and analysis when using interpretive exercises	Memory, recall, and comprehension; thinking and reasoning behaviors like organizing ideas, defending positions, and integrating points
Major advantages	1. Items can be answered quickly so a broad sample of instructional topics can be surveyed on a test. 2. Items are easy and objective to score. 3. Test constructor has complete control over the stem and responses so the effect of writing ability is controlled.	1. Preparation of items relatively easy; only a few questions are needed. 2. Affords pupils a chance to construct their own answers; only way to test behaviors such as organizing and expressing information. 3. Lessens chance that pupils can guess the correct answer to items.
Major disadvantages	1. Time-consuming to construct; most time spent constructing items. 2. Many items must be constructed for a test. 3. Guessing is a problem.	1. Time-consuming to score; most time spent scoring items. 2. Covers small sample of instructional topics. 3. Bluffing is a problem.

Table 3.5 also shows that while supply and selection items consume approximately the same amount of total time to construct and score, each format allocates its time differently. Selection items are time-consuming to construct, but can be scored quite quickly. Supply items are less time-consuming to construct, but are much more time-consuming to score.

Selection items are most useful when application and problem-solving skills are assessed.

Higher-Level Test Items

There is a growing emphasis on teaching and assessing pupils' higher-level thinking behaviors. As the following quotes show, teachers recognize the importance of pupils learning how to manipulate and apply their knowledge. They know that knowledge takes on added meaning when it can be used in real-life situations.

The kids need to go beyond the facts and rote learning. You can't survive in society unless you can think, reason, and apply what you know.

It would be so boring to only teach facts. Some memorization is needed, of course, but day after day of memorization work would be demeaning to me and the pupils. I have to make room for thinking and reasoning skills.

What is more exciting for a pupil and her teacher than that moment when the pupil's eyes light up with recognition that they can solve a new problem or apply a new idea. That excitement doesn't come very often when instruction is focused on rote, memorization behaviors.

Any test question that demands more from a pupil than memory is a higher-level item.

Many people believe that essay questions are the only way to test higher-level thinking, but that is not the case. Any test question that demands more from a pupil than memory is a higher-level item. Thus, any true-false, short-answer, or multiple-choice item that requires the pupil to solve a problem, interpret a chart, or identify the relationship between two phenomena qualifies as a higher-level thinking item. Similarly, any assessment that requires pupils to demonstrate their ability to carry out an activity (e.g., give an oral talk, construct a mobile, or read an unfamiliar foreign language passage aloud) also qualifies as a higher-level performance.

Interpretive Exercise

Interpretive exercises assess higher-level skills because the pupils must interpret or apply given information.

The **interpretive exercise** is a common form of multiple-choice item that can assess higher-level thinking. An interpretive exercise gives pupils some information or data and then asks a series of selection-type questions based on that information. Item number 3 on page 96 is an example of an interpretive exercise. Generally, multiple-choice items that ask for interpretations of graphs, charts, reading passages, pictures, or tables (e.g., What is the best title for this story? According to the chart, which year had the largest decline?) are classified as interpretive exercises. These exercises can assess such higher-level behaviors as recognizing the relevance of information, identifying warranted and unwarranted generalizations, recognizing assumptions, interpreting experimental findings, and explaining pictorial materials.

To answer the questions posed, pupils have to interpret, comprehend, analyze, apply, or synthesize the information presented. Interpretive exercises assess higher-level skills because they contain all the information needed to answer the questions posed. Thus, if a pupil answers incorrectly, it is because he or she cannot do the thinking or reasoning required by the question, not because the pupil failed to memorize background information.

The principle of testing pupils' higher-level skills by providing them with necessary information and then asking questions that require them to use that information can be applied beyond the realm of interpretive exercises. Compare what might be tested in these two versions of the same question.

Version 1

In one or two sentences, describe what Henry Wadsworth Longfellow is telling the reader in the first two verses of his poem "A Psalm of Life," which we read in class but did not discuss.

Version 2

In one or two sentences describe what Henry Wadsworth Longfellow is telling the reader in these verses of his poem "A Psalm of Life."

Tell me not, in mournful numbers,
   Life is but an empty dream!—
For the soul is dead that slumbers,
   And things are not what they seem.

Life is real! Life is earnest!
   And the grave is not its goal;
Dust thou art, to dust returnest,
   Was not spoken of the soul.

If a pupil does poorly on the first version, the teacher does not know whether the pupil failed to remember the poem or, remembering the poem, could not interpret what Longfellow was trying to say. In the second version, memory is made irrelevant by providing the needed verses, and inability to interpret the poem's message is the most plausible explanation for a pupil doing poorly. Removing the need to memorize pertinent information in order to answer a higher-level thinking question permits a purer assessment of the higher-level behavior of interest. However, this approach is only useful when memorization is not a focus of the test. If a teacher wants pupils to memorize poems, formulas, rules, and the like, it makes no sense to provide them on the test.

Here are five general guidelines for constructing or judging interpretive exercises.

1. *Relevance.* The exercise must be related to the instruction provided pupils. If not, it should not be used.
2. *Similarity.* The material presented in the exercise should be new to the pupils but similar to material presented during instruction.
3. *Brevity.* There should be sufficient information for pupils to answer the questions, but the exercises should not become a test of general reading ability.
4. *Answers not provided.* The correct answers should not be found directly in the material presented. Interpretation and analysis should be needed.
5. *Multiple questions.* Include more than one question in each interpretive exercise to make most efficient use of time.

Like the essay question, the interpretive exercise is a useful way to assess higher-level behaviors. However, unlike the essay question, interpretive exercises cannot show how pupils organize their ideas when solving a problem or how well they can produce their own answers to questions.

GENERAL GUIDELINES FOR WRITING AND CRITIQUING TEST ITEMS

Whether writing your own test items or selecting those prepared by others, there are three general guidelines that help insure good tests: (1) cover important objectives; (2) write clearly and simply; and (3) review items before testing. This section discusses and illustrates these guidelines.

Cover Important Objectives

Test items should reflect important topics and skills emphasized during instruction, should be stated briefly and clearly, and should be self-contained.

One important guideline to keep in mind when preparing tests is not to focus exclusively on trivial knowledge and skills. Studies have examined the nature of the test items that classroom teachers write and have found that the vast majority assessed memory-level behaviors (Crooks, 1988; Fleming and Chambers, 1983; Marso and Pigge, 1989, 1991). From elementary school to the university, items that stress recall and memory are much more extensively used than items which assess higher-level thinking and reasoning. The reason for this is that it is much easier to write a short-answer or multiple-choice question about factual knowledge than it is to write a question which probes pupils' general understanding. In far too many instances the richness of instruction is undermined by the use of test items that trivialize the breadth and depth of the concepts and skills taught.

Each example below shows an objective taught, the test item used to assess it, and an alternative item that would have provided a more suitable assessment of the objective. Note that the poor items trivialized a higher-level objective by assessing it with a memory item.

1. *Objective:* Given a description of a literary form, the pupils can classify the form as fable, mystery, folktale, or fantasy.
   Poor item: What kind of stories did Aesop tell? _____
      A. fables   B. mysteries   C. folktales   D. fantasies
   Better item: A story tells about the year A.D. 2020 and the adventures of a young Martian named Zik, who traveled to other worlds to capture strange creatures for the zoo at Martian City. This story is best classified as a
      A. fable   B. mystery   C. folktale   D. fantasy

2. *Objective:* The pupils can describe similarities and differences in chemical compounds and elements.
   Poor item: Chlorine and Bromine are both members of a chemical group called the _____.
   Better item: Chlorine and Bromine are both halogens. What similarities do they possess that makes them halogens? What are two differences in their chemical properties?

3. *Objective:* The pupils can explain how life was changed for the Sioux Indians when they moved from the forests to the grasslands.
   Poor item: What animal did the Sioux hunt on the grasslands?
   Better item: What are three changes in the life of the Sioux that happened when they moved from the forests to the grasslands?

There are two main reasons for ensuring that the questions in an achievement test reflect the important topics and skills that were emphasized during instruction. First, if there is not a good match between instruction and the test questions, pupils' performance on the test will be a poor indication of their actual learning. Pupils may have learned what was taught but were unable to show their mastery due to an invalid test. Furthermore, the low grades that usually accompany such invalid tests often diminish pupils' academic aspirations and expectations.

Test items that do not reflect the important topics of instruction are not a valid indicator of student achievement.

Second, tests that do not match instruction will have little positive influence in motivating and focusing pupil study. If pupils find little relationship between instruction and test content, they will undervalue instruction. Each of us can remember instances when we prepared well for a test based upon the teacher's instruction and review, only to find that the test contained many questions that focused either on picky, isolated details or on types of problems that were not discussed in class. Recall how you felt when you tried to prepare for the next test given by that teacher.

The problem of mismatch between tests and instruction can be overcome to a large degree by thinking about testing earlier than the day before the test is to be given. With relatively little advanced planning, tests that assess the important aspects of instruction can be prepared.

Write Clearly and Simply: Six Rules

If test questions use ambiguous words or sentence structure, contain inappropriate vocabulary, or contain clues to correct answers, the test will not be a valid indicator of pupil achievement and will not be useful for grading or other decision making. The most important skill in writing or selecting good test items is the ability to express oneself clearly and succinctly. Test items should be: (1) briefly stated so pupils do not spend a disproportionate amount of time reading, (2) clearly expressed so pupils will understand their task, and (3) capable of standing alone since each item provides a separate measurement.

The following sections contain some confusing test items. The teachers who prepared these items knew the content they wanted to test and were convinced that they had clearly stated their intent. Unfortunately, this was not the case.

Rule 1

Avoid wording and sentence structure that are ambiguous and confusing. Test questions must be understood by pupils. If the wording or sentence structure is confusing and prevents pupils from figuring out what they are being asked, pupils will not have an opportunity to demonstrate their learning. Consider the following test items:

Example 1 All but one of the following is not an element. Which one is not?

    A. carbon   **B.** salt   **C.** sugar   **D.** plastic

Example 2 Maine is not the only state which does not have a border with a neighboring state.   T F

In examples 1 and 2, the wording and sentence construction is awkward and confusing. The pupil has to sort through multiple negatives to figure out what is being asked. It is better, therefore, to phrase questions briefly, directly, and in the positive voice, as shown in these edited versions.

Which one of these is an element?

A. carbon   **B.** salt   **C.** sugar   **D.** plastic

Maine has a common border with another state.   T F

Other items, such as examples 3 and 4, are more than just confusing, they are virtually incomprehensible.

Example 3 What is the relative length of the shortest distance between Chicago and Detroit and Sacramento? _____

Example 4 The _____ produced by the _____ is used by the green _____ to change _____ and _____ into _____. This process is known as _____.

What would be a reasonable answer to each? Example 4 is so mutilated by blank spaces that a pupil has to be a mind reader just to figure out what is being asked. No pupil should be confronted by such a question. Taken individually, the words in example 3 are not overly difficult, but their sequencing makes their intent altogether unclear. Pupils will get items like 3 and 4 wrong regardless of how well they have mastered the information and skills taught them. The following changes overcome the problems in examples 3 and 4:

Test items should be brief, clearly written, and free of ambiguous words so that comprehension is not an issue.

Which is closer to Sacramento, Chicago or Detroit?

The process in which green plants use the sun's energy to turn water and carbon dioxide into food is called _____.

If a pupil answers the revised items incorrectly, it is because the pupil did not know the desired answer. That is acceptable. Remember, the purpose of a test item is not to guarantee correct answers but to give pupils a *fair* chance to show how much they know about the things they were taught. To do this, test items must be readily comprehended.

Another factor which prevents pupils from being able to focus quickly and clearly on the question being posed is the use of ambiguous words or phrases. Read items 5, 6, and 7 and try to identify a problem in each of them that could cause pupils difficulty in deciding how to answer:

Example 5 Shakespeare was the world's greatest playwright.   T   F

Example 6 The most important city in the southeast United States is
          A. Atlanta   B. Miami   C. New Orleans   D. Tuscaloosa

Example 7 Write an essay in which you consider the future of atomic energy.

Each example contains an ambiguous term that might be puzzling to pupils and make their choice of an answer difficult. The true-false example contains the undefined word "greatest." Did the teacher mean that Shakespeare wrote more plays than any other playwright? That more of his plays are still being performed than those of any other playwright? That his plays are required reading in more American classrooms than any other playwright's? Until pupils know what the teacher means by "greatest," they will have difficulty responding. Example 6 has the same fault. What does the phrase "most important" mean? Each of these cities is important in many ways. Words like *greatest, most important, best,* and similar ambiguous words should be replaced by more specific language, regardless of the type of test item used. Note the rewritten versions of examples 5 and 6.

More of William Shakespeare's plays are required reading in American classrooms than those of any other playwright.   T   F

The main transportation center for train and airplane traffic in the southeast United States is
A. Atlanta   B. Miami   C. New Orleans   D. Tuscaloosa

In example 7 the teacher wants the pupils to "consider" the future of atomic energy. Does the teacher mean compare and contrast atomic energy to fossil fuel, discuss the relative merits of fission versus fusion as a means of generating energy, or explain the positive and negative consequences of increased use of atomic energy? It is not clear. The item needs to be more specific for the pupils to respond in the way the teacher desires.

Describe the advantages and disadvantages of increased use of atomic energy in the automobile manufacturing process.

In most cases, the teachers who wrote examples 1 to 7 knew what they wanted to ask pupils but were unable to write items that clearly conveyed their intents. Teachers must say precisely what they mean, not assume or hope that their pupils will interpret their test items in the ways intended.

Rule 2

Use appropriate vocabulary. The difficulty level of test questions can be influenced dramatically by their vocabulary. If pupils cannot understand the vocabulary used in test questions, their test scores will reflect their vocabulary deficiencies rather than how much they have learned from instruction, and thus be invalid. Every teacher should take into account the vocabulary level of his or her pupils when writing or selecting the items for achievement tests. Note the difference in the following two ways of writing a true-false question to assess pupils' understanding of capillary action, a principle which explains how liquids rise in narrow passages.

1. The postulation of capillary effectuation promotes elucidation of how pliant substances ascend in incommodious veins.   T F

2. The principle of capillary action helps explain how liquids rise in small passages.   T F

Clearly, vocabulary level can affect pupils' ability to understand what is being asked in a test question.

Rule 3

Questions should be short, specific, and written to pupils' vocabulary level.

Keep questions short and to the point. Items should quickly focus pupils on the question being asked. Examine these questions.

Example 8 Switzerland
    A. is located in Asia
    B. produces large quantities of gold
    C. has no direct access to the ocean
    D. is a flat arid plain

Example 9 Billy's mother wanted to bake an apple pie for his aunt and uncle who were coming for a visit. Billy had not seen them for many months. When Billy's mother saw that she had no apples in the house, she sent Billy to the store to buy some. Her recipe called for 8 apples to make a pie. If apples at the store cost 30 cents for two, how much money will Billy need to buy eight apples?
    A. $0.30   **B.** $0.90   **C.** $1.20   **D.** $2.40

In example 8, the stem does not clearly set a problem for pupils. That is, after pupils read the item stem "Switzerland," they still have no idea of the question being asked. Only after reading the stem *and* all the options does the point of the item begin to become clear. The item could be more directly stated as follows:

Which of the following statements about the geography of Switzerland is true?
A. It is located in Asia.
B. It is a flat arid plain.
C. It has no direct access to an ocean.
D. It has a tropical climate.

Example 9 seeks to find out whether the pupil can correctly determine the cost of some apples. The information about the aunt and uncle's visit, how long it had been since Billy last saw them, or the lack of apples in the house is not important, can be distracting, and takes time away from relevant items. A better way to state the item is

To make an apple pie Billy's mother needed 8 apples. If apples cost 30 cents for 2, how much will 8 apples cost?
A. $0.30   B. $0.90   C. $1.20   D. $2.40

In short-answer or completion items the blanks should come at the end of the sentence so pupils know what kind of a response is required. Compare these two items and notice how placing the blank at the end helps one to get a quicker grasp of what the item is about:

_____ and _____ are the names of two rivers that meet in Pittsburgh.

The names of two rivers that meet in Pittsburgh are _____ and _____.

Matching items can also be written to help focus pupils more quickly on the questions being asked. Look over example 10 and suggest a change that would help focus pupils more clearly on the questions they have to answer.

Example 10 Draw a line to match the President in Column A with his accomplishment in Column B.

Column A	Column B
G. Washington	Signed the Emancipation Proclamation
T. Jefferson	President during the New Deal
U. Grant	First President of the United States
F. Roosevelt	Head of Northern troops in Civil War
	Main author of the Declaration of Independence

Most matching items can be improved by placing the column with the lengthier descriptions on the left and the column with the shorter descriptions on the right, as shown below.

Draw a line to match the President in Column B with his accomplishment in Column A. One accomplishment will not be used.

Column A
Signed the Emancipation Proclamation
President during the New Deal
First President of the United States
Head of Northern troops in Civil War
Main author of the Declaration of Independence

Column B
G. Washington
T. Jefferson
U. Grant
F. Roosevelt

Rule 4

With the exception of
essays, most test items
should have only one
correct answer.

Write items that have one correct answer. With the exception of essay questions, most paper-and-pencil test items are designed to have pupils select or supply one best answer. With this goal in mind, read examples 11, 12, and 13. See how many correct answers you can provide for each item.

Example 11 Who was George Washington?

Example 12 Ernest Hemingway wrote _____.

Example 13 Where is Dublin located?
A. south of Scotland   B. near England   C. Ireland   D. in the Irish Sea

Each of these items has more than one correct answer. George Washington was the first President of the United States, but he also was a member of the Continental Congress, commander of the Continental Army, a Virginian, a surveyor, a slaveowner, and a man with false teeth. Faced with such an item, pupils ask themselves, "Which of the many things I know about George Washington should I answer?" Similarly, Ernest Hemingway wrote short stories and letters as well as famous novels such as *The Old Man and the Sea*.

Examples 11, 12, and 13 can be restated so that pupils know precisely what is being asked of them. Notice how each question asks for something specific, thus indicating to pupils the nature of the expected correct answer.

What was the name of the first President of the United States?

The name of the author of *The Old Man and the Sea* is _____.

In what country is Dublin located?
A. England   B. France   C. Germany   D. Ireland   E. Spain

Items with more than one correct answer occur much more often in short-answer and completion items than in selection items. Unless short-answer or completion items are stated specifically and narrowly, the teacher can expect many different responses. The dilemma for the teacher then becomes whether to give credit for answers that are technically correct but not the desired one. Stating the short-answer or completion item narrowly at the start will prevent such dilemmas.

Rule 5

Give information about the nature of the desired answer. While the failure to properly focus pupils is common to all types of test items, it is most often seen in essay items. Despite pupils' freedom to structure their own responses, essay questions should still require pupils to demonstrate mastery of key ideas, principles, or concepts that were taught. An essay, like any other type of test item, should be constructed to find out how well pupils have learned the things they were taught.

Here are a few typical essay questions written by classroom teachers:

Example 14 Compare and contrast the north and south in the Civil War. Support your views.

Example 16 Describe what happened to art during the Renaissance.

Example 16 Why should you study science?

In each of these questions, the pupil's task is not clearly defined. When pupils encounter global questions such as these, they may have little idea of what the teacher is looking for and may end up with a poor grade because they guessed wrong about the teacher's intent. This practice is unfair to pupils and produces test results that do not reflect pupils' achievement.

In order to determine whether pupils have learned what was taught, essay questions should be narrowed to focus pupils on the areas of interest. Pupils should be informed about the anticipated nature and scope of their answer. While essay questions should provide the pupil freedom to select, organize, state, and defend positions, they should not afford pupils total freedom to write whatever they want. Obviously, to develop a well-focused essay question the teacher must give considerable thought to the purpose and scope of the question before actually writing it.

Essay questions should focus students' answers on the major points covered by instruction.

Below, examples 14, 15, and 16 have been rewritten to reflect more precisely the teacher's intent. Notice how the vague and ambiguous directions ("Support your views," and "Describe") are made clearer to pupils in the revised questions.

Example 14 What forces led to the outbreak of the Civil War? Indicate in your discussion economic conditions, foreign policies, and social conditions in both the north and the south before the war. Which two factors were most influential in the start of the Civil War? Give two reasons to support your choice of each factor. Your answer will be graded on your discussion of the differences between the north and the south at the start of the war and the strength of the arguments you advance to support your choice of the two factors most influential in the start of the war. (thirty minutes)

Example 15 Compare art during the Renaissance to art prior to the Renaissance in terms of the portrayal of the human figure, use of color, and emphasis on religious themes. Your essay will be judged in terms of the distinctions you identify between the two periods and the explanations you provide to account for the differences.

Example 16 Give two reasons a third-grade pupil should study science. What are some things that studying science teaches us? What are some jobs that use science? Write your answer in at least five complete sentences.

Certainly these are not the only ways that these essay items could have been rewritten, but these revisions point out the need for focus in essay questions. When pupils approach these revised items, they have a clear sense of what is expected of them; they no longer have to guess regarding the desired scope and direction of their answers. Note also that it is much more difficult for the pupil to bluff an answer to the revised items than it is to the initial, broadly stated items. The revised items call for answers that are specifically related to instruction and, therefore, test what was taught. In order to write such items, however, the teacher must have a clear sense of what he or she is trying to assess.

For all types of test items, pupils should have a clear sense of what is expected of them.

To summarize, regardless of the particular type of test item used, pupils should be given a clear idea of what their task is. In the case of multiple-choice items, this may mean elaborating a stem in order to clarify the options. In matching items, it may involve putting the longer options in the left column. In short-answer or completion items, it may mean placing the blank at the end of the statement or specifying precisely the nature of the desired answer. In essay questions, it may mean elaborating the question to include information about the scope, direction, and scoring criteria for a desired answer. In all cases, the intent is to allow the pupil to respond most validly and efficiently to the items.

Rule 6

Writers of test items should take care not to provide grammatical clues, implausible option clues, or specific determiner clues.

Do not provide clues to the correct answer. The item-writing rules discussed thus far have all been aimed at problems that inhibited pupils from doing their best. However, the opposite problem arises when teachers' items contain clues that help pupils answer questions correctly even though they have not learned the content being tested. Many types of clues may appear in items: grammatical clues, "implausible option" clues, and "specific determiner" clues. Try to identify the clues in examples 17 and 18.

Example 17 A figure that has eight sides is called an

     A. pentagon   **B.** quadrilateral   **C.** octagon   **D.** ogive

Example 18 As compared to autos of the 1960s, autos in the 1980s

     A. bigger interiors
     B. to use less fuel
     C. contain more safety features
     D. was less constructed in foreign countries

These examples contain grammatical clues to the correct answer. In example 17, using the article "a" or "an" at the end of the question or stem indicates to pupils what letter will begin the next word. The "an" before the blank tells the pupil that the next word must begin with a vowel, so the options "pentagon" and "quadrilateral" cannot be correct. There are two ways to correct this problem: replace the single article with the combined "a(n)" or get rid of the article altogether by writing the question in the plural form.

Figures that have eight sides are called

A. pentagons   **B.** quadrilaterals   **C.** octagons   **D.** ogives

In example 18, only option C grammatically fits the stem. Regardless of pupils' knowledge, they can select the correct answer because of the grammatical clue. Now try to find the clues in examples 19 and 20.

Example 19 Which of the following best describes an electron?

     A. negative particle   **B.** neutral particle
     C. positive particle   **D.** a voting machine

Example 20 Match the correct phrase in Column A with the term in Column B. Write the <u>letter</u> of the term in Column B on the line in front of the correct phrase in Column A.

Column A	Column B
_____ 1. Type of flower	**A.** Cobra
_____ 2. Poisonous snake	**B.** Fission
_____ 3. How amoeba reproduce	**C.** Green
_____ 4. Color of chlorophyll	**D.** Hydrogen
_____ 5. Chemical element	**E.** Rose

Example 19 contains a clue that is less obvious than those in examples 17 and 18 but which is quite common in multiple-choice items. One of the options is inappropriate or implausible and therefore is immediately dismissed by the pupils. Choice D, "a voting machine," will be dismissed as an unlikely answer by all but the most careless readers. As much as possible, options in test questions should be realistic and reasonable choices. A useful rule of thumb to follow is to have at least three incorrect (but reasonable) options, or **distractors,** in each multiple-choice item.

A distractor is a reasonable but incorrect option in a multiple-choice item.

The more choices pupils have, the less likely it is that they can guess the correct answer. Understanding this, teachers sometimes write three or four good options for an item and then add on a fourth or fifth option such as "none of the above" or "all of the above." It is usually better to avoid these options.

Example 20 is a very easy item. The reason for this is because the topics to be matched are so different from one another that many of the options in Column B are implausible matches to the statements in Column A. The item does not test one homogeneous subject area. Consider the following matching item which tests pupils' knowledge of a single, homogeneous topic. Note the difficulty in answering this item compared to example 20.

A matching item should test the students' knowledge of a single, homogeneous topic.

Match the names of the animals in Column A to their correct classification in Column B. Write the letter of the correct classification on the line in front of each animal name. The choices in Column B may be used more than once.

Column A	Column B
_____ 1. Alligator	A. Amphibian
_____ 2. Condor	B. Bird
_____ 3. Frog	C. Fish
_____ 4. Porpoise	D. Mammal
_____ 5. Snake	E. Reptile
_____ 6. Salamander	

The revised item is a better test of pupils' knowledge in two ways. First, it does not include the obvious matches and mismatches that occur when many unrelated topics are contained in the same item. The revised version focuses on a single topic, classification of animals into groups. Second, unlike example 20, the revised item has an unequal number of entries in Columns A and B. Unequal entries in the two columns of a matching item prevent pupils from getting the last match correct by a process of elimination.

Look for the clues in examples 21 and 22:

Example 21 Some people think the moon is made of green cheese.   **T F**

Example 22 One should never phrase a test item in the negative.   **T F**

These items contain clues that are called **specific determiners.** In true-false questions, words such as *always, never, all,* and *none* tend to appear in statements that are false and testwise pupils tend to answer accordingly. Conversely, words like *some, sometimes,* and *may* tend to appear in statements that are true. Thus, in example 21, it is reasonable to assume that *some* people think the moon is made of green cheese, so example 21 should be marked T. On the other hand, example 22 must be marked F if one can think of even a single situation in which a test item can reasonably be stated in the negative (e.g., Which one of these is *not* an example of democracy?).

Table 3.6 provides a list of common item-writing rules that pertain to each of the various item types discussed in this chapter. These rules supplement the more general item-writing principles just considered.

Review Items before Testing

The single best piece of advice that can be given to improve most classroom tests is to review them before reproducing and administering them to pupils. Having written or selected the items for a chapter or unit test, wait one day and reread them. If one has a colleague, spouse, or friend who is willing to review the items critically, this is very desirable.

Have a colleague or friend critique your test items before the test is administered to students.

We have now examined most of the links in the chain of achievement testing. We have discussed the importance of providing pupils with good instruction, the decisions that must be made in planning achievement tests, the instructional review that should precede testing, and the construction or selection of test items that give pupils a fair chance to demonstrate their learning. Two final links which influence the adequacy of achievement tests are assembling and administering the test and scoring the test.

TABLE 3.6   SUGGESTIONS FOR PREPARING TEST ITEMS

Multiple Choice
- Set pupils' task in the item stem.
- Include repeated words in the stem.
- Avoid grammatical clues.
- Use positive wording if possible.
- Include only plausible options.
- Avoid using "all of the above" or "none of above."

Matching
- Use a homogeneous topic.
- Put longer options in left column.
- Provide clear direction.
- Use unequal numbers of entries in the two columns.

Essay
- Use several short-essay questions rather than one long one.
- Provide a clear focus for pupils in questions.
- Indicate scoring criteria to pupils.

True-False
- Make statements clearly true or false.
- Avoid specific determiners.
- Do not arrange responses in a pattern.
- Do not select textbook sentences.

Completion and Short Answer
- Provide a clear focus for the desired answer.
- Avoid grammatical clues.
- Put blanks at the end of the item.
- Do not select textbook sentences.

ASSEMBLING THE TEST

Once items have been reviewed and revised, they must be arranged into a test. If one uses a textbook test, the items will already be arranged and ready for copying. In assembling one's own test, similar types of items should be grouped together and kept separate from other item types. Grouping items by type (1) avoids the necessity of pupils shifting from one response mode to another as they move from item to item, (2) means that a single set of directions can be used for all of the items in that test section, and (3) makes scoring easier.

Another important consideration in assembling the test is the order in which the item types are presented to pupils. Place selection items first and supply items last so that pupils will not devote a disproportionate amount of time to these latter items. Within the supply section, short-answer or completion questions should be placed before essay questions.

Finally, in arranging items on the test, remember these common-sense practices.

1. Little pupils write big, so leave enough space, especially on essay tests, for young pupils to write their answers.
2. Don't split a multiple-choice or matching item across two different pages of the test.
3. Place multiple-choice options on a new line below the stem.
4. Number test items, especially if pupils must record answers on a separate answer sheet or in a special place on the test.

Each section of the test should have directions that focus pupils on what to do, how to respond, and where to place their answer. For older pupils, it is also helpful to indicate the number of points that will be given to each test section so they can make decisions about how to allocate their time. Lack of directions is one of the most common faults in teachers' tests. Here are some sample directions.

♦ Items 1 to 15 are multiple-choice items. Read each item carefully and write the <u>letter</u> of your answer on the line in front of the question number.

♦ Answer each question by writing the correct answer in the space below the question. No answer should be longer than one sentence.

♦ Mark each statement true or false. <u>Circle</u> the letter (T or F) of your choice.

The test should be reproduced so that each pupil has his or her own copy. Writing the test questions on the blackboard can be time-consuming, create problems for pupils with poor vision, and encourage pupils to look around the room during test taking. Orally read questions place a pre-

TABLE 3.7   GUIDELINES FOR ASSEMBLING A TEST

- Organize the test by item type: selection before supply, essay last.
- Allow sufficient space for written responses, especially for young children's essay items.
- Don't split multiple-choice or matching items across two pages; separate stem from options in multiple-choice questions.
- Number test items.
- Provide clear directions for each section of the test; for older pupils, indicate value of each section or question.
- Provide enough questions to assure reliability.

mium on listening ability and prevent pupils from working at their own pace. They should be avoided unless one is assessing listening skills.

Tests that promote valid decisions also need to be reliable. The main factors in attaining reliable achievement tests are (1) the number and representativeness of the items included on the test and (2) the objectivity of scoring. In general, the more items on the test the higher its reliability, because the test allows a teacher to look at a larger sample of pupil performance. Which of the following spelling tests do you think would produce the more stable and consistent information about a pupil's spelling achievement? Test 1, which consists of a single word selected from a 100-word list, or Test 2, which contains a sample of 15 words selected from the same 100 word list? Table 3.7 summarizes guidelines for assembling tests.

The more items on a test the higher its reliability, because the teacher can look at a larger sample of pupil performance.

ADMINISTERING THE TEST

Test administration is concerned with the physical and psychological setting in which pupils take the test. The aim is to establish both a physical and psychological setting that permits pupils to maximize their test performance.

Physical Setting

Pupils should have a quiet, comfortable environment in which to take the test. Interruptions should be minimized by posting a sign on the door indicating testing is going on. When an interruption does occur, the teacher must make a judgment about whether it is fair for pupils to continue with testing. Obviously a one-minute interruption is less disruptive than a

One way to minimize interruptions during testing is to post a sign on the door indicating testing is being conducted.

fifteen-minute fire drill, which gives pupils an opportunity to talk to one another about the test. If it is judged that an interruption was sufficiently disruptive to diminish pupils' ability to provide a fair and representative indication of their achievement, testing should be terminated.

Occasionally typographical errors or problems with items are not detected until testing has begun, usually when a pupil points out a problem. In such situations, an announcement should be made to the whole class informing them of the problem (e.g., "Please correct item 17 in the following way" or "Option B in item 29 should be changed to . . . "). A general rule of thumb is not to aid a pupil by providing a clue to the correct answer. In the end, the decision of whether and how to answer pupil questions rests with the individual teacher. This is appropriate as long as the teacher is consistent in responding to all pupils who ask questions.

Psychological Setting

Test anxiety is diminished by giving students advance notice of the test, an opportunity to prepare for it, and by conducting a test review.

Establishing a productive psychological setting that reduces pupil anxiety and sets a proper atmosphere for testing is as important as providing a comfortable physical environment. Giving pupils advance notice about the test, giving them an opportunity to prepare for it, and providing a good chapter or unit review will help diminish test anxiety. Even so, it is probably impossible to completely allay all pupils' test anxiety.

The line between overemphasizing the importance of the test, thereby heightening pupil anxiety, and underemphasizing the test, thereby diminishing pupil motivation, is hard to define. Tests should be taken seriously by pupils and they should be encouraged to do their best. The appropriate middle ground between over- and underemphasizing the importance of tests will vary with the age and characteristics of pupils. Each teacher must find the middle ground for his or her class knowing that whatever preparations are chosen, there will usually be some pupils who will be very anxious about their performance and some who will not care.

Cheating

Unfortunately, cheating on tests is a fairly common occurrence that has a variety of motives. Pupils may experience external pressure from teachers or parents to do well; they may fail to prepare for tests and rely upon cheating to get them through; they may be in an intensively competitive classroom where the teacher's policy is one of grading on the curve; or they may be confused about what is acceptable behavior in a classroom where "everybody else does it."

The forms of cheating vary from looking at another's paper to bringing crib sheets to an exam to hiring someone to take one's test (Ebel and Fris-

---

TABLE 3.8   STRATEGIES TO PREVENT CHEATING

Strategies prior to Testing

- Teach well; be sensitive to pupils' instructional needs and misunderstandings.
- Announce the test ahead of time; give pupils ample opportunity to prepare.
- Describe for pupils the general nature and content of the test.
- Identify for pupils what constitutes cheating and explain the consequences if caught.

Strategies during Testing

- Have pupils remove all unneeded materials from their desktop.
- Space pupils about the room; have them sit in alternating seats.
- Watch students during testing; move about the room quietly.
- Forbid sharing of materials like erasers, calculators, and charts.
- Prepare different test forms or arrange pages in varying orders.
- Enforce established cheating rules.

---

bie, 1991). No matter how or why it is done, cheating is dishonest and unacceptable behavior. It is the teacher's responsibility to discourage cheating by seating arrangements, careful proctoring, and other activities (Bushway and Nash, 1977; Slavin, 1994). Table 3.8 presents suggestions to control cheating, both before and during testing.

Teachers can discourage cheating through seating arrangements, careful proctoring, and swift punishment of those who do cheat.

If some pupils do cheat, those who don't are unfairly penalized for their appropriate and ethical behavior. Teachers should discourage cheating and penalize pupils caught doing it, because it is both an immoral activity and provides a distorted, invalid picture of a pupil's achievement. It is, however, important to have strong evidence to support charges of cheating, since pupils have certain due process rights when accused (Hills, 1981). Table 3.9 summarizes important concerns in test administration.

TABLE 3.9   GUIDELINES FOR ADMINISTERING A TEST

- Provide a quiet, comfortable setting.
- Try to anticipate and avoid questions through good directions.
- Provide a good psychological setting: Provide advance notice, review, and encouragement for pupils to do their best.
- Discourage cheating through seating arrangements, circulating around the room, and enforcement of rules and penalties.
- Help pupils keep track of time.

SCORING TESTS

Measurement is the process of representing an individual's performance level by a number.

After administering a test, the teacher is left with a stack of papers that represent each pupil's performance. In order to use this information, the teacher must first summarize it, and scoring is the most common way of doing this. The process of scoring a test involves **measurement,** that is, representing an individual's performance level in terms of a number. In achievement tests, performance on the test items is translated into a score that is used in making decisions about the pupil.

Of course, when pupil achievement is measured by test scores, each pupil should be measured in exactly the same way. Whatever rules are used for scoring one pupil should also be applied to all other pupils. It would be unfair to give Jessica 5 points for getting an item correct and Ron or Arthur only 2 points for their equally correct answer to the same item. Thus, good measurement requires that common rules be used when assigning those numbers.

Scoring Selection Items

Selection items can be scored objectively because they are usually brief and have only one correct answer.

Selection-type items are easiest to score, short-answer and completion items next easiest, and essays most difficult. On selection items, pupils respond by writing, circling, or marking the letter of their response. Scoring selection items is essentially a clerical task that involves comparing each pupil's answers to a **key** showing the correct answers. The number of matches indicates the pupil's score on the test.

Scoring selection test items is usually quite objective, meaning that independent scorers will arrive at the same or very similar scores. The main reason that selection items produce objective scores is because answers are brief and there is one clearly correct answer to each item. However, as pupils' responses to questions become more lengthy and complex, and as the clarity of what is a correct or incorrect answer blurs, test scoring becomes more subjective and time-consuming. **Subjectivity** refers to those tests where independent scorers would not arrive at the same or similar scores. In subjective tests, a pupil's performance depends as much on *who* scores the test as on the pupil's answers. It has long been known that even when the same person scores the same essay test twice, there is no guarantee that the scores will be the same or similar (Starch and Elliott, 1912; Starch and Elliott, 1913). If we are to have confidence in a test score, it is important that the score be objective.

Subjective test scores are those where independent scorers have difficulty arriving at the same or similar scores.

To have confidence in a test score, it is important that the score be as objective as possible.

Scoring Short-Answer and Completion Items

As long as short-answer and completion items are clearly written, focus pupils on their task, and call for a short response such as a word, phrase, date, or number, scoring is not difficult and quite objective. However, as such items require lengthier pupil responses, subjectivity of scoring will increase because more interpretations of what pupils knew or meant to say will have to be made.

No matter how well a teacher has prepared and reviewed test items of any kind, he or she never knows how an item will work until *after* it is administered to pupils. Inevitably, there are occasions when pupils' responses to a carefully constructed item reveal that most pupils misinterpreted it. The pupils' answers are correct given their interpretation, but incorrect given the teacher's intention. How should such occurrences be handled in scoring?

In scoring unexpected responses, teachers must decide if wrong answers are the result of faulty test items or a lack of student learning.

How a teacher interprets pupils' unexpected responses influences their test scores and grades. For example, suppose that one item in a 10-item achievement test reveals many unexpected responses. If the teacher simply marks these responses wrong because they do not match the answer key, he or she may be penalizing pupils for his or her own faulty test item. This 10 percent deduction could make a big difference in a pupil's eventual grade.

In reviewing unexpected responses, the teacher must decide if wrong answers are the result of faulty items or a lack of pupil learning. Test scores should not automatically be raised simply because many pupils got an item wrong, but the teacher must make a judgment about the likely source of the problem and how it will be rectified, if at all. Recognize, however, that if problem items are not examined and analyzed, no reasonable decision can be made.

In the end, scoring decisions rest with the teacher. Teachers must decide who is at fault when pupils misinterpret an item and whether pupils should lose credit for wrong answers on items that were not discussed in class. Two principles should be considered in making such decisions. First, since the test scores should reflect pupils' achievement on the chapter or unit being tested, the scores should deal only with topics that were taught and with items that are clearly written. If points are deducted for things not taught or for misinterpreting ambiguous questions, the score will not reflect true achievement. Second, whatever decision is made regarding the scoring of poor or untaught items, it should be applied uniformly to all pupils.

Test scores that reflect ambiguous or untaught items are less valid indicators of student achievement.

Scoring Essay Items

Essay questions represent the ultimate in scoring complexity because they permit pupils to construct their own unique responses to the question. Therefore, interpretation of the responses is necessary. Moreover, the answer to an essay question is presented in a form that contains many distractions that contribute to subjective scoring.

Think of an essay answer you have written. Remember what it looked like spread out over the page. Keep in mind that the purpose of the question was to determine how well you understood and could manipulate information you had been taught. However, the person who scored your essay was probably influenced by many of the following characteristics:

♦ Handwriting
♦ Writing style, including sentence structure and flow
♦ Spelling and grammar
♦ Neatness
♦ Fatigue of the scorer
♦ Identity of the pupil
♦ Location of one's test paper in the pile of test papers

Many types of scorer subjectivity can influence how an essay item is scored.

Each of these factors can influence a teacher's reaction to an essay answer, although none of them has anything to do with the actual content of the pupil's response. For example, a pupil whose penmanship is so poor that it forces the teacher to figure out what each scribbled word means will frustrate the teacher and divert attention away from the content of the answer. The essay likely will get a lower score than that of another pupil who provides exactly the same answer in more legible handwriting. A pupil whose answer flows smoothly and interestingly from point to point likely will get a better score than a pupil who states the same points in a string of simple, declarative sentences. Poor grammar and misspelled words create a negative impression and may also divert a teacher's attention away from the content of the pupil's response. And neatness does make a good impression on teachers.

Scoring essays is also a time-consuming and tiring task, and scores may be influenced by how alert the teacher was when the essays were read. After the teacher has read the same general response twenty or so times, boredom and fatigue begin to set in, and pupils who provide essentially the same answer may get scores different from those whose essays were read earlier.

In almost all essay questions there is at least one point when the reader must interpret what the pupil meant to say because the pupil expressed his or her thoughts ambiguously. Knowledge of whose answer is being read often influences the teacher's interpretation. For example, Roger and Alicia have each answered an essay question and included some statements that were ambiguous. The teacher knows that Roger is an interested, able pupil who always does well on tests and in class discussions. The teacher reasons, "Although Roger didn't make this point clearly, he probably knew the answer even though it didn't come out right. I'll give him the credit." The teacher also knows that Alicia generally does poorly in school and remembers her indifference during a recent class discussion. The teacher thinks, "Since Alicia is a poor student and doesn't care about this subject, she probably had no idea of what was correct here. She will get no credit." One way to avoid such biased scoring is to identify papers by number or have pupils put their names on the last page of a test. Notice that knowing the pupil's identity is not a problem in scoring selection items, because scoring involves little interpretation and few distractions.

Lastly, consider the following situation. At the end of an essay exam your teacher allows you to put your test paper anywhere you wish in the pile of pupil papers to be graded. The instructor tells you that she or he will start with the top paper and work down through the pile in order. Where would you place your test paper? Could your placement make a difference in your score? If you think it could, what does this say about the potential subjectivity of essay tests? If essay scores are to represent pupils' achievement and be used as a basis for grading or making other decisions about pupils, it is important that a teacher have confidence that their scores are as objective as possible.

Holistic versus Analytic Scoring

Teachers typically use two approaches to scoring essay questions: holistic and analytic (Tindal and Marston, 1990). **Holistic scores** give a teacher's *overall impression* of the whole essay by providing a single score or grade. **Analytic scoring,** on the other hand, views the essay as being made up of many components and provides *separate scores* for each one. Thus, an essay that is scored analytically might result in separate scores for factual accuracy, organization, supporting arguments, and grammar and spelling. Analytic scoring provides more detailed feedback that pupils can use to improve their essays. Consequently, it is especially useful when scoring initial drafts of essays. However, attempting to score more than three or four separate features often makes scoring confusing and time-consuming. In both holistic or analytic scoring, helpful or encouraging suggestions written on pupils' tests are recommended.

Holistic scores provide a single, overall impression of the complete essay. Analytic scores provide a separate score for each component of the essay.

Steps to Ensure Objectivity

Regardless of whether a teacher uses holistic or analytic scoring, certain steps should be followed to ensure that pupils' essays are scored objectively. Although the following suggestions are time-consuming, they are necessary if scores are to be valid for decision making.

1. *Define what constitutes a good answer before administering an essay question.* The less focused an essay question is, the broader the range of pupil responses that will be written, and the more difficult it will be to apply uniform scoring criteria. Including information about the pupil's specific task, the scope of the essay, and the scoring criteria in the essay directions has numerous benefits. First, it helps pupils respond to a precise set of teacher expectations. This in turn will diminish scoring subjectivity. Second, by writing questions which clearly indicate the characteristics of a good answer, the teacher has to confront the issue of scoring before testing. The criteria that focus pupils' responses are also the basic criteria that will be used in scoring the pupils' answers.

A well-focused essay item will include scoring criteria and specific information about the pupils' task.

2. *In multiple-essay tests, score all pupils' answers to the first question before moving to the second question.* If it is difficult to score a single essay question objectively, it is more difficult to score two or three different essay questions in succession. Scoring all the answers to a single essay question at one time ensures against the "carryover effect": the tendency to let one's reaction to a pupil's initial essay influence one's perception of succeeding essays written by that same pupil.

3. *Read essay answers a second time after initial scoring.* The best way to check for objectivity in essay scoring is to have a second individual read and score pupils' papers using the same criteria as the teacher used to score them. Since this is usually impractical, except when making very important decisions (e.g., awarding a scholarship, selecting for an honor society), an acceptable procedure is for the teacher to reread and, if necessary, rescore a sample of papers before finalizing the scores. Two scorings by the same person, even if done quickly and on only a sample of papers, are better than a single scoring and lead to more objective decision making.

Essay questions permit the assessment of many thought processes that can be assessed in no other way. When such thought processes are part of the instructional objectives and are actively taught to pupils, they should be assessed to obtain a representative picture of pupil learning. Nevertheless, when using essay questions, one must realize the difficulty inherent in scoring them and the dangers of scoring them improperly. A teacher should use essay questions if they are the best way to assess what has been taught, but time should be set aside to score them objectively so that their results can be used with confidence. Table 3.10 summarizes guidelines to follow when scoring tests.

Before scores of essay items are finalized, check for objectivity by rereading and, if necessary, rescoring a sample of papers.

TABLE 3.10   GUIDELINES FOR SCORING A TEST

- Test scores should be based upon topics that were taught and items that are clearly written.
- Make sure the same rules are used to score all pupils.
- Be alert for the following distractors that may impede the objectivity of essay scores: writing style, grammar and spelling, neatness, scorer fatigue, prior pupil performance, and carryover effects.
- Define what constitutes a good answer before administering an essay question.
- Score all answers to the first essay question before moving on to score the succeeding question.
- Read essay questions a second time after initial scoring.
- Carry out post-test review in order to locate faulty test items and, when necessary, to make scoring adjustments.

DISCUSS TEST RESULTS WITH PUPILS

Pupils want information about their test performance. Teachers can provide this information through comments written on papers, tests, or projects which indicate to pupils what they did well and how they might improve. It also is helpful to go over the results of a test with pupils. This is especially useful when the pupils have their marked tests in front of them during the review. The teacher should pay special attention to items that a large proportion of the class got wrong in order to clear up misconceptions and to indicate the nature of the desired answer. For older pupils it also is helpful to explain how the tests were scored and graded. Finally, opportunity should be provided for shy pupils to discuss the test in private with the teacher.

Going over test results when pupils have the graded test in front of them is useful.

CHAPTER SUMMARY

◆ Official assessments help teachers make summative decisions such as assigning grades, recommending pupils for promotion, placing pupils in groups, and referring pupils to special education services.

◆ Official assessments are taken very seriously by pupils, parents, school administrators, and the public at large because they are public and can have tangible consequences for pupils.

◆ The methods used to assess pupil learning depend on the objectives and instruction provided. Methods that permit the pupils to show the behaviors taught are essential for valid assessment. Use multiple-choice, matching, or true-false questions when pupils are taught to "choose" or "select" answers; short-answer or essay questions when pupils are taught to "explain," "construct," or "defend" answers; and actual performances when pupils are taught to "demonstrate" or "show." The most basic requirement for official assessments is that they assess what pupils were taught.

◆ The decision whether to construct one's own test or use a textbook test depends upon how closely instruction followed the lead of the textbook. The more a teacher supplements or omits from the textbook, the less likely the textbook test will be a valid indication of pupils' learning.

◆ Preparing pupils for official assessments requires careful teacher thought and planning. First and foremost, teachers should provide the best instruction possible prior to assessment. Good instruction should be followed up by a review that gives pupils a chance to ask questions and practice important behaviors and skills that will be tested. Pupils, especially those in early elementary grades, should be given practice with item formats that they are not familiar with before testing. Pupils should be informed in advance of the time, nature, coverage, and format of the test.

◆ In preparing pupils for testing, teachers should discuss items and examples similar but not identical to the actual test items.

- Paper-and-pencil tests can be composed of two types of questions: selection (multiple choice, true-false, and matching) and supply (short answer, completion, and essay). Both types of questions can assess higher- and lower-level thinking.

- Selection items can be answered quickly, cover a broad sample of instructional topics, and are scored objectively. However, they are time-consuming to construct, and guessing is a problem. Supply items can be prepared easily, afford pupils opportunity to construct their own answers, and discourage guessing. However, they are difficult and time-consuming to score and tend to cover a limited amount of instructional topics.

- Teachers should try to include higher-level thinking questions in both their instruction and formal assessments. The interpretive exercise is a useful way to incorporate higher-level skills into paper-and-pencil assessments.

- When writing or selecting paper-and-pencil test questions, three general guidelines should be followed: Cover important topics and behaviors, write clearly and simply, and review items before testing.

- Most of the items in teacher and textbook tests are at the recall or memory level of thinking, because such items are easiest to write. However, if tests are to be valid, they should reflect all the content and behaviors taught, both lower and higher level.

- Six rules that guide item writing are: (1) Avoid wording that is ambiguous and confusing; (2) use appropriate vocabulary and sentence structure for pupils; (3) keep questions short and to the point; (4) write items that have one correct answer; (5) give pupils information about the desired answer; and (6) do not provide clues to the correct answer.

- In assembling items into a test, similar item types should be grouped together. Selection items should be placed at the start of the test and supply items at the end. Short-answer items should be placed before essay items.

- Each section of the test should have directions that tell pupils what to do, how to respond, and where to place their answers. Older pupils may also be helped by knowing how much each item is worth. Each pupil should have his or her own copy of the test.

- Providing advanced warning of a test, reviewing important objectives, and encouraging pupils to do their best without exerting undo pressure will help set a suitable psychological climate in which pupils can perform their best.

- Cheating is an unacceptable, dishonest testing behavior. It is the teacher's responsibility to establish conditions that reduce cheating by pupil seating arrangements, constantly circulating around the classroom, forbidding pupils to share materials, and enforcing cheating rules and penalties.

- An objective test item is one that independent scorers would score the same or similarly. A subjective item is one where independent scorers would not score the item the same. Factors that contribute to subjectivity include handwriting, style, grammar, and knowledge of the pupils.

- Selection items are usually easy to score objectively because they involve comparing a pupil's response to an answer key. Supply items become increasingly subjective as pupils are given more freedom to construct their own answers. Essay items are the most subjective kind of item.

- The two principal methods of scoring essay tests are holistic scoring, which produces a single overall score for an essay, and analytic scoring, which produces a number of scores corresponding to particular features of the essay (e.g., organization and style).

♦ In order to make essay scoring objective, a teacher should: decide what factors constitute a good answer, explain those factors in the test item, read all responses to a single essay question before reading other questions, and reread essays a second time to corroborate initial scores.

♦ After a test is scored, review items that show unusual answers or response patterns to see if faulty items or pupil learning is responsible. If faulty items are judged to be responsible, a scoring adjustment may be in order.

QUESTIONS FOR DISCUSSION

1. What are some things that a teacher can do to help prepare students for classroom testing? What are some dangers of test preparation that must be avoided?

2. If higher-level thinking requires pupils to work with material and concepts they have not been taught specifically, what are some ways to prepare pupils to take tests that include higher-level items?

3. What are some of the differences between a good teacher and an effective teacher? How could you tell whether you were seeing good, effective, or good and effective teaching?

4. What are some objectives that are best assessed using supply items? Using selection items?

5. How are sizing-up assessment, lesson plans, and instruction linked to formal assessments of pupils' learning?

6. What factors should a teacher consider when deciding whether to use a textbook test or one of her own?

7. Do teachers and parents have the same view of formal testing? Why or why not?

8. What harm could result if a teacher's achievement test produced invalid information about pupil learning?

REFLECTION EXERCISE

Think back over your school career and consider all the assessments you have taken. What was the best test or assessment you ever took? What characteristics made it the best? What was the worst assessment you ever took? What made it the worst?

In reflecting on these questions consider not just the test or assessment itself, but also the instruction that preceded it, the information about the test you were given, the conditions of administration, the way the test was scored, and the grade you received. How did all these factors influence your perception of the good and bad test?

ACTIVITIES

1. Each of the following nine test items has at least one fault. Read each item, identify the fault(s), and rewrite the item to correct the fault(s). When you have finished rewriting the items, organize them into a test to be given to students. Include directions for items and group items of a similar type together.

   1. What do you consider to be the most important objective in education?
      A. The student can read with comprehension.
      B. The student can correctly perform basic computations.
      C. The student gets along well with his or her peers.
      D. The student upholds democratic ideals in her or his actions.

   2. Minor differences among organisms of the same kind are known as
      A. heredity   B. variations   C. adaptation   D. natural selection

   3. The recall of factual information can best be assessed with a _____ item.
      A. matching   B. objective   C. essay   D. short answer

   4. Although experimental research completed, particularly that by Hans-mocker, must be considered too equivocal and the assumptions viewed as too restrictive, most testing experts would recommend that the easiest method of significantly improving pencil and paper achievement test reliability would be to
      A. increase the size of the group
      B. increase the weighting of items
      C. increase the number of items
      D. increase the amount of testing time

   5. F. Scott Fitzgerald wrote

   6. Boston is the most important city in the Northeast.   T   F

   7. An electric transformer can be used
      A. for storing up electricity
      B. to increase the voltage of alternating current (correct answer)
      C. it converts electrical energy into direct current
      D. alternating current is changed to direct current

   8. Most of South America was settled by colonists from Spain. How would you account for the large number of Spanish colonists settling there?
      A. They were adventurous.
      B. They searched for wealth. (correct answer)
      C. They wanted low taxes.
      D. They were seeking religious freedom.

   9. The only way to improve a skill is through practice.   T   F

2. Below are five educational objectives. For each objective write one test item of the type specified in the parentheses following the objective.

1. The student can match the symbols of chemical elements to their names. (matching)
2. The student can identify the nouns in a sentence that contains more than one noun. (multiple choice)
3. The student can indicate whether a statement about the Constitution is true or false. (true-false)
4. The student can state the name of the Speaker of the House of Representatives. (short answer)
5. The student can write the correct definition of an adverb. (short answer)

For objectives 4 and 5, indicate the minimum answer that would receive full credit.

3. Rewrite the following essay question to make it more focused for pupils. Then state a set of criteria you would use to judge the quality of your pupils' answers. Compare the Democratic and Republican Parties.

REVIEW QUESTIONS

1. What is the fundamental purpose of assessing pupils' achievement? What decisions must teachers make when they are preparing to assess their pupils' achievement?
2. How should the validity of an achievement test be determined?
3. What are some differences between selection and supply items? What are the advantages and disadvantages of each? What are common faults in each type?
4. What is the difference between objective and subjective scoring? What factors make it difficult to score essay questions objectively? What steps can a teacher take to make essay scoring more objective?
5. What is the difference between teaching the test and teaching to the test?
6. What guidelines should be followed in arranging the items in a test?
7. What are some strategies that can be used to defeat cheating on tests?
8. How do holistic and analytic scoring differ? When should each be used?
9. What is the relationship among educational objectives, instruction, and achievement testing?

REFERENCES

Airasian, P. W. (1988). Symbolic validation: The case of state-mandated, high-stakes testing. *Educational Evaluation and Policy Analysis, 10*(4), 301-313.

_____(1989). Classroom assessment and educational improvement. In L. W. Anderson (Ed.), *The effective teacher* (pp. 333-342). New York: Random House.

Annis, L. F. (1983). *Study techniques.* Dubuque, IA: William C. Brown.

Berliner, D. C. (1987). Simple views of effective teaching and a simple theory of classroom instruction. In D. C. Berliner and B. V. Rosenshine (Eds.), *Talks to teachers* (pp. 93-110). New York: Random House.

Bushway, A., and Nash, W. R. (1977). School cheating behavior. *Review of Educational Research, 47,* 623-632.

Canner, J., Fisher, T., Fremer, J., Haladyna, T., Hall, J., Mehrens, W., Perlman, C., Roeber, E., and Sandifer, P. (1991). *Regaining trust: Enhancing the credibility of school testing programs. A report from a National Council on Measurement in Education Task Force.* Mimeo, April 1991.

Crooks, T. J. (1988). The impact of classroom evaluation practices on students. *Review of Educational Research, 58*(4), 438-481.

Ebel, R. E., and Frisbie, D. A. (1991). *Essentials of educational measurement.* Englewood Cliffs, NJ: Prentice Hall.

Fleming, M., and Chambers, B. (1983). Teacher-made tests: Windows to the classroom. In W. E. Hathaway (Ed.), *Testing in the schools* (pp. 29-47). San Francisco, CA: Jossey-Bass.

Frisbie, D. A. (1992). The multiple true-false item format: A status review. *Educational Measurement: Issues and Practice, 11*(4), 21-26.

Hills, J. R. (1981). *Measurement and evaluation in the classroom.* Columbus, OH: Charles E. Merrill.

Marso, R. N., and Pigge, F. L. (1989). Elementary classroom teachers' testing needs and proficiencies: multiple assessments and inservice training priorities. *Educational Review, 13,* 1-17.

Marso, R. N., and Pigge, F. L. (1991). The analysis of teacher-made tests: Testing practices, cognitive demands and item construction errors. *Contemporary Educational Psychology, 16,* 179-286.

Millman, J., and Pauk, W. (1965). *How to take tests.* New York: McGraw-Hill.

Sarnacki, R. E. (1979). An examination of test-wiseness in the cognitive domain. *Review of Educational Research, 49,* 60-79.

Scriven, M. (1967). The methodology of evaluation. In R. W. Tyler (Ed.), *Perspectives of curriculum evaluation* (pp. 39-83). Chicago: Rand McNally.

Slavin, Robert E. (1994). *Educational psychology: Theory and practice.* Boston: Allyn and Bacon.

Starch, D., and Elliott, E. (1912). Reliability of the grading of high-school work in English. *School Review, 20,* 442-457.

Starch, D., and Elliott, E. (1913). Reliability of grading work in mathematics. *School Review, 21,* 254-259.

Tindal, G. A., and Marston, D. B. (1990). *Classroom-based assessment.* Columbus, OH: Merrill.

CHAPTER 4

PERFORMANCE ASSESSMENT

PERFORMANCE ASSESSMENT IN SCHOOLS AND CLASSROOMS
Performance-Oriented Subjects
Early Childhood and Special Needs Pupils

DEVELOPING PERFORMANCE ASSESSMENTS
Define the Purpose of Assessment
Identify Performance Criteria
Cautions in Developing Performance Criteria
Developing Observable Performance Criteria
Provide a Setting to Elicit and Observe the Performance
Scoring or Rating Performance
Anecdotal Records
Checklists
Rating Scales and Rubrics

USES OF PERFORMANCE ASSESSMENTS
Self-Assessment and Peer Review
Linking Assessment and Instruction
Grading

PORTFOLIO ASSESSMENT
Purpose of Portfolio
Performance Criteria
Setting
Scoring and Judging

VALIDITY AND RELIABILITY OF PERFORMANCE ASSESSMENTS
Clarity of Purpose
Preparing Pupils for Performance Assessment
Improving Performance Assessments

CHAPTER SUMMARY

T he following situations describe common classroom assessment practice.

1. Ms. Landers taught her ninth-grade science class a unit on microscopes. She taught her pupils how to set up, focus, and use a microscope. Each pupil used a microscope to identify and draw pictures of three or four objects on glass slides. At the end of the unit, she tested the pupils' achievement by giving a paper-and-pencil test that asked them to label parts of a diagrammed microscope and answer multiple-choice questions about the history of the microscope.

2. In Mr. Cleaver's third-grade class, oral reading skills are strongly emphasized, and he devotes a great deal of energy to helping pupils use proper phrasing, vocal expression, and clear pronunciation when they read aloud. All of the tests that Mr. Cleaver uses to grade his pupils' reading achievement are paper-and-pencil tests that assess pupils' paragraph comprehension and word recognition.

3. Mrs. Wilkes included a unit on cardiopulmonary resuscitation (CPR) in her eleventh-grade health class. Pupils were introduced to CPR and shown a movie on how to perform it. An emergency medical technician from the local fire department came to class with a practice dummy and instructed each pupil in the technique using the dummy as an imaginary victim. Mrs. Wilkes tested her pupils' achievement on the unit with a 25-item true-false test on CPR technique.

Most paper-and-pencil tests measure knowledge of performance, not performance itself.

These examples illustrate an important limitation of paper-and-pencil tests: they allow teachers to assess many, but not all, important school learning outcomes. In each of these classrooms, the teacher relied solely on paper-and-pencil tests, which measured *knowledge of performance,* but not ability to actually *perform the skill* itself.

There are many classroom assessment situations in which valid assessment requires that teachers gather formal information about pupils' performances or products. Examples include pupil products such as stories, paintings, lab reports, and science fair projects, and pupil performances such as giving a speech, holding a pencil, typing, and cooperating in groups. Table 4.1 contrasts the selection and supply items discussed in the prior chapter with typical examples of performance and product assessments.

Performance assessments allow pupils to demonstrate what they know and can do in a real situation.

Assessments in which pupils carry out an activity or produce a product in order to demonstrate their knowledge and skill are called **performance assessments.** Performance assessments permit pupils to show what they can do in a real situation (Fitzpatrick and Morrison, 1971; Wiggins, 1992). The distinction between being able to describe how a skill should be performed (knowledge) and being able to actually perform it (performance) is important in classroom assessment (Wolf, Bixby, Glen, and Gardner, 1991). Teachers recognize this distinction, as the following comments illustrate:

TABLE 4.1 A FRAMEWORK OF ASSESSMENT APPROACHES

Selection	Supply	Product	Performance
Multiple choice	Completion	Essay, story, or or poem	Musical, dance, or dramatic perfor- mance
True-false	Label a diagram	Research report	Science lab demon- stration
Matching	Short answer	Writing portfolio	Typing test
	Concept map	Diary or journal	Athletic competition
		Science fair project	Debate
		Art exhibit or portfolio	Oral presentation
			Cooperation in groups

SOURCE: Adapted from S. Ferrara and J. McTighe, "Assessment: A Thoughtful Practice". In A. Costa, J. Bellanca, and R. Fogarty (Eds.), *If Minds Matter: A Forward to the Future, Vol II.* © 1992 IRI/Skylight Publishing, Inc., Palatine, IL. Reprinted with permission.

I want my pupils to learn to do math for its own intrinsic value, but also because math is so essential for everyday life. Making change, balancing check-books, doing a budget, and many other practical, real world, activities require that pupils know how to use their math knowledge.

The kids need to learn to get along in groups, be respectful of others' property, and wait their turns. I don't want kids to be able to recite classroom rules, I want them to practice them. These behaviors are just as important for kids to learn in school as reading, writing, and math.

Some types of paper-and-pencil test items can be used to provide information about the thinking processes that underlie pupils' perfor-mance. For example, a math problem in which pupils have to show their work provides insight into the mental processes used to solve the prob-lem. An essay question shows pupils' organizational skills, thought processes, and application of capitalization and punctuation rules. Whereas these two forms of paper-and-pencil test items can be used to assess performance, the majority of paper-and-pencil test questions reveal little about the mental processes a pupil goes through to arrive at an answer. With most selection and supply questions, the teacher observes the *result* of the pupil's intellectual process but not the thinking that produced the result. If the pupil gets a multiple-choice, true-false, matching, or completion item correct, the teacher assumes that the pupil must have followed the correct process, but there is little direct evidence to support this assumption, since the only evidence of the pupil's thought process is a letter circled or a single word written. On the other hand, essays and other extended response items provide a product that shows how pupils think about and construct their responses. They permit the teacher to see the logic of arguments, the manner in which the response is organized, and the conclusions drawn by the pupil. Thus, paper-and-pencil assessments like essays, stories, reports, or "show your work" problems are also performance assessments. Table 4.2 shows some of the differences among objective test items, essay questions, oral questions, and performance assessments.

Some paper-and-pencil assessments such as essays and reports are also performance assessments.

TABLE 4.2 COMPARISON OF VARIOUS TYPES OF ASSESSMENTS

	Objective Test	Essay Test	Oral Question	Performance Assessment
Purpose	Sample knowledge with maximum efficiency and reliability	Assess thinking skills and/or mastery of how a body of knowledge is structured	Assess knowledge during instruction	Assess ability to translate knowledge and understanding into action
Pupil's response	Read, evaluate, select	Organize, compose	Oral answer	Plan, construct, and deliver an original response
Major advantage	Efficiency—can administer many items per unit of testing time	Can measure complex cognitive outcomes	Joins assessment and instruction	Provides rich evidence of performance skills
Influence on learning	Overemphasis on recall encourages memorization; can encourage thinking skills if properly constructed	Encourages thinking and development of writing skills	Stimulates participation in instruction, provides teacher immediate feedback on effectiveness of teaching	Emphasizes use of available skill and knowledge in relevant problem contexts

SOURCE: Adapted from R. J. Stiggins, "Design and Development of Performance Assessments," *Educational Measurement: Issues and Practice,* 1987, *6*(3) p. 35. Copyright 1987 by the National Council on Measurement in Education. Adapted by permission of the publisher.

Chapter 2 discussed how teachers observe their pupils' performance in order to size them up and obtain information about the moment-to-moment success of their instruction. Such observations are primarily informal and spontaneous. In this chapter, we are concerned with assessing more formal, structured performances and products, those which the teacher plans in advance, helps each pupil to perform, and formally judges. The assessment can take place during normal classroom instruction (e.g., oral reading activities, setting up laboratory equipment) or in some special situation set up to elicit a performance (e.g., giving a speech in an auditorium, demonstrating CPR on a dummy). In either case, the activity is formally structured; the teacher arranges the conditions in which the performance or product occurs and is judged. Such assessments permit each pupil to show his or her mastery of the same process or task, something that is impossible during informal observation of spontaneous classroom events.

Formal performance assessments permit each pupil to show mastery of the same process or task.

This chapter will identify instructional areas that lend themselves to formal performance assessments. Procedures and problems unique to such assessments will be discussed, and practical suggestions that lead to valid and reliable classroom performance assessment will be described.

PERFORMANCE ASSESSMENT IN SCHOOLS AND CLASSROOMS

Recently, a great deal of attention has been focused on performance assessment in schools. The amount of attention would lead one to believe that performance assessment is new and untried in classrooms and that it can solve all the problems of classroom assessment. Neither of these beliefs is true. Performance assessment has been used extensively in classrooms for as long as there have been classrooms. Table 4.3 provides examples of common performances that have long been assessed in schools.

Three factors account for the growing popularity of performance assessment. First, it is now being proposed or mandated as part of formal statewide assessment programs. Thus, thirty-six states currently assess pupils' writing performance, while twenty-six states assess such things as speaking and listening skills (Office of Technology Assessment, 1992). Second, recent emphasis on pupils' problem solving, higher-order thinking, and "real-world" reasoning strategies have led to a focus on performance and product assessments as the most appropriate ways for pupils to demonstrate such outcomes. Third, it is felt that performance assessments will allow pupils who do poorly on selection-type tests an opportunity to show their achievement in alternative ways.

Performance assessments reflect the recent emphasis on real-world problem solving.

TABLE 4.3   FIVE COMMON DOMAINS OF PERFORMANCE ASSESSMENT

Communication Skills	Psychomotor Skills	Athletic Activities	Concept Acquisition	Affective Skills
Writing essays	Holding a pencil	Shooting free throws	Constructing open and closed circuits	Sharing toys
Giving a speech	Setting up lab equipment	Catching a ball	Selecting proper tools for shop tasks	Working in cooperative groups
Pronouncing a foreign language	Using scissors	Hopping	Identifying unknown chemical substances	Obeying school rules
Following spoken directions	Dissecting a frog	Swimming the crawl	Generalizing from experimental data	Maintaining self-control

Performance-Oriented Subjects

All schools expect pupils to demonstrate communication skills, so reading, writing, and speaking are perhaps the most common areas of classroom performance assessment. Likewise, simple psychomotor skills, such as being able to sit in a chair or hold a pencil, as well as more sophisticated skills, such as setting up laboratory equipment or using tools to build a birdhouse, are a fundamental part of school life, especially in the preschool and primary years. Closely related are the athletic performances that are taught in physical education classes.

There also is a growing emphasis on using performance assessment to determine pupils' acquisition of the concepts they are taught in school (Wiggins, 1992). The argument made is that if pupils really grasp a concept, they can *use* it to solve real-life problems. For example, after teaching pupils about money and making change, the teacher may assess learning by having pupils count out the money needed to purchase objects from the classroom "store" or act as storekeeper and make change for other pupils' purchases. Rather than giving a multiple-choice test on the chemical reactions that help identify unknown substances, the teacher could give each pupil an unknown substance and have them go through the process of identifying it. These kinds of hands-on demonstrations of concept mastery are growing in popularity.

Assessing students' understanding of a concept through hands-on demonstrations is becoming more common.

Finally, teachers constantly assess pupils' feelings, values, attitudes, and emotions. When a teacher checks the "satisfactory" rating under the category "works hard" or "obeys school rules" on a pupil's report card, the teacher bases this judgment on observations of the pupil's performance. Teachers rely upon observations of pupils' performance to collect evidence about important behaviors such as getting along with peers, working independently, following rules, and self-control.

Most teachers do recognize the importance of balancing supply and selection assessments with performance and product assessments as indicated in the following comments:

> It's not reasonable to grade reading without including the pupil's oral reading skills. I always spend some time when it's grading time listening to and rating my pupils' oral reading quality.

> My kids know that a large part of their grade depends on how well they follow safety procedures and take proper care of the tools they use. They know I'm always on the lookout for times when they don't do these things and that it will count against them if I see them.

> I wouldn't want anyone to assess my teaching competence solely on the basis of my students' paper-and-pencil test scores. I would want to be seen interacting with the kids, teaching them, and attending to their needs. Why should I confine my assessments of my pupils solely to paper-and-pencil methods?

It is important for teachers to balance supply and selection assessments with performance and product assessments.

Early Childhood and Special Needs Pupils

While performance assessment cuts across subject areas and grade levels, it is heavily used in early childhood and special education. Because preschool, kindergarten, and primary school pupils are limited in their communication ability and are still in the process of being socialized into the school culture, much information is obtained by observing their performances. Instruction at this age is focused on gross and fine motor development, verbal and auditory acuity, and visual development (Guerin and Maier, 1983), as well as social acclimation behaviors. Table 4.4 illustrates some of the important early childhood behaviors that teachers assess by performance-based means. There are other behaviors that fit within these five domains (Guerin and Maier, 1983; McLoughlin and Lewis, 1990), but these examples provide a sense of how heavily the early childhood curriculum is weighted toward performance outcomes.

Special needs pupils, especially those who exhibit multiple handicaps, are similar in some ways to early childhood pupils (McLoughlin and Lewis, 1990; Salvia and Ysseldyke, 1991). For pupils who are severely limited in their cognitive, affective, and/or psychomotor development, school instruction is typically focused on so-called "self-help" skills such as getting oneself dressed, brushing one's teeth, making a sandwich, and operating a vacuum cleaner. Pupils are taught to carry out these performances through many, many repetitions. Observation of pupils as they perform these activities is the main assessment technique special education teachers use to identify performance mastery or areas needing further work.

To summarize, performance assessment gathers evidence about pupil learning by observing and rating pupils' performance or products. Appro-

Early education teachers rely heavily on performance-based assessments because of their students limited communication skills.

> **TABLE 4.4   COMMON EARLY CHILDHOOD BEHAVIOR AREAS**
>
> **Gross motor development.** Roll over, sit erect without toppling over, walk a straight line, throw a ball, jump on one or two feet, and skip
>
> **Fine motor development.** Cut with scissors, trace an object, color in the lines, draw geometric forms (circles, squares, triangles, etc.), penmanship, left-to-right progression in reading and writing, and eye-hand coordination
>
> **Verbal and auditory acuity.** Identify sounds, listen to certain sounds and ignore others (tune out distractions), discriminate between sounds and words that sound alike (e.g., fix–fish), remember numbers in sequence, follow directions, remember the correct order of events, and pronounce words and letters
>
> **Visual development.** Find a letter, number, or object similar to one shown by the teacher, copy a shape, identify shapes and embedded figures, reproduce a design given by the teacher, and differentiate objects by size, color, and shape
>
> **Social acclimation.** Listen to the teacher, follow a time schedule, share, wait one's turn, and respect the property of others

Performance assessments are especially useful in performance-oriented subjects like art, music, shop, and foreign language.

priate to all grade levels, it is especially useful in subjects such as art, music, public speaking, shop, foreign language, and physical education, all of which emphasize observable performances of some kind. It is also very useful with early childhood and special needs pupils whose lack of basic communication, psychomotor, and social skills forces the teacher to rely upon pupil performances to assess instructional success.

DEVELOPING PERFORMANCE ASSESSMENTS

A diving competition is an instructive example of a skill that is best demonstrated by a performance. Submitting a written essay describing how one would perform various dives, or answering a multiple-choice test about diving rules, are hardly appropriate ways to assess diving *performance.* Rather, a valid assessment of diving performance requires seeing the diver actually perform and, to make the assessment reliable, the observer must see a series of dives, not just one.

Diving judges rate dives using a scale that has 21 possible numerical scores that can be awarded (e.g., 0.0, 0.5, 1.0, . . ., 5.5, 6.0, 6.5, . . ., 9.0, 9.5, 10.0). They observe a very complicated performance made up of many body movements that together take about two seconds to complete. They do not have the benefit of slow motion or instant replay to review the performance and they cannot discuss the dive with one another. If their attention strays for even a second, they miss a large portion of the performance. Yet when the scores are flashed on the scoreboard, the judges inevitably are in very close agreement. Rarely do all judges give a dive the exact same score, but rarely is there more than a one-point difference between any two judges' scores. This is amazing agreement among observers for such a short, complicated performance.

With this example in mind, let's consider the four essential features of all formal performance assessments, whether it is a diving competition, an oral speech, a book report, a typing exercise, or a science fair project (Stiggins, 1987). This overview will then be followed by a more extensive discussion of each feature. Briefly, every performance assessment should:

- ◆ *Have a clear purpose* which identifies the decision to be made from the performance assessment
- ◆ *Identify observable aspects* of the pupil's performance or product that can be judged
- ◆ *Provide an appropriate setting* for eliciting and judging the performance or product
- ◆ *Provide a judgment or score to describe performance*

Define the Purpose of Assessment

In a diving competition, the *purpose* of the assessment is to rank the divers' performance in order to identify the best divers. Each dive receives a score and the highest total score wins the competition. Suppose, however, that dives were being performed during practice prior to a competition. The diver's coach would be the judge for the practice dives. The coach's concern would be less with the overall score for a dive than with the specific performance criteria that judges will score during a competition. Consequently, the coach would "score" the practice dive not with a single overall judgment, but formatively, with a separate judgment about each part of the dive. Thus, a dive would produce not one judgment, but a series of diagnostic judgments corresponding to each of many specific performances that it involves. Those areas in which the diver was weak would likely be emphasized in practice.

Performance assessments are particularly suited to *diagnosis* because they can provide information about how a pupil performs each of the specific parts that make up a more general performance or product. This part-by-part assessment makes it easy to identify the strong and weak points of a pupil's performance. When the performance criteria are stated in terms of observable pupil behaviors or product characteristics, as they should be, remediation is made easy. Each suggestion for improvement can be described in specific terms—e.g., "report to group project area on time," "wait your turn to speak," "do your share of the group work." Teachers indicate that they use performance assessment for many purposes: grading pupils, constructing portfolios of pupil work, diagnosing pupil learning, helping pupils recognize the important steps in a process or the important characteristics of a product, and providing concrete examples of pupil work for parent conferences. Whatever the purpose of performance assessment, it should be specified at the beginning of the assessment process so that proper kinds of performance criteria and scoring procedures can be established.

Recognizing a specific purpose for performance assessment is necessary so that proper criteria and scoring procedures can be established.

Identify Performance Criteria

Performance criteria are the specific behaviors a pupil should perform to properly carry out a performance or produce a product. They are at the heart of successful performance assessment, yet they are the area in which most problems occur.

When teachers first think about assessing performance, they tend to think in terms of global performances such as oral reading, giving a speech, safety in the laboratory, penmanship, producing a book report, organizing ideas, fingering a keyboard, or getting along with peers. In reality, such performances cannot be assessed until they are broken down into the more specific behaviors or characteristics that comprise them. These specific behaviors and characteristics are the performance criteria that will be observed and judged by the teacher.

Performances and products are normally broken down into specific, observable criteria, each of which can be judged independently.

Performance assessments are particularly suited to diagnosis because they provide information about how pupils perform each specific criterion in a general performance.

Table 4.5 shows two sets of criteria for assessing pupils' performance when (1) working in cooperative groups and (2) playing the piano. These criteria focus teachers' observations of pupils' performance in the same way that diving judges have criteria to judge diving performance. Notice how important performance criteria are in clearly identifying the important aspects of the performance or product being assessed. Well-stated performance criteria are at the heart of successful efforts at performance assessment.

Performance criteria can focus on processes, products, or both.

In order to define performance criteria, a teacher must first decide if a process or a product will be observed. Will processes such as typing or oral reading be assessed, or will products such as a typed letter or book report be assessed? In the former case, criteria are needed to judge the pupil's actual performance (typing, reading aloud), while in the latter, criteria are needed to judge the end product (typed letter, book report). In some cases, both process and product can be assessed. For example, a first-grade teacher assessed both process and product when she (1) observed a pupil writing to determine how the pupil held the pencil, positioned the paper, and manipulated the pencil and (2) judged the finished, handwritten product to assess how well the pupil formed his letters. Notice that the teacher observed different things according to whether she was interested in the

TABLE 4.5   EXAMPLES OF PERFORMANCE CRITERIA FOR WORKING IN GROUPS AND PIANO PLAYING

Working in Groups	Piano Playing
_____ Reports to group project area on time	_____ Sits upright with feet on floor (or pedal, when necessary)
_____ Starts work on own	
_____ Shares information	_____ Arches fingers on keys
_____ Contributes ideas	_____ Plays without pauses or interruptions
_____ Listens to others	_____ Maintains even tempo
_____ Waits turn to speak	_____ Plays correct notes
_____ Follows instructions	_____ Holds all note values for indicated duration
_____ Courteous to other group members	_____ Follows score dynamics (forte, crescendo, descrescendo)
_____ Helps to solve group problems	
_____ Considers viewpoints of others	_____ Melody can be heard above other harmonization
_____ Carries out share of group-determined activities	_____ Phrases according to score (staccato and legato)
_____ Completes assigned tasks on time	_____ Follows score pedal markings

pupil's handwriting *process* or handwriting *product*. It is for this reason that teachers must know what they want to observe before performance criteria can be identified.

The key to identifying performance criteria is to break down the overall performance or product into its component parts. It is these parts that will be observed and judged. Consider, for example, a product assessment of eighth graders' written paragraphs. The purpose of the assessment is to judge pupils' ability to write a six- to ten-sentence paragraph on a topic of their choice. In preparing to judge the completed paragraph, a teacher initially listed the following performance criteria for a well-organized paragraph:

♦ First sentence
♦ Appropriate topic sentence
♦ Good supporting ideas
♦ Good vocabulary
♦ Complete sentences
♦ Capitalization
♦ Spelling
♦ Conclusion
♦ Handwriting

These performance criteria do identify important areas of a written paragraph, but the areas are vague and poorly stated. What, for example, is meant by "first sentence." What is an "appropriate" topic sentence or "good" vocabulary? What should be examined in judging "capitalization," "spelling," and "handwriting"? Performance criteria need to be specific enough to focus the teacher on well-defined characteristics of the performance or product. They must also be specific enough to permit the teacher to explain to pupils, in terms they can understand, the specific features that make up a well-written paragraph. Once defined, the criteria permit consistent teacher assessments of performance and consistent communication with pupils about their learning.

If a teacher cannot answer these questions for himself or herself, how can he or she provide suitable examples or instruct pupils on the proper way to construct a well-organized paragraph? A general rule of thumb says that performance criteria are clearly stated when another teacher at your grade level could use your performance criteria without you being there to explain them. The list below shows a revised version of the performance criteria for a well-organized paragraph. Note the difference in clarity and how the revised version focuses the teacher (and students during instruction) on very specific features of the paragraph that are important and will be assessed:

- ◆ Indents first sentence
- ◆ Topic sentence sets main idea of paragraph
- ◆ Following sentences support main idea
- ◆ Sentences arranged in logical order
- ◆ Uses age-appropriate vocabulary
- ◆ Writes in complete sentences
- ◆ Capitalizes proper nouns and first words in sentences
- ◆ Makes no more than three spelling errors
- ◆ Conclusion follows logically from prior sentences
- ◆ Handwriting is legible

Cautions in Developing Performance Criteria

A few words of caution are appropriate here. First, it is important to recognize that the above list of performance criteria is not the only one that describes the characteristics of a well-written paragraph. Different teachers might identify other criteria that they feel are more important than some of the ones shown. Thus, emphasis should not be on identifying the "best" or "only" set of criteria for a performance or product, but rather on stating criteria that are meaningful and important for your pupils and that clearly describe the performance or product to be assessed.

Performance criteria should be specific, observable, and clearly stated.

Clearly stated performance criteria should be useable by other teachers without instructions.

Second, it is possible to break down most school performances and products into many very specific steps, behaviors, or characteristics. However, a too lengthy list of performance criteria becomes unusable because teachers rarely have the time to observe a large number of detailed performance criteria for each pupil. Too many criteria make the observation process intrusive, with the teacher hovering over the pupil, rapidly checking off behaviors, and often interfering with a pupil's performance.

In short, numerous detailed performance criteria are useful only when the observer has the time to carry out in-depth observation of a single pupil. Since these conditions are rare in most classrooms, it is counterproductive to spend great amounts of time listing performance criteria that cannot be observed and assessed. For classroom performance assessment to be manageable and meaningful, a balance must be established between specificity and practicality. The key to attaining this balance is to identify the *essential* criteria associated with a performance or product. About ten to fifteen performance criteria is a manageable number for most classroom teachers to use.

Third, the process of identifying performance criteria is an ongoing one that is rarely completed on the first attempt. As with most writing assignments, initial performance criteria will need to be revised and clarified in order to provide the focus needed for valid and reliable assessment. To aid this process, teachers should think about the performance or product they wish to observe and reflect on its key aspects. They also can examine a few actual products or performances as a basis for revising their initial list of criteria.

The following list shows the initial set of performance criteria a teacher wrote to assess pupils' oral reports:

- ◆ Speaks clearly and slowly
- ◆ Pronounces correctly
- ◆ Makes eye contact
- ◆ Exhibits good posture when presenting
- ◆ Exhibits good effort
- ◆ Presents with feeling
- ◆ Understands the topic
- ◆ Exhibits enthusiastic attitude
- ◆ Organizes

Note the lack of specificity in many of the criteria: "slowly," "correctly," "good," "understands," and "enthusiastic attitude." These criteria hide more than they reveal about what to observe, making it hard to explain to pupils precisely what is expected of them and leading to assessments that are invalid and unreliable. After reflecting on and observing a few oral presentations, the teacher revised and sharpened the performance criteria as shown below. Note that the teacher first divided the general performance

Very long lists of performance criteria (over 10 to 15) become unmanageable and intrusive.

Like other writing assignments, good performance criteria need to be revised and sharpened over time.

into three areas (physical expression, vocal expression, and verbal expression) and then identified a few important performance criteria within each of these areas:

I. Physical Expression
- ♦ Stands straight and faces audience
- ♦ Changes facial expression with changes in tone of the report
- ♦ Maintains eye contact with audience

II. Vocal Expression
- ♦ Speaks in a steady, clear voice
- ♦ Varies tone to emphasize points
- ♦ Speaks loudly enough to be heard by audience
- ♦ Paces words in an even flow
- ♦ Enunciates each word

III. Verbal Expression
- ♦ Chooses precise words to convey meaning
- ♦ Avoids unnecessary repetition
- ♦ States sentences with complete thoughts or ideas
- ♦ Organizes information logically
- ♦ Summarizes main points at conclusion

Developing Observable Performance Criteria

The value of performance assessments depends on identifying performance criteria that can be observed and judged.

The value and richness of performance and product assessments depend heavily on identifying performance criteria that can be observed and judged. The following guidelines should prove useful for this purpose.

1. *Select the performance or product to be assessed and either perform it yourself or imagine yourself performing it.* Think to yourself, "What would I have to do in order to complete this task? What steps would I have to follow?" You may also observe pupils performing the task and identify the important elements in their performance. Finally, you can actually carry out the performance yourself, recording and studying your performance or product.

2. *List the important aspects of the performance or product.* What specific behaviors or attributes are most important to the successful completion of the task? What behaviors have been emphasized in instruction? The specific behaviors or attributes identified will become the performance criteria that guide instruction, observation, and assessment.

3. *Try to limit the number of performance criteria, so they can all be observed during a pupil's performance.* This is less important when one is assessing a product, but even then, it is better to assess a limited number of key criteria than a large number that vary widely in their importance.

Remember, you will have to observe and judge performance on each of the criteria identified. A good rule of thumb is to limit the number of performance criteria to about ten to fifteen.

4. If possible, have groups of teachers think through the important behaviors included in a task. Since all first-grade teachers assess oral reading in their classrooms and since the criteria for successful oral reading do not differ much from one first-grade classroom to another, a group effort at defining performance criteria will likely save time and produce a more complete set of criteria than that produced by a single teacher. Similar group efforts are useful for other common performances or products such as book reports, science fair projects, and the like. It is useful and reinforcing for pupils when teachers within and across grades in a school utilize similar criteria in assessing performances and projects.

When teachers within a school develop similar performance criteria across grade levels, it is reinforcing to pupils.

5. Express the performance criteria in terms of observable pupil behaviors or product characteristics. The performance criteria should direct attention to things the pupil is doing or characteristics of a product that the pupil has produced. Be specific when stating the performance criteria. Don't write "The child works"; write instead, "The child remains focused on the task for at least four minutes." Don't write "Organization"; write instead "Information is presented in a logical sequence." Note how each performance criterion is expressed in terms of an observable pupil behavior in the revised lists on pages 142 and 144.

6. Don't use ambiguous words that cloud the meaning of the performance criteria. The worst offenders in this regard are adverbs that end in *-ly*. Other words to avoid are *good* and *appropriate*. Thus, criteria such as *appropriate organization, speaks correctly, writes neatly,* and *performs gracefully* are ambiguous and leave interpretation up to the observer. The observer's interpretation may vary from time to time and pupil to pupil, diminishing the fairness and usefulness of the assessment. Instead of "organizes adequately" one might substitute "has an identifiable beginning, middle, and end" or "presents ideas in a logical order." Instead of "speaks correctly," one might substitute "enunciates each word," "can be heard in all parts of the room," or "does not run sentences together." The particular criteria will depend upon the teacher and his or her instruction, but the criteria should be stated in terms of observable behaviors and product characteristics, preferably ones that pupils and other teachers could understand. Review and revise criteria as necessary based upon experience using them.

7. Arrange the performance criteria in the order in which they are likely to be observed. This will save time when observing and will maintain primary focus on the performance.

8. Check for existing performance criteria before defining your own. The performance criteria associated with giving an oral speech, reading aloud, using a microscope, writing a persuasive paragraph, cutting with scissors, and the like have been thought about and listed by many people. No one who reads this book will be the first to try to assess these and other common school performances. The moral here is that one need not reinvent the wheel every time a wheel is needed. Many texts contain examples of performance criteria for many school skills, and these should be used and modified as needed (e.g., Carey, 1988; Cartwright and Cartwright, 1984; Ebel and Frisbie, 1991; Gronlund and Linn, 1990; Borich, 1993; Sax, 1989). Table 4.6 summarizes the foregoing guidelines.

Regardless of the particular performance or product assessed, clearly stated performance criteria are critical to the success of both instruction and assessment. The criteria define the important aspects of a performance or product, guide what pupils should be taught, and produce a focus for both the teacher and pupil when assessing performance. Although performance and product assessments are widely used in most classrooms, they are frequently used in the absence of well-articulated performance criteria. If the teacher doesn't know what makes a good essay response or a good science fair project, how are pupils to be guided during instruction and how are they to be assessed fairly? Clear performance criteria are needed.

Provide a Setting to Elicit and Observe the Performance

Once the performance criteria are defined, a setting in which to observe the performance or product must be selected or established. Depending on the nature of the performance or product, the teacher may observe

---

TABLE 4.6   GUIDELINES FOR STATING PERFORMANCE CRITERIA

1. Identify the steps or features of the performance or task to be assessed by imagining yourself performing it, observing pupils performing it, or inspecting finished products.
2. List the important criteria of the performance or product.
3. Try to keep the number of performance criteria small enough so that they can be reasonably observed and judged. Ten to fifteen criteria is a good number to use.
4. Arrange the criteria in the order in which they are likely to be observed.
5. Express the criteria in terms of observable pupil behaviors or product characteristics.
6. Avoid vague and ambiguous words like *correctly, appropriately,* and *good.*
7. Check for existing performance assessment instruments to use or modify before constructing one's own.

behaviors as they naturally occur in the classroom or set up a specific situation in which the pupils must perform. There are two considerations in deciding whether to observe naturally occurring behaviors or to set up a more controlled exercise: (1) the frequency with which the performance naturally occurs in the classroom and (2) the seriousness of the decision to be made.

Teachers may observe and assess naturally occurring classroom behaviors or set up situations in which they assess carefully structured performances.

If the performance occurs infrequently during normal classroom activity, it may be more efficient to structure a situation in which pupils must perform the desired behaviors. For example, in the normal flow of classroom activities, pupils rarely have the opportunity to give a planned five-minute speech, so the teacher should set up an exercise in which each pupil must develop and give a five-minute speech. Oral reading, on the other hand, occurs frequently enough in many elementary classrooms that pupils' performance can be observed as part of the normal flow of reading instruction.

Formally structured performance assessments are needed when teachers are dealing with low-frequency behaviors and making important decisions.

The importance of the decision to be made from a performance assessment also influences the context in which observation takes place. In general, the more important the decision, the more structured the assessment environment should be. A course grade, for example, represents an important decision about a pupil. If performance assessments contribute to grading, evidence should be gathered under structured, formal circumstances so that every pupil has a fair and equal chance to exhibit his or her achievement. The validity of the assessments is likely to be improved when the setting is similar and familiar to all pupils.

Regardless of the nature of the assessment, evidence obtained from a single assessment describes only one example of a pupil's performance. For a variety of reasons such as illness, home problems, or other distractions, pupil performance at a single time may not provide a reliable indication of the pupil's true achievement. To be certain that one has an accurate indication of what a pupil can and cannot do, multiple observations are useful. If the different observations produce similar performance, a teacher can have confidence in the evidence and use it in decision making. If different observations contradict one another, more information should be obtained.

Multiple observations of pupil performance provide more reliable and accurate information.

Scoring or Rating Performance

The final step in performance assessment is to score the pupil's performance. As in previous steps, the nature of the decision to be made influences the judgmental system used. Scoring a performance assessment can be holistic or analytic, just like scoring an essay question. In situations such as group placement, selection, or grading, holistic scoring is most useful. To make such decisions, a teacher seeks to score individuals using a single, overall score. On the other hand, if the assessment purpose is to diagnose pupil difficulties or certify pupil mastery of each individual

Holistic scoring (a single overall score) is good for such things as group placement or grading; analytic scoring (scoring individual criteria) is useful in diagnosing student difficulties.

performance criterion, then analytic scoring, with a separate score or rating on each performance criterion, is appropriate. In either case, the performance criteria underlie the scoring or rating approach that is adopted.

In most classrooms, the teacher is both the observer and scorer. In situations where an important decision is to be made, additional observers/scorers may be added. Thus, it is common for performance assessments in athletic, music, debate, and art competitions to have more than a single judge in order to make scoring fairer.

Anecdotal records, checklists, rating scales, and portfolios are options available to record and collect observations of pupils.

A number of options exist for collecting and recording observations of pupil performance: anecdotal records, checklists, rating scales, and portfolios.

Anecdotal Records

Anecdotal records are written accounts of significant pupil events and behaviors the teacher has observed.

Written accounts of significant individual-pupil events and behaviors the teacher has observed are called **anecdotal records.** Only those observations that have special significance and cannot be obtained from other classroom assessment methods should be included in an anecdotal record (Cartwright and Cartwright, 1984; Gronlund and Linn, 1990). Figure 4.1 shows an example of an anecdotal record. Notice that it provides information about the learner, date of observation, name of teacher observing, and a factual description of the event.

Most teachers have difficulty identifying particular events or behaviors that merit inclusion in an anecdotal record. What is significant and important in the life of a pupil is not always apparent at the time an event or behavior occurs. From the hundreds of observations made each day, how is a teacher to select the one that might be important enough to write down? It may take many observations over many days to recognize which events really are significant. Moreover, anecdotal records are time-consuming to prepare and need to be written up soon after the event or

FIGURE 4.1
Anecdotal Record for Lynn Gregory

PUPIL *Lynn Gregory*   DATE *12/3/94*

OBSERVER *J. Ricketts*

    All term Lynn has been quiet and passive, rarely interacting w/classmates in class or on the playground. Today Lynn suddenly "opened up" and wanted continual interaction w/classmates. She could not settle down, kept circulating around the room until she became bothersome to me and her classmates. I tried to settle her down, but was unsuccessful.

behavior is observed, while it is fresh in the teacher's mind. This is not always possible. For these reasons, anecdotal records are not extensively used by teachers. This does not mean that teachers do not observe and judge classroom events; we know that they do. It simply means that they seldom write down descriptions of these events.

Checklists

A **checklist** is a written list of performance criteria. As a pupil's performance is observed or product judged, the scorer determines whether the performance or the product meets each performance criterion. If it does, a checkmark is placed next to that criterion indicating that it was observed; if it does not, the checkmark is omitted. Figure 4.2 shows a completed

FIGURE 4.2

Checklist Results for an Oral Presentation

NAME *Rick Gray*   DATE *Nov. 11, 1996*

  I. Physical Expression

    ✓ A. Stands straight and faces audience

    _____ B. Changes facial expressions with changes in tone of the presentation

    ✓ C. Maintains eye contact with the audience

  II. Vocal Expression

    ✓ A. Speaks in a steady clear voice

    ✓ B. Varies tone to emphasize points

    _____ C. Speaks loudly enough to be heard by the audience

    ✓ D. Paces words in an even flow

    _____ E. Enunciates each word

  III. Verbal Expression

    _____ A. Chooses precise words that convey meaning

    ✓ B. Avoids unnecessary repetition

    ✓ C. States sentences with complete thoughts or ideas

    ✓ D. Organizes information logically

    ✓ E. Summarizes main points at conclusion

A checklist, which is a written list of performance criteria, can be used repeatedly over time to diagnose strengths, weaknesses, and changes in performance.

checklist for Rick Gray's oral presentation. The performance criteria for this checklist were presented on page 144.

Checklists are diagnostic, reusable, and capable of charting pupil progress. They provide a detailed record of pupils' performances, one that can and should be shown to pupils to help them see where improvement is needed. Rick Gray's teacher could sit down with him after his presentation and point out both the behaviors he performed well and the ones he needs to improve. Because it focuses on the specific behaviors of a performance, a checklist provides diagnostic information. The same checklist can be reused, with different pupils or with the same pupil over time. In fact, using the same checklist more than once is an easy way to obtain information about a pupil's improvement over time.

There are, however, disadvantages associated with checklists. One important disadvantage is that it gives the teacher only two choices for each criterion: performed or not performed. A checklist provides no middle ground for scoring. Suppose that Rick Gray stood straight and faced the audience most of the time during his oral presentation, or paced his words evenly except in one brief part of the speech when he spoke too quickly and ran his words together. How should his teacher score him on these performance criteria? Should Rick receive a check because he did them most of the time, or should he not receive a check because his performance was slightly flawed? Sometimes this is not an easy choice. A checklist forces the teacher to make an absolute decision for each performance criterion, even though a pupil's performance is somewhere between these extremes.

Checklists cannot record gradations in performances.

A second disadvantage of checklists is the difficulty of summarizing a pupil's performance into a single score. We saw how useful checklists can be for diagnosing pupils' strengths and weaknesses. But what if a teacher wants to summarize performance across a number of criteria to arrive at a holistic score for grading purposes? There are three basic ways to summarize performance across all criteria on a checklist. At this point we shall discuss only two of them. The third, called a scoring rubric, will be discussed shortly.

One way to summarize Rick's performance into a single score would be to translate the number of performance criteria he successfully demonstrated into a percentage. For example, there were thirteen performance criteria on the oral presentation checklist and Rick demonstrated nine of them during his presentation. Assuming each criterion is equally important, Rick's performance translates into a score of 69 percent: $(9 \div 13) \times 100 = 69$). Thus, Rick demonstrated 69 percent of the desired performance criteria. (In Chapter 5 we will discuss the way scores like Rick's 69 percent are turned into grades.)

Summarizing performance from a checklist can be done by setting up rating standards or by calculating the percentage of criteria accomplished.

A second way to summarize performance would be for the teacher to set up standards for rating pupils' performance. Suppose Rick's teacher set up the following standards:

Excellent	12 or 13 performance criteria shown
Good	9 to 11 performance criteria shown
Fair	5 to 8 performance criteria shown
Poor	5 or less performance criteria shown

These standards allow the teacher to summarize performance on a scale that goes from excellent to poor. The scale could also go from a grade of A to one of D. The same standard would be used to summarize each pupil's performance. Rick performed nine of the thirteen criteria, and the teacher's standard indicates that his performance should be classified as "good" or "B." Of course, there are many such standards that can be set up and the one shown is only an example. In establishing standards, it is advisable to keep the summarizing rules as simple as possible.

Rating Scales and Rubrics

Although they are similar to checklists, **rating scales** allow the observer to judge performance along a continuum rather than as a dichotomy. Both checklists and rating scales are based upon a set of performance criteria, and it is not unusual for the same set of performance criteria to be used in both a rating scale and a checklist. However, a checklist gives the observer two categories for judging, while a rating scale gives more than two.

Three of the most common types of rating scales are the numerical, graphic, and descriptive scales. Figure 4.3 shows an example of each of these scales as applied to two specific performance criteria for giving an oral presentation. In numerical scales, a number stands for a point on the rating scale. Thus, in the example, "1" corresponds to the pupil *always* performing the behavior, "2" to the pupil *usually* performing the behavior, and so on. Graphic scales require the rater to mark a position on a line divided into sections based upon a scale. The rater marks an "X" at that point on the line that best describes the pupil's performance. Descriptive rating scales, also called **scoring rubrics,** require the rater to choose among different descriptions of actual performance. In descriptive rating scales, different levels of performance are stated and the teacher chooses the one that the pupil's performance came closest to.

The three most common types of rating scales are numerical, graphic, and descriptive (also called scoring rubrics).

Scoring rubrics, or descriptive rating scales, require the rater to choose among different descriptions of actual performance.

Regardless of the type of rating scale one chooses, a couple of general rules will improve their use. First, limit the number of rating categories. There is a tendency to think that the greater the number of rating categories to choose from, the better the rating scale. In practice, this is not the case. Few observers can make reliable discriminations in pupil performance across more than five rating categories, and more categories on a rating scale is likely to make the ratings unreliable. Stick to three to five well-defined and distinct rating scale points as shown in Figure 4.3.

Second, strive to use the same rating scale for each performance criterion. This is not usually possible in descriptive rating scales where the descriptions vary with each performance criterion. However, for numerical and graphic scales, it is best to select a single rating scale and to use that scale for all performance criteria. Using many different rating categories requires the observer to change focus frequently and will decrease rating accuracy by distracting the rater's attention from the performance.

Figure 4.4 shows Sarah Jackson's completed numerical rating performance for her oral presentation. Note that the performance criteria for the rating scale shown in Figure 4.4 are identical to those in the checklist shown in Figure 4.2. The only difference between the checklist and the rating scale is in the way performance is scored.

While rating scales provide more categories for assessing a pupil's performance, thereby providing detailed diagnostic information, the multiple rating categories complicate the process of summarizing performance across criteria to arrive at an overall pupil score. With a checklist, summarization reduces to giving credit for criteria checked and no credit for criteria not checked. One cannot do this with a rating scale because performance is judged in terms of *degree,* not presence or absence. A teacher must treat ratings of "always," "usually," "seldom," and "never" differently from each other, or there is no point to having the different rating categories.

Numerical summarization is the most straightforward and commonly used approach to summarizing performance on rating scales. It assigns a point value to each category in the scale and sums the points across the performance criteria. For example, consider Sarah Jackson's ratings in Figure 4.4. To obtain a summary score for Sarah's performance, one can assign 4 points to a rating of "always," 3 points to a rating of "usually," 2 points to a rating of "seldom," and 1 point to a rating of "never." The numbers 4, 3, 2, and 1 match the four possible ratings for each performance criterion with 4 representing the most desirable response and 1 the least desirable. Thus, high scores indicate good performance. Note, that before summarizing Sarah's performance into a single score, it is important that the teacher identify areas of weakness so that Sarah can be guided to improve her oral presentations.

Sarah's total score, 39, can be determined by adding the circled numbers. The highest possible score on the rating scale is 52; if a pupil was rated "always" on each performance criterion, the pupil's total score would be 52 (4 points × 13 performance criteria). Thus, Sarah got a score of 39 out of a possible 52 points. In this manner, a total score can be determined for each pupil rated. This score can be turned into a percentage by dividing it by 52, the total number of points available: (39 ÷ 52) × 100 = 75).

Having too many different scales tends to distract the rater from the performance, making the ratings unreliable.

Whereas checklists measure only the presence or absence of some performance, a rating scale measures the degree to which the performance matches the criteria.

Numerical Rating Scale

Directions: Indicate how often the pupil performs each of these behaviors while giving an oral presentation. For each behavior circle **1** if the pupil **always** performs the behavior, **2** if the pupil **usually** performs the behavior, **3** if the pupil **seldom** performs the behavior, and **4** if the pupil **never** performs the behavior.

Physical Expression

A. Stands straight and faces audience.

       1   **2**   **3**   **4**

B. Changes facial expression with change in the tone of the presentation.

       1   **2**   **3**   **4**

Graphic Rating Scale

Directions: Place an **X** on the line which shows how often the pupil did each of the behaviors listed while giving an oral presentation.

Physical Expression

A. Stands straight and faces audience.

always   **usually**   **seldom**   **never**

B. Changes facial expressions with change in tone of the presentation.

always   **usually**   **seldom**   **never**

Descriptive Rating Scale

Directions: Place an **X** on the line at the place which best describes the pupil's performance on each behavior.

Physical Expression

A. Stands straight and faces audience.

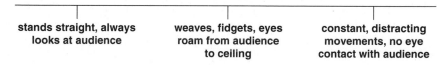

| **stands straight, always looks at audience** | **weaves, fidgets, eyes roam from audience to ceiling** | **constant, distracting movements, no eye contact with audience** |

B. Changes facial expressions with change in tone of the presentation.

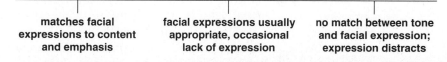

| **matches facial expressions to content and emphasis** | **facial expressions usually appropriate, occasional lack of expression** | **no match between tone and facial expression; expression distracts** |

FIGURE 4.3
Types of Rating Scales

NAME *Sarah Jackson*   DATE *Nov. 11, 1996*

Directions: Indicate how often the pupil performs each of these behaviors while making an oral presentation. For each behavior **circle 4** if the pupil **always** performs that behavior, **3** if the pupil **usually** performs that behavior, **2** if the pupil **seldom** performs that behavior, and **1** if the pupil **never** performs that behavior.

I. Physical Expression

(4) 3 2 1   A. Stands straight and faces audience

4 3 (2) 1   B. Changes facial expression with changes in tone of the presentation

4 (3) 2 1   C. Maintains eye contact with the audience

II. Vocal Expression

(4) 3 2 1   A. Speaks in a steady clear voice

4 (3) 2 1   B. Varies tone to emphasize points

4 3 (2) 1   C. Speaks loudly enough to be heard by the audience

4 (3) 2 1   D. Paces words in an even flow

4 3 (2) 1   E. Enunciates each word

III. Verbal Expression

4 3 (2) 1   A. Choose precise words that convey meaning

4 (3) 2 1   B. Avoids unnecessary repetition

(4) 3 2 1   C. States sentences with complete thoughts or ideas

(4) 3 2 1   D. Organizes information logically

4 (3) 2 1   E. Summarizes main points at conclusion

FIGURE 4.4
*Rating Scale Results
for an Oral
Presentation*

*Rubrics are used to
provide an indication of
the overall level at which
a pupil performs.*

Descriptive summarization, or a *scoring rubric,* provides a second way to summarize performance on checklists and rating scales. Scoring rubrics are brief, written descriptions of different levels of pupil performance. Rubrics can be used to summarize both pupil performances and products. The rubric below is one developed to summarize performance on the oral presentation checklist and rating scale shown previously. Notice that this rubric is a summarization of the performance criteria at different levels of performance. Often, as below, a teacher may label the various descriptions as "excellent," "good," "fair," and "poor" or with particular grades to summarize the performance. However, since these one-word labels do not meaningfully describe pupil performance, the full rubric is also needed to represent the performance observed.

Excellent   Pupil consistently faces audience, stands straight, and maintains eye contact; voice projects well and clearly; pacing and tone variation appropriate; well-organized, points logically and completely presented; brief summary at end.

Good   Pupil usually faces audience, stands straight, and makes eye contact; voice projection good, but pace and clarity vary during talk; well-organized but repetitive; occasional poor choice of words and incomplete summary.

Fair   Pupil fidgety; some eye contact and facial expression change; uneven voice projection, not heard by all in room, some words slurred; loosely organized, repetitive, contains many incomplete thoughts; little summarization.

Poor   Pupil body movements distracting, little eye contact or voice change; words slurred, speaks in monotone, does not project voice beyond first few rows, no consistent or logical pacing; rambling presentation, little organization with no differentiation between major and minor points; no summary.

To use the scoring rubric, teachers judge which of the descriptions comes closest to the pupil's performance based on the results of a checklist or rating scale. Sometimes teachers use descriptive rating scales in conjunction with a pupil's numerical ratings, seeking to judge which description comes closest to the pupil's numerically rated performance. If we look at Sarah Jackson's numerical ratings and try to describe her overall performance in terms of the descriptions above, it is clear that Sarah is neither excellent nor poor. Her performance is either good or fair. The teacher would have to make a judgment as to which of these categories best describes Sarah's performance. The fact that Sarah had more 4's and 3's than 2's and 1's led Sarah's teacher to place her performance in the "good" category.

Table 4.7 shows a scoring rubric for group performance in communication of ideas, knowledge and use of history, and critical thinking for eleventh-grade history–social science. Note how each category in the rubric contains different performance levels of the performance criteria for each of the three areas scored.

Note the difference between checklists and rating scales, which can provide specific diagnostic information about pupil strengths and weaknesses, and scoring rubrics, which summarize performance in a general way that provides much less specific diagnostic information. Rubrics are especially useful for setting pupil achievement targets and for obtaining a summative, single-score representation of pupil performance.

Rubrics summarize performance in a general way, whereas checklists and rating scales can provide specific diagnostic information about pupil strengths and weaknesses.

	Level I Minimal Achievement	Level II Rudimentary Achievement
Communication of ideas **20**	(1–4) Position is vague. Presentation is brief and includes unrelated general statements. Overall view of the problem is not clear. Statements tend to wander or ramble.	(5–9) Presents general and indefinite position. Only minimal organization in presentation. Uses generalities to support position. Emphasizes only one issue. Considers only one aspect of problem.
Knowledge and use of history **30**	(1–6) Reiterates one or two facts without complete accuracy. Deals only briefly and vaguely with concepts or the issues. Barely indicates any previous historical knowledge. Relies heavily on the information provided.	(7–12) Provides only basic facts with only some degree of accuracy. Refers to information to explain at least one issue or concept in general terms. Limited use of previous historical knowledge without complete accuracy. Major reliance on the information provided.
Critical thinking **30**	(1–6) Demonstrates little understanding and only limited comprehension of scope of problem or issues. Employs only the most basic parts of information provided. Mixes fact and opinion in developing a viewpoint. States conclusion after hasty or cursory look at only one or two pieces of information. Does not consider consequences.	(7–12) Demonstrates only a very general understanding of scope of problem. Focuses on a single issue. Employs only the information provided. May include opinion as well as fact in developing a position. States conclusion after limited examination of evidence with little concern for consequences.

Level III Commendable Achievement	Level IV Superior Achievement	Level V Exceptional Achievement
(8–12) Takes a definite but general position. Presents a somewhat organized argument. Uses general terms with limited evidence that may not be totally accurate. Deals with a limited number of issues. Views problem within a somewhat limited range.	(13–16) Takes a clear position. Presents an organized argument with perhaps only minor errors in the supporting evidence. Deals with the major issues and shows some understanding of relationships. Gives consideration to examination of more than one idea or aspect of the problem.	(17–20) Takes a strong, well-defined position. Presents a well-organized, persuasive argument with accurate supporting evidence. Deals with all significant issues and demonstrates a depth of understanding of important relationships. Examines the problem from several positions.
(13–18) Relates only major facts to the basic issues with a fair degree of accuracy. Analyzes information to explain at least one issue or concept with substantive support. Uses general ideas from previous historical knowledge with fair degree of accuracy.	(19–24) Offers accurate analysis of the documents. Provides facts to relate to the major issues involved. Uses previous general historical knowledge to examine issues involved.	(25–30) Offers accurate analysis of the information and issues. Provides a variety of facts to explore major and minor issues and concepts involved. Extensively uses previous historical knowledge to provide an in-depth understanding of the problem and to relate it to past and possible future situations.
(13–18) Demonstrates a general understanding of scope of problem and more than one of the issues involved. Employs the main points of information from the documents and at least one general idea from personal knowledge to develop a position. Builds conclusion on examination of information and some consideration of consequences.	(19–24) Demonstrates clear understanding of scope of problem and at least two central issues. Uses the main points of information from the documents and personal knowledge that is relevant and consistent in developing a position. Builds conclusion on examination of the major evidence. Considers at least one alternative action and the possible consequences.	(25–30) Demonstrates a clear, accurate understanding of the scope of the problem and the ramifications of the issues involved. Employs all information from the documents and extensive personal knowledge that is factually relevant, accurate, and consistent in the development of a position. Bases conclusion on a thorough examination of the evidence, an exploration of reasonable alternatives, and an evaluation of consequences.

USES OF PERFORMANCE ASSESSMENTS

The preceding sections described the steps in developing and scoring performance and product assessments and emphasized the importance of clearly stated performance criteria. In this section we shall examine some of the different ways performance criteria and assessments are being used in schools. The examples that follow do not exhaust all the rich and creative ways teachers are implementing performance assessments, but they do suggest the possibilities. In reviewing these examples note especially how critical the identification of suitable performance criteria is to their success.

Figure 4.5 shows a Book Knowledge Survey for use with beginning readers. Although laid out in a format different from those shown above, this instrument is essentially a checklist. It is meant to chart each pupil's progress towards acquiring skills needed for reading, and provides a section for teacher comments on pupil performance.

Self-Assessment and Peer Review

Self-assessments and peer reviews help pupils understand the performance criteria and can become the basis for class discussion and analysis.

Many teachers include both the definition and the criterion being rated in their performance assessments as a means of: (1) reminding themselves of the areas being assessed and (2) helping pupils critique their own and others' work. Figure 4.6 is a rating scale intended to assess high school pupils' creative writing. After the pupils have completed a creative writing assignment, the teacher may use the rating scale to rate the assignment herself or ask each pupil to **self-assess** his or her own assignment using the scale. Often, reviewing one's work with the performance criteria as a guide helps identify weaknesses in the work.

Alternatively, teachers may engage the pupils in **peer review,** during which pupils exchange assignments and discuss and rate each other's assignment using the creative writing rating instrument. This process allows a pupil to see and judge another pupil's work using the performance criteria. Often this approach helps the pupils doing the rating to thoroughly learn the performance criteria and also provides them with a model against which to compare their own work. Peer review, in conjunction with the performance criteria, can also become the basis for class discussion and analysis of pupils' work, a discussion that can be based upon the desired performance criteria, not unsupported pupil opinion. The teacher may then allow the pupils an extra day to revise their assignment based upon the self- or peer-assessments.

FIGURE 4.5 *(on facing page)*
Book Knowledge Survey
SOURCE: L. Bushnell and M. Lescher, Westwood Public Schools, Westwood, MA, March 29, 1993.

BOOK KNOWLEDGE SURVEY

Student: _____

Date: _____   # of Questions Correct:

Grade: _____

Assessor: _____   # of Survey Questions: 17

Text: _____

Directions: * The book should have illustrations and 1-2+ sentences per page.
   * Ask the questions listed below as they relate to the text.
   * If the student has previously displayed mastery of a line item, the "Previously Demonstrated" column may be checked without repeating the "Survey Question."

Previously Demon.	Survey Questions	Answered Correctly	Comments
	Give student book upside down & backward. Say: "Show me the front cover."		
	"Show me the title."		
	"What is an author?"		
	"What is an illustrator?"		
	"Show me the title page."		
	On a page with both text and illustrations, ask: "Where do we read the story from?"		
	"Point to the words as I read them."		
	When text is written on both left & right pages, ask: "Which page should we read first?"		
	"Find the word _____ ."		
	"Find the capital letter _____ ."		
	"Find the lowercase letter _____ ."		
	"Show me the first letter of a word."		
	"Show me the last letter of a word."		
	Point to a period. Ask: "What is this called?" "What is it for?"		
	Point to a comma. Ask: "What is this called?" "What is it for?"		
	Point to an exclamation mark. Ask: "What is this called?" "What is it for?"		
	Point to quotation marks. Ask: "What are these called?" "What are they for?"		

This rating scale is to help you and me to assess your creative writing. Each work of creative writing you produce will be assessed in terms of the criteria in this scale. Sometimes I will assess your work and other times you or a classmate will be asked to assess your work.

Criteria
VOICE: Voice refers to the ability to express words and images in a distinct, individual manner.

The voice of the student in this piece is distinct and clear, and gives an impression of the kind of person doing the writing.
　　　　always　　　sometimes　　　rarely　　　never

TONE: Tone refers to the attitude and feeling the author conveys regarding her or his subject. If the subject is a tragic one, does the author convey a tone of despair or sadness? If the subject is a joyful one, is a sense of happiness conveyed?

The tone of the piece is clear; it is obvious what type of feeling the author is trying to convey.
　　　　always　　　sometimes　　　rarely　　　never

FOCUS: Focus refers to the writer's ability to concentrate on a particular situation, conflict, or character without introducing unnecessary material that serves to distract the reader.

The focus of the piece is maintained; the author brings the reader into his or her world and retains the reader's attention.
　　　　always　　　sometimes　　　rarely　　　never

DEVELOPMENT: Development refers to the progression of a piece of writing. A piece should have a clear beginning, middle, and end. The characters should also be developed to give the reader a sense of how they think, act, and respond to situations.

The story line and characters are convincingly developed as the piece progresses.
　　　　always　　　sometimes　　　rarely　　　never

MECHANICS: Mechanics refer to the technical aspects of writing, like grammar, spelling, sentence structure, and usage.

The piece is free from mechanical errors,
　　　　always　　　sometimes　　　rarely　　　never

FIGURE 4.6
Creative Writing
Rating Scale
Source: Adapted from
Creative Writing Rating
Form, Mason Miller,
Boston College, 1994. Used
with permission.

Linking Assessment and Instruction

Note that self- or peer-review brings assessment and instruction very close to one another. In fact, it is often difficult to tell whether assessment or instruction is taking place. When students are using the performance criteria to review their own or another pupil's writing, they are neither solely assessing nor solely learning, they are using assessment as a means of learning. Also note that this kind of self- or peer-review and the learning that comes from it would not be possible with most types of paper-and-pencil test items.

Performance assessment can also link instruction and assessment in other ways. For example, rather than having the teacher tell pupils what the important criteria for a performance or product are, the teacher can involve the pupils in the process of identifying important performance criteria. This can be accomplished through class discussion or by providing pupils with good and poor examples of the performance or product and having them identify those characteristics that make the example good or poor. The identified characteristics will become the performance criteria. Involving pupils in this way gives them "ownership" of the criteria and provides them with concrete examples of what are good and poor performances or products. Of course, the teacher must have a prior idea of what the important criteria are in order to select useful examples to show the pupils.

Involving students in developing performance criteria helps them understand what is important about a performance or product.

Teachers often include performance criteria in assignments or exercises to remind the pupils of what is expected of them. In Chapter 3 we saw how essay questions can be made clearer by including the criteria that will be used to score pupils' answers. To focus and clarify pupils' laboratory reports a science teacher included the following performance criteria in the laboratory directions: state the basic problem the lab focuses on; list steps needed to investigate the problem; produce and list reasonable estimates of data values; apply formulas related to the problem; state a conclusion based on the data gathered and analyzed. Informing the pupils of the criteria of a good product or performance in the assignment itself helps focus pupils on the desired criteria when completing the assignment.

Grading

What are essentially scoring rubrics are being widely used in report cards, especially those in the early elementary grades. Figure 4.7 illustrates a rubric that first grade teachers in the Ann Arbor, Michigan Public Schools use to assign grades to pupils. The entire report card is five pages long and contains simplified versions of rubrics such as the ones

NOT YET - 1	2	DEVELOPING - 3	4	ACHIEVING - 5		EXTENDING

Such as: May demonstrate one or _more_ of following:
 	
Identifies the topic but does not identify any details from the book.
Cites information incorrectly.
Draws only from personal experience rather than from evidence in the book.
Identifies details but not topic.
		Such as: May demonstrate one or _more_ of following:
		
		Identifies topic and one (1) detail from the book.
		Identifies several details, but needs prompting to clearly state the main topic.
				Criteria: Demonstrates _all_ of following:
				
				Identifies from an informational book:
				  topic of book,
				  two or more supporting details.
				
				Such as:
				"_This book is about whales. The blue whale is the largest animal on earth. Whales have babies that are born alive — not hatched._"
						Identifies main ideas.
						Identifies background knowledge.
						Distinguishes between what s/he already knew and what was just learned.
						Identifies topic and details of an informational book <u>read by student.</u>

FIGURE 4.7
Scoring Rubric Used in First Grade Report Form
Used with permission of Ann Arbor Michigan Public Schools.

shown in Figure 4.7, as well as a cover page sent home to explain the report cards to parents. The outcomes reported to parents are the language arts and mathematics outcomes the district has identified as most crucial for teachers to monitor and for students to achieve. Notice that each desired outcome is defined by specific performances or products at each of the three rubric levels: not yet, developing learner, and achieving learner.

PORTFOLIO ASSESSMENT

Portfolios are carefully selected collections of a student's performances or products that show accomplishments or improvements over time.

An important addition to the growing uses of performance assessment is **portfolio assessment,** an approach that is gaining widespread use in schools and classrooms (Mitchell, 1992; O'Neil, 1993; Office of Technology Assessment, 1992; Wolf, 1989). A portfolio is a collection of a pupil's performances or products. The term derives from an artist's portfolio, which is a collection of the artist's work designed to show his or her style and range. As used in classrooms, portfolios have the same basic purpose: to collect a series of pupil performances or products that show the pupil's accomplishments or improvement over time. Portfolios are more than folders that hold all of a pupil's work. They contain a consciously selected sample of a pupil's work that is intended to show growth and development towards some important curriculum goal. The basic aim of collecting pupils' work into portfolios is to support instruction and learning. Without a link to instruction and learning, the use of portfolios is a fruitless activity.

A portfolio can be made up of many different pupil performances or products; for example, writing samples, lists of books read, journal entries, photographs, videotapes of musical or dramatic performances, science laboratory reports, handwriting samples, recordings of foreign language pronunciation, solved math word problems, and poems. In one school, first-grade teachers kept a portfolio of tape recordings of their pupils' oral reading. Every three weeks, each pupil read a passage onto his or her own portfolio tape. The tapes were shared with parents and used with pupils to identify areas that needed improvement.

At the middle and high school levels teachers typically have pupils maintain a writing or science portfolio which contains various writing assignments or laboratory experiments that have been done. Often these portfolios contain both rough drafts and finished products to show pupils and the teacher the progression of the work.

As the above examples show, portfolios can be used for many purposes. Whatever the use, it is important that they be guided by a specific purpose, because that purpose will influence what information is collected and how it is used. Too often, teachers defer the question, "What should I do with all this information?" until *after* they have collected large amounts of pupil work into portfolios. Table 4.8 shows the most common purposes for pupil portfolios.

Perhaps the greatest contribution of portfolios is to give pupils a chance to revisit and reflect upon their products and performances. For most pupils, life in school is an ongoing sequence of papers, performances, assignments, and productions. Each day a new batch of these is produced, and the previous day's productions are tossed away, both mentally and physically. Collecting pupils' work in a portfolio retains it for subsequent

Portfolios allow students to revisit and reflect upon their performances and products.

TABLE 4.8 COMMON PURPOSES FOR PUPIL PORTFOLIOS

- ♦ Makes pupils part of the assessment process by requiring them to revisit, reflect on, and judge their own work
- ♦ Gives teachers, parents, and pupils information about pupil progress over time
- ♦ Reinforces the importance of performances and products, not just selection assessments
- ♦ Provides concrete examples of pupils work for parent conferences
- ♦ Permits diagnosis of pupil performances and products
- ♦ Encourages pupils to think about what constitutes good performance in a subject area
- ♦ Grades pupils
- ♦ Gives pupils a chance to reflect on and assess prior work

pupil review and reflection. With suitable guidance, pupils can be encouraged to think about and compare their work over time, an opportunity rarely provided in the absence of portfolios. Pupils might be asked, Which of these portfolio items shows the most improvement? Which did you enjoy most and why? From which did you learn the most? In what areas have you made the most progress over the year? Pupils are allowed to see their progress and judge their work from the perspective of time and personal development.

Portfolio assessment involves the same four steps as other forms of performance assessment: a clear purpose, appropriate performance criteria, a suitable setting, and rating or scoring criteria.

Unfortunately, many teachers view portfolio assessment simply as the collection of all pupil performances. But there is a great deal more to successful portfolio assessment than collecting pupils' work. Portfolio assessment is dependent upon the same four steps as all other types of performance assessment: (1) a clear purpose, (2) appropriate performance criteria, (3) a suitable setting, and (4) rating or scoring criteria. A discussion of each follows.

Purpose of Portfolio

The items that go into a portfolio, the criteria used to judge those items, and the frequency with which items are added or deleted all depend on the portfolio's purpose. Thus, if the purpose of a portfolio is to illustrate for parents a pupil's typical work in some subject area, its contents would likely be more wide-ranging than if its purpose is to assess the pupil's improvement in written composition or oral reading over a single marking period. In the latter case, written compositions or tape recordings of oral readings would have to be obtained periodically throughout the marking period, while in the former, a collection of papers from one day or week of school would suffice.

It is important to determine the purpose and general guidelines for what goes into a portfolio before compiling it. Is it to grade, group, instruct, or diagnose pupils?

If a portfolio is intended to show a pupil's best performance in an area, the contents of the portfolio would change as more samples of performance became available; if the purpose is to show improvement, earlier performances would have to be retained as the portfolio grew. If a purpose is to have pupils reflect on their work, the teacher would need to prepare prompts or questions that would focus the pupils' reflections. Purpose is a crucial issue to consider in carrying out portfolio assessment, and it is important to determine the purpose and general guidelines for the pieces that will go into the portfolio *before* compiling it.

Allowing students to help determine what goes into their portfolios gives them a sense of ownership over it.

In order to promote pupil ownership of their portfolios, it is important to allow pupils to make at least some of the choices as to what pieces will go into their portfolio. Some teachers develop portfolios that contain two types of pieces, those required by the teacher and those selected by the pupil. However, all pupil selections ought to be accompanied by an explanation of why he or she feels that piece belongs in the portfolio. This latter information will require the pupil to reflect on the characteristics of the piece and why it belongs in the portfolio.

Performance Criteria

Performance criteria are needed to assess the individual pieces that make up a portfolio. Without such criteria, assessment cannot be consistent within and across portfolios. The nature and process of formulating such criteria is the same as when formulating them for checklists and rating scales. In fact, the individual pieces in the portfolio will probably be judged using a checklist or rating scale similar to ones discussed earlier. Thus, depending upon the type of performance contained in a portfolio, many of the performance criteria discussed earlier in this chapter could be used to assess individual portfolio pieces.

Performance criteria are needed to evaluate each of the individual pieces within a portfolio.

If portfolios in a targeted subject area are to be kept by all teachers in a school or are to be passed from one teacher to the next as a pupil progresses through the grades, it is advisable for all the affected teachers to cooperate in formulating a common set of performance criteria. Such cooperative practice is useful because it involves groups of teachers in the process of identifying important performance criteria, helps produce common instructional emphasis within and between grades, and fosters discussion and sharing of materials among teachers (Herbert, 1992). It is also reassuring for pupils to have some consistency in both instruction and teacher expectations as they pass through the grade levels.

As with individual checklists and rating scales, it is valuable for teachers and pupils to identify jointly the portfolio performance criteria. This gives pupils a sense of ownership over their performance and helps them think through the portfolio pieces they will produce. Beginning a lesson with joint discussion of what makes a good book report, oral reading, science lab, or sonnet is a useful way to initiate instruction because it gets pupils thinking about the characteristics of the performance or product. Such discussions illustrate how performance assessments can serve both instructional and assessment functions.

There is another, very important, reason why performance criteria are needed for portfolio assessment. The performances or products that make up a portfolio should, like all forms of assessment, reflect the instruction provided to pupils. Performance criteria become the teacher's instructional objectives, identifying the important performances or criteria pupils need to learn. Without explicit criteria, instruction may not provide all the experiences necessary to carry out the desired performance or product, thereby reducing the validity of the portfolio. Of course, once stated, per-

The performance criteria used in evaluating portfolios should align with a teacher's instructional objectives.

formance criteria can be amended and extended. Often, after examining the first few pieces in pupils' portfolios, the need to add, delete, or modify criteria becomes clear.

Setting

In addition to a clear purpose and performance criteria, portfolio assessments must take into account the setting in which pupils' performances will be gathered. In cases involving written portfolios, the performances will usually be gathered by an in-class or out-of-class writing assignment. When portfolios are to be made up of oral or physical performances, science experiments, artistic productions, and the like, special equipment or arrangements may be needed to properly collect the desired pupil performance. Many teachers underestimate the time it will take to collect the performances and products that make up portfolios, as well as the management and record keeping needed to maintain them. In higher grades, pupils can be made responsible for their own portfolios, with periodic teacher checks. This is more difficult to do in lower grades.

Scoring and Judging

Scoring portfolios is a time-consuming process that involves judging each individual piece and the portfolio as a whole.

Lastly, portfolio assessments require methods for scoring and judging pupils' performances. It is important to note that scoring portfolios is a time-consuming task, since not only does each individual piece have to be judged, but also the collected pieces often must be summarized and assessed as a whole. Moreover, the complexity of the performances and products that make up the portfolio (e.g., written stories, tape recordings, laboratory write-ups) requires considerable attention to detail, which further increases scoring time.

When the purpose of a portfolio is only to provide descriptive information about pupil performance to next year's teacher or to parents at a parent-teachers night, no scoring or summarization of the portfolio contents is necessary. The contents themselves provide the desired descriptive information. However, when the purpose of a portfolio is to diagnose, chart improvement, judge the success of instruction, encourage pupils to reflect on their work, or grade pupils, some form of summarization or scoring is required. Individual portfolio pieces are typically scored using the methods discussed earlier in this chapter: checklists, rating scales, and rubrics. Thus, each story, tape recording, lab report, handwriting sample, or cooperative group product can be judged using performance criteria assembled into a checklist, rating scale, or rubric.

Individual portfolio pieces are normally judged using performance criteria that have been assembled into some form of checklist, rating scale, or rubric.

The teacher does not always have to be the one who assesses a portfolio piece. It is desirable and instructive to allow the pupil to self-assess some pieces in order to provide practice in critiquing his or her own work in terms of the performance criteria. Figure 4.8 shows a self-assessment sheet a teacher used to encourage pupils to reflect on their work, revise it, and self-assess the revision. Notice how the teacher let the pupil select the piece to be rewritten but asked the pupil to describe why she chose this particular piece from her writing portfolio and what were its strong and weak points.

Allowing students to self-assess their own portfolio encourages pupil reflection and learning.

FIGURE 4.8
Self-Assessment Sheet

Choose a story from your writing folder that you wish to rewrite. Answer the following questions.

I chose this story because

The best feature of this story is

The things that need improvement in this story are

Rewrite the story, making the improvements you believe are needed. Do your best work. After you have finished rewriting, judge what you have written. Circle the number that describes your story

Spelling, grammar, punctuation
    1 = few capitals, many misspellings, incorrect punctuation
    2 = some errors in spelling, grammar, and punctuation
    3 = amost no errors in spelling, grammar, and punctuation

Organization
    1 = story switches topics, contains unneeded ideas, and is hard to follow
    2 = story usually stays focused on a single topic or idea
    3 = story is focused on a single topic or idea and is easy to follow

Word Usage
    1 = mostly simple words used, few descriptive words
    2 = some imaginative and descriptive words, but only in some parts
    3 = imaginative and descriptive words used throughout

Language and Details
    1 = simple sentence structure used throughout; few details included
    2 = mix of sentence structures in some places; details in some parts
    3 = varied sentence structures and details provided throughout

Story Line
    1 = no central problem or goal; little action or plot development
    2 = story problem or goal stated; story lacks action and development
    3 = story problem or goal stated; plot developed; keeps readers' interest

Then, after rewriting the piece, the pupil was provided performance criteria in the form of a series of rubrics to rate the revised piece.

Consider how much more involved in the writing process this pupil is than when an assignment is given, passed in to the teacher, graded, returned to the pupil, and soon forgotten. Note also the way that this kind of assessment encourages pupil reflection and learning. Even without a formal instrument such as shown in Figure 4.8, it is useful for teachers to develop questions that will focus pupils reflection on their portfolio pieces: Which piece was most difficult and why? Which shows your best work and why? Which are you most proud of and why?

Performance criteria used to assess an entire portfolio are different from those used to assess individual portfolio items.

The performance criteria used to assess an entire portfolio for purposes such as assigning a grade or recommending a pupil placement are usually different from the criteria used to assess individual portfolio items. Such holistic portfolio assessment requires developing a set of summarizing criteria. For example, improvement in writing might be judged by comparing early pieces to later pieces in terms of: (1) number of spelling, capitalization, and punctuation errors; (2) variety of sentence structures used; (3) use of supporting detail; (4) appropriateness of detail to purpose; (5) ability to emphasize and summarize main ideas; (6) link and flow between paragraphs; and (7) personal involvement in written pieces. Alternatively, a teacher might rate earlier written pieces with a general scoring rubric and compare the level of early performances to later performances using the same rubric.

Different portfolios with different purposes require different summarizing criteria. For example, how would you summarize a portfolio containing a number of tape recordings of a pupil's Spanish pronunciation? What indicators would you use to judge *overall* progress or performance?

The contents of a portfolio can also be reported in terms of a summarizing narrative as illustrated in Figure 4.9. The top portion of the narrative shows what the portfolio contains: a history of the pupil's writing productions that includes the date produced, the literary genre, the topic addressed, the reason the piece was written, its length, and the number of drafts produced. The bottom part of the narrative shows the teacher's summary of the pupil's performance, including both descriptions and supporting illustrations. Such narratives are useful in describing a pupil's portfolio, but they are quite time-consuming to construct.

To summarize, assessments of performances, products, and portfolios broaden considerably the information teachers can gather about pupil achievement. Moreover, they involve pupils in their own learning in a deeper, more reflective manner than most paper-and-pencil assessments. Consequently they blur the line between instruction and assessment. Table 4.9 summarizes their main advantages and disadvantages. Because of the time they consume, teachers should begin implementing performance assessments slowly, focusing initially on only one or two particular performances, until everyone, including pupils, becomes comfortable with the demands of these kinds of assessment.

Date	Genre	Topic	Reason	Length	Drafts
9/??	Self-Reflection	Thinking About Your Writing	Requested	1 page	1 draft
10/17	Narrative/Dramatic	Personal Monologue	Important	1 page	2 drafts
1/16	Response to Literature	On *The Lord of the Flies*	Unsatisfying	1 page	4 drafts
2/??	Self-Reflection	Response to Parent Comments	Requested	1 page	1 draft
2/28	Narrative/Dramatic	"The Tell-Tale Heart"	Free Pick	3 pages	2 drafts
5/22	Response to Literature	On *Animal Farm*	Satisfying	5 pages	2 drafts
6/??	Self-Reflection	Final Reflection	Requested	2 pages	1 draft

As a writer, Barry shows substantial growth from the beginning of the year in his first personal monologue to his last piece, a response to *Animal Farm*. Initially, Barry seems to have little control over the flow and transition of his ideas. His points are not tied together, he jumps around in his thinking, and he lacks specificity in his ideas. By January, when Barry writes his response to *The Lord of the Flies*, he begins a coherent argument about the differences between Ralph's group and Jack's tribe, although he ends with the unsupported assertions that he would have preferred to be "marooned on a desert island" with Ralph. Barry includes three reasons for his comparison, hinges his reasons with transition words, but more impressively, connects his introductory paragraph with a transition sentence to the body of his essay. In the revisions of this essay, Barry makes primarily word and sentence level changes, adds paragraph formatting, and generally improves the local coherence of the piece.

By the end of February when he writes his narrative response to Poe's "The Tell-Tale Heart," Barry displays a concern for making his writing interesting. "I like the idea that there are so many twists in the story that I really think makes it interesting." He makes surface level spelling changes, deletes a sentence, and replaces details, although not always successfully (e.g., "fine satin sheets and brass bed," is replaced with the summary description "extravagant furniture"). Overall, it is an effective piece of writing showing Barry's understanding of narrative form and his ability to manipulate twists of plot in order to create an engaging story.

Barry's last selection in his portfolio is an exceptional five-page, typed essay on Orwell's *Animal Farm*. The writing is highly organized around the theme of scapegoating. Using supporting details from the novel and contemporary examples from politics and sports, Barry creates a compelling and believable argument. The effective intertextuality and the multiple perspectives Barry brings to this essay result largely from an exceptional revision process. Not only does he attempt to correct his standard conventions and improve his word choices; he also revises successfully to the point of moving around whole clumps of text and adding sections that significantly reshape the piece. This pattern of revision shows the control Barry has gained over his writing.

In Barry's final reflection he describes his development, showing an awareness of such issues as organizing and connecting ideas, choosing appropriate words and details, and making his writing accessible to his readers. "I had many gaps in my writing. One problem was that I would skip from one idea to the next and it would not be clear what was gong on in the piece. . . . Now, I have put in more details so you don't have to think as much as you would. I also perfect my transitions and my paragraph form. . . . My reading . . . has improved my vocabulary and it helped me organize my writing so it sounds its best and makes the most sense possible. . . .There are many mistakes I have made throughout the year, but I have at least learned from all of them." I agree with him.

FIGURE 4.9

Narrative Description of Pupil's Writing Portfolio
SOURCE: P. A. Moss, et al., "Portfolios, Accountability, and an Interpretive Approach to Validity," *Educational Measurement: Issues and Practice*, 1992, *11*(3), p. 18. Copyright 1992 by the National Council on Measurement in Education. Reprinted by permission of the publisher.

TABLE 4.9   ADVANTAGES AND DISADVANTAGES OF PERFORMANCE, PRODUCT, AND PORTFOLIO ASSESSMENTS

Advantages

- Chart pupil performance over time
- Conduct pupil self-assessment of own products and performances
- Conduct peer review of products and performances
- Provide diagnostic information about performances and products
- Integrate assessment and instruction
- Promote learning through assessment activities
- Give pupils ownership over their learning and productions
- Clarify lesson, assignment, and test expectations
- Report performance to parents in clear, descriptive terms
- Permit pupil reflection and analysis of work
- Provide concrete examples for parent conferences
- Assemble cumulative evidence of performance
- Reinforce importance of pupil performances

Disadvantages

- Most disadvantages associated with performance, product, and especially portfolio assessments involve the time they require:
  - To prepare materials, performance criteria, and scoring formats
  - To manage, organize, and record-keep
  - For teachers and pupils to become comfortable with the use of performance assessments and the change in teaching and learning roles they involve
  - To score and provide feedback to pupils

VALIDITY AND RELIABILITY OF PERFORMANCE ASSESSMENTS

Since formal performance assessments are used to make decisions about pupils, it is important that they be valid and reliable. This section describes steps that can be taken to obtain high-quality performance assessments, ones which can be trusted and used confidently in making such decisions. Three general areas are considered: clarity of purpose, pupil preparation, and improving validity and reliability.

Clarity of Purpose

The purpose of a formal performance assessment influences how it is carried out and scored. Thus, one's method of observation and how one summarizes those observations will differ according to whether the purpose is to grade, group, or diagnose pupils. Without knowledge of the decision to be made, useful assessments cannot be planned. Identify one or two major goals in advance, and try to focus only on them. Too many purposes will detract from good assessment of any single one.

Preparing Pupils for Performance Assessment

The pupil performances that classroom teachers collect and judge should have been taught and practiced prior to being assessed. The overall purpose of performance assessment is the same as other methods of classroom assessment: to determine how much pupils have learned from instruction. The difference between performance assessment and most paper-and-pencil tests is in the ways they gather information about the pupil's learning.

The purpose of performance assessment, like all classroom assessment, is to determine how much pupils have learned from instruction.

Chapter 3 discussed how teachers get their pupils ready for assessment. First and foremost, they must provide good instruction on whatever objectives their pupils are expected to learn. Just as teachers should avoid testing pupils on concepts they were not taught, so too they should avoid performance assessments of untaught behaviors and performances. Furthermore, the instruction should be guided by clearly identified performance criteria.

Pupils learn to set up and focus microscopes, build bookcases, write book reports, give oral speeches, measure with a ruler, perform musical selections, and speak French the same way they learn to solve simultaneous equations, find countries on a map, write a topic sentence, or balance a chemical equation. They are given instruction and practice. Achievement depends upon pupils being taught the things on which they are being assessed. One of the advantages of the various performance assessment methods is that their guiding criteria can be used to identify and remediate specific weaknesses.

In preparing pupils for performance assessment, the teacher should inform them of the performance criteria on which they will be judged. In many classrooms, teachers and pupils jointly discuss and define criteria for a desired performance or product (Herbert, 1992). This helps them to understand what is expected of them by identifying the important dimensions of the performance or product. Another, less interactive way to do this is for the teacher to give pupils a copy of the checklist or rating form that will be used during their assessment. If performance criteria are not made clear to pupils, they may perform poorly not because they are incapable but because they were not aware of the teacher's expectations and the criteria for a good performance. In such cases, the performance ratings do not reflect the pupil's true ability to perform, and the grade received could lead to invalid decisions about the pupil.

Unless students are informed about the performance criteria upon which they will be judged, they may not perform up to their abilities.

Improving Performance Assessments

Judging a pupil's performance involves three distinct actions: observing, responding, and rating.

There are three distinct aspects to judging a pupil's performance: observing, responding, and rating (Almi and Genishi, 1979). When teachers observe, they see how their pupils look, watch what they do, and hear what they say. However, as they observe, teachers also respond to what they see. They are pleased or annoyed by the pupil's appearance, performance, and attention to the task; they feel sympathy for the pupil who is trying very hard but can't seem to pull off a successful performance. Teachers rarely can be completely dispassionate observers of what their pupils do because they know their pupils too well and have a set of built-in predispositions for each one. Although teachers are encouraged to ignore such feelings because they get in the way of objective pupil assessments, in reality, it is almost impossible to do so. However, teachers must at least recognize these feelings and try to judge performance in terms of the established criteria. Clearly, inattentive observation or overemphasis on feelings rather than actual pupil performance diminishes the validity of the assessment and, in turn, the appropriateness of decisions based on it.

The process of observing, responding to, and rating pupil performance is similar to the process of constructing, reading, and scoring essay questions. In each case, there are many irrelevant and distracting factors that can influence the teacher's judgments. The key to improving rating or scoring skills is to try to eliminate the distracting factors so that the assessment will more closely reflect the pupil's actual performance. In performance assessments, the main source of error is the observer who judges both what is happening during a performance and the quality of the performance. Any distractions or subjectivity that arise during the observation or judging process can introduce error into the assessment, thereby reducing its validity and reliability.

Distractions and personal feelings can introduce error into either the observation or judging process, thereby reducing the validity and reliability of the assessment.

Validity

Validity is concerned with whether the information obtained from an assessment permits the teacher to make a correct decision about a pupil's learning. We have already seen that either failure to instruct pupils regarding desired performances or the inability to control personal expectations can produce invalid information and decision making. Another factor which can reduce the validity of formal performance assessment is **bias.** When some factor such as native language, prior experience, gender, or race differentiates the scores of one group of pupils from those of another, we say the scores are biased. That is, judgments regarding the performance of one group of pupils are influenced by the inclusion of irrelevant, subjective criteria.

When irrelevant, subjective factors differentiate the scores of one group of pupils from another, the scores are said to be biased.

Suppose that oral reading performance was being assessed in a second-grade classroom. Suppose also that within the classroom there was a group of pupils whose first language was Spanish. The oral reading assessment involved reading aloud from a storybook written in English. When the teacher reviewed her notes of the pupils' performances, she saw that the Spanish-speaking pupils as a group did very poorly. Would the teacher be correct in saying that the Spanish-speaking pupils have poor oral reading skills? Would this be a valid conclusion to draw from the assessment evidence?

A more reasonable interpretation would be that the oral reading assessment was measuring the Spanish-speaking pupils' familiarity with the English language rather than their oral reading performance. How might the English-speaking pupils have performed if the assessment required reading in the Spanish language? In essence, the assessment provided different information about the two groups (oral reading proficiency versus facility in the English language). It would be a misinterpretation of the evidence to conclude that the Spanish-speaking pupils had poorer oral reading skills without taking into account the fact that they were required to read and pronounce unfamiliar English words.

When an assessment provides information that is irrelevant to the decisions it was intended to help make, the assessment is invalid. Thus, in all forms of assessment, but especially performance assessment, a teacher must select and use procedures, performance criteria, and settings that do not give an unfair advantage to some pupils because of cultural background, language, or gender (Linn, Baker, and Dunbar, 1991). Other sources of error that commonly affect the validity of performance assessments are teachers' reliance on mental rather than written record keeping, and being influenced by prior perceptions of a pupil (Gronlund and Linn, 1990). Each of these errors threatens the validity of interpretations and subsequent decisions. A word about each follows.

Teachers should select performance criteria and settings that do not give an unfair advantage to any group of students.

It is advisable to write down the results of performance assessments at the time they are observed. Failure to do so forces a teacher to rely upon memory when ratings are finally recorded. The longer the interval between the observation and the written rating, the more likely the teacher is to forget important features of pupil performance. Moreover, when a number of pupils are consecutively performing, it is difficult to remember and differentiate clearly among the performances at some later point. In short, failure to record observations and judgments at the time of the performance introduces memory error into the ratings or scores that are awarded later.

Teachers should write down performance assessments at the time they are observed in order to avoid memory error.

Ideally, judgments or ratings should be based solely on the pupil's performance of the desired behaviors. Unfortunately, teachers' prior knowledge of their pupils often lessens the objectivity of their ratings. Factors such as personality, effort, work habits, cooperativeness, and the like are all part of a teacher's perception of the pupils in his or her class. Often, these prior perceptions influence the rating a pupil is given: the likable, cooperative pupil with the pleasant personality may receive a higher rating than the standoffish, belligerent pupil, even though they performed

Assessing pupils on the basis of their personal characteristics rather than on their performance lowers the validity of the assessment.

similarly. Assessing pupils on the basis of their personal characteristics rather than their performance lowers the validity of the assessment.

Reliability

Reliability is concerned with the stability and consistency of assessments. Hence, the logical way to obtain information about the reliability of pupil performance is to observe the performance more than once. Doing this, however, is not reasonable for those school performances that require special settings or equipment. Since each pupil must perform individually, few teachers can afford the class time necessary to obtain multiple observations of each pupil. On the other hand, some performances such as holding a pencil, tracing, cutting with scissors, speaking a foreign language, or measuring with a ruler can be observed and judged quickly, often in the natural flow of classroom instruction. Such behaviors are not difficult to observe repeatedly and therefore permit multiple assessments of pupils' performances.

Reliability is also affected when performance criteria or rating categories are vague and unclear. This forces the teacher to interpret them, and because interpretations often vary, can introduce inconsistency into the assessment. One way to eliminate much of this inconsistency is to be explicit about the purpose of a performance assessment and to state the performance criteria and rating categories in terms of observable pupil behaviors. The objectivity of an observation can be enhanced by having several individuals independently observe and rate a pupil's performance, as in a diving competition. In situations where a group of teachers cooperate in developing criteria for a pupil performance, product, or portfolio, it would not be difficult to have more than one teacher observe and judge a few pupils in order to see whether assessments are objective across teachers. This is a practice followed in performance assessments such as the College Board English Achievement Essay and in most statewide writing assessments.

Many factors reduce the validity or reliability of performance assessments by distorting either observations or scores. They produce assessments that are based upon irrelevant characteristics that have nothing to do with a pupil's actual performance. One remedy for these problems is to cut down the number of distractions that a teacher must face when carrying out a performance assessment. The following guidelines, if conscientiously followed, will minimize such distractions and provide more valid and reliable performance assessments.

- ◆ Know the purpose of the assessment before beginning.
- ◆ Teach and give pupils practice on the performance criteria.
- ◆ State the criteria in terms of observable behaviors and avoid using adverbs such as *appropriately, correctly,* or *well* in performance crite-

Observing a performance more than once increases the reliability of the assessment but is time-consuming.

Unclear or vague performance criteria increase teacher interpretation, which introduces inconsistency into the assessment.

Having more than one person observe and rate a performance increases the objectivity of the assessment.

ria because their interpretation may shift from pupil to pupil. Use overt, well-described behaviors that can be seen by an observer and, therefore, are less subject to interpretation. Inform pupils of these criteria and focus instruction on them.

◆ Select performance criteria that are at an appropriate level of difficulty for the pupils. The criteria used to judge the oral speaking performance of third-year debate pupils would likely be more detailed than those used to judge first-year debate pupils. We would not expect first-year accordion players to perform the same pieces as fifth-year players, or first-grade readers to read as fluently as sixth-grade readers. Make the performance criteria realistic for the pupils' level.

Performance criteria should be realistic in terms of the students' developmental level.

◆ Limit the number of performance criteria to a manageable number. A large number of criteria make observation difficult and cause errors that reduce the validity of the assessment information.

◆ Maintain a written record of pupil performance. Inevitably when a teacher observes many pupils perform and tries to keep a mental record of each pupil's performance, things are forgotten and mistakes made, thereby lowering the validity of the assessments. Checklists and rating scales are the easiest method of recording pupil performance on the important criteria, although more descriptive narratives are often desirable and informative. Tape recordings or video tapes may be used to provide a record of performance, so long as their use does not upset or distract the pupils. If a formal instrument cannot be used to record judgments of pupil performance, then make informal notes of its strong and weak points.

In the end, performance assessments are like essay questions in that it is impossible to eliminate all subjectivity from the scoring process. While this is the reality of the situation, it also is true that performance assessment is the only method that can gather appropriate evidence about many important school outcomes. This reality should not be used to excuse sloppy and error-laden assessment. In this respect, performance assessment is no different from the other assessment techniques that have been discussed. In all cases, problems can be reduced by following suggested practices. It is better to use evidence from imperfect performance assessments than it is to make uninformed decisions about pupil achievement of important school outcomes.

CHAPTER SUMMARY

◆ Performance assessments require pupils to demonstrate their knowledge by creating an answer, carrying out a process, or producing a product, rather than by selecting an answer. Performance assessments complement paper-and-pencil tests in classroom assessments.

♦ Performance assessments are useful for determining pupil learning in performance-oriented areas such as communication skills (oral reading, writing, and speaking); psychomotor skills (tracing, cutting with scissors, dissecting); athletic activities (jumping, throwing a ball, swimming); concept acquisition (demonstrating knowledge of concepts by using them to solve real problems); and affective characteristics (cooperation in groups, following rules, self-control).

♦ Performance assessments have many uses. They can chart pupil performance over time, provide diagnostic information about pupil learning, give pupils ownership over their learning, integrate the instructional and assessment processes, foster pupils' self-assessment of their work, and assemble into portfolios both cumulative evidence of performance and concrete examples of pupils' work. The main disadvantage of performance assessments is the time it takes to prepare for, implement, and score them.

♦ Successful performance assessment requires the following: a well-defined purpose for assessment; clear, observable performance criteria; an appropriate setting in which to elicit performance; and a scoring or rating method.

♦ The specific behaviors a pupil should display when carrying out a performance or the characteristics a pupil product should possess are called performance criteria. These criteria define the aspects of a good performance or product. They should be shared with pupils and used as the basis for instruction.

♦ The key to identifying performance criteria is to break down a performance or product into its component parts since it is these parts that will be observed and judged. It is often useful to involve pupils in identifying the criteria of products or performances. This provides them with a sense of involvement in learning and introduces them to important components of the desired performance.

♦ Try to keep the number of performance criteria small, between ten and fifteen, in order to focus on the most important aspects of performance and simplify the observation process. If possible, work collaboratively with other teachers on common assessment areas or performances.

♦ Avoid using ambiguous words that cloud the meaning of performance criteria (e.g., adequately, correctly, appropriate); state specifically what should be looked for in the performance or product. The criteria should be stated explicitly, so another teacher could use them independently.

♦ Performance assessments may be scored and summarized either qualitatively or quantitatively. Anecdotal records and teacher narratives are qualitative descriptions of pupil characteristics and performances. Checklists, rating scales, and scoring rubrics are quantitative assessments of performance. Portfolios may include either qualitative, quantitative, or both kinds of information about pupil performance.

♦ Checklists and rating scales are developed from the performance criteria for a performance or product. Checklists provide the observer only two choices in judging each performance criterion: present or absent. Rating scales provide the observer with more than two choices in judging: for example, always, sometimes, never or excellent, good, fair, poor, failure. Rating scales may be numerical, graphic, or descriptive. Performance can be summarized across performance criteria numerically or with a scoring rubric.

◆ Portfolios are collections of pupils' work in an area that show change and progress over time. Portfolios may contain pupil products (essays, paintings, lab reports) or pupil performances (reading aloud, foreign language pronunciation, using a microscope).

◆ Portfolios have many uses: focusing instruction on important performance activities; reinforcing the point that performances are important school outcomes; providing parents, pupils, and teachers with a perspective on pupil improvement; diagnosing weaknesses; allowing pupils to revisit, reflect on, and assess their work over time; grading pupils; and integrating instruction with assessment.

◆ Portfolio assessment is a form of performance assessment and thus involves these four factors: definition of purpose, identification of clear performance criteria, establishment of a setting for performance, and construction of a scoring or rating scheme. In addition to performance criteria for each individual portfolio piece, it is often necessary to develop a set of performance criteria to assess or summarize the entire portfolio.

◆ To ensure valid performance assessment, pupils should be instructed on the desired performance criteria before being assessed.

◆ The validity of performance assessments can be improved by: stating performance criteria in observable terms; setting performance criteria at an appropriate difficulty level for pupils, limiting the number of performance criteria to be observed; maintaining a written record of pupil performance; and checking to determine whether extraneous factors (native language, cultural experience) influenced a pupil's performance.

◆ Reliability can be improved by multiple observations of performance or by checking for agreement among those people observing the same performance, product, or portfolio and using the same criteria.

QUESTIONS FOR DISCUSSION

1. What types of objectives would be most suitably assessed using performance assessment?

2. How do formal and informal performance assessment differ in terms of pupil characteristics assessed, validity and reliability of the information obtained, and usefulness for teacher decision making?

3. What are the advantages and disadvantages of performance assessments for teachers? For pupils?

4. How should a teacher determine the validity of a performance assessment?

5. How might instruction differ when a teacher desires to assess pupils' performances and products rather than their responses to selection-type tests?

6. What are some examples of how performance assessment can be closely linked to instruction? For example, how can performance assessment be used to involve pupils in the instructional process?

REFLECTION EXERCISES

1. Suppose you had to construct a teaching portfolio that would show a prospective employer your qualifications for a teaching position. What performance or product evidence would you want to include in your portfolio? Why would you want each of these performances or products included?

2. Think back over the last three years of your schooling. During that time, what types of performance or product assessments have you been required to complete? In what subject areas? What proportion of all the assessments you have taken do you estimate to be nonselection assessments? What weaknesses can you recall in the way the performances or products were presented, explained, or graded? How could they have been improved?

ACTIVITIES

1. Select a subject area you might like to teach and identify one objective in that subject that cannot be assessed by selection or essay questions. Construct a performance or product assessment instrument to assess this objective. Provide the following information: (a) the objective and a brief description of the behavior or product you will assess and the grade level at which it is taught; (b) a set of at least 10 observable performance criteria for judging the performance or product; (c) a method to score pupil performance; and (d) a method to summarize performance into a single score. The assessment procedure used may be in the form of a checklist or a rating scale. A two- to three-page document should be sufficient to provide the needed information. Be sure to focus on the clarity and specificity of the performance criteria and on the clarity and practicality of the scoring procedure.

2. Rewrite in clearer form the following performance criteria for assessing a pupil's poem. Remember, what you are trying to do is write performance criteria that most people would understand and interpret the same way.

   ♦ Poem is original
   ♦ Meaningfulness
   ♦ Contains rhymes
   ♦ Proper length
   ♦ Well focused
   ♦ Good title
   ♦ Appropriate vocabulary level

REVIEW QUESTIONS

1. How do performance assessments differ from other types of assessment? What are the benefits of using performance assessment?

2. What four steps have to be attended to in carrying out performance assessment? What happens at each of these steps?

3. Why are performance criteria so important to performance assessment? How do they help the assessor not only with judging pupils' performance and products but also with planning and conducting instruction?

4. What is the difference between a checklist and a rating scale? How does a portfolio differ from a checklist or rating scale?

5. What are the main threats to the validity of performance assessments? How can validity be improved?

6. What are the major disadvantages of performance assessment?

7. In what ways is scoring performance assessments similar to scoring essay questions?

REFERENCES

Almi, M., and Genishi, C. (1979). *Ways of studying children.* New York: Teachers College Press.

Borich, G. D. (1993). *Observation skills for effective teaching.* Columbus, OH: Charles E. Merrill.

Carey, L. M. (1988). *Measuring and evaluating school learning.* Boston: Allyn & Bacon.

Cartwright, C. A., and Cartwright, G. P. (1984). *Developing observational skills* (2nd ed.). New York: McGraw-Hill.

Ebel, R. L., and Frishie, D. A. (1991). *Essentials of educational measurement.* Englewood Cliffs, NJ: Prentice-Hall.

Fitzpatrick, R., and Morrison, E. J. (1971). Performance and product evaluation. In R. L. Thorndike (Ed.), *Educational measurement* (pp. 237-270). Washington, DC: American Council on Education.

Gronlund, N. E., and Linn, R. (1990). *Measurement and evaluation in teaching.* New York: Macmillan.

Guerin, G. R., and Maier, A. S. (1983). *Informal assessment in education.* Palo Alto, CA: Mayfield.

Herbert, E. A. (1992). Portfolios invite reflection—from both students and staff. *Educational Leadership, 49* (8), 58-61.

Linn, R., Baker, E., and Dunbar, S. (1991). Complex performance based assessment: Expectations and validation criteria. *Educational Researcher, 20* (8), 15-21.

McLoughlin, J. A., and Lewis, R. B. (1990). *Assessing special students.* Columbus, OH: Merrill.

Mitchell, R. (1992). *Testing for learning.* New York: Free Press.

Office of Technology Assessment, U.S. Congress (1992). *Testing in American schools—asking the right questions.* Washington, DC: Government Printing Office.

O'Neil, J. (1993). The promise of portfolios. *ASCD Update, 35* (7), 1-5.

Salvia, J., and Ysseldyke, J. E. (1991). *Assessment in special and remedial education* (third ed.). Boston: Houghton Mifflin Co.

Sax, G. (1989). *Principles of educational and psychological measurement and evaluation.* Belmont, CA: Wadsworth Publishing Co.

Stiggins, R. J. (1987). Design and development of performance assessments. *Educational Measurement: Issues and Practice, 6*(3), 33-42.

Wiggins, G. (1992). Creating tests worth taking. *Educational Leadership, 49* (8), 26-33.

Wolf, D. P. (1989). Portfolio assessment: Sampling student work. *Educational Leadership, 46* (7), 35-36.

Wolf, D. P., Bixby, J., Glen, J., and Gardner, H. (1991). To use their minds well: Investigating new forms of student assessment. In G. Grant (Ed.), *Review of Research in Education, 17* (pp. 31-74). Washington, DC: American Educational Research Association.

CHAPTER 5

GRADING PUPIL PERFORMANCE

GRADING: ITS RATIONALE AND DIFFICULTIES
Why Grade?
The Difficulty of Grading

GRADING AS JUDGMENT

STANDARDS OF COMPARISON
Comparisons with Other Pupils
Comparison to Predefined Standards
Comparison to a Pupil's Ability
Comparison to Pupil Improvement
Grading in Cooperative Learning

SELECTING PUPIL PERFORMANCES
Academic Achievement
Affective Considerations

SUMMARIZING DIFFERENT TYPES OF ASSESSMENT
What Should Be Included in a Grade?
Selecting Weights for Assessment Information
Combining Different Assessment Information
Computing Pupils' Overall Scores

ASSIGNING GRADES
A Criterion-Referenced Example
A Norm-Referenced Example

OTHER METHODS OF REPORTING PUPIL PROGRESS
Parent-Teacher Conferences
Other Reporting Methods

CHAPTER SUMMARY

W e have seen that teachers use a variety of techniques to gather information about their pupils' learning. But classroom teachers must do more than just describe pupils' performances; they must also make judgments about them. The process of judging the quality of a pupil's performance is called **grading.** It is the process by which scores and descriptive assessment information are translated into marks or letters that indicate the quality of each pupil's performance and learning. Assigning **grades** to pupils is a most important professional responsibility, one a teacher carries out many times during the school year and one that has important consequences for pupils.

Grading is the process of judging the quality of a pupil's performance by comparing it to some standard of good performance.

Teachers assign grades both to individual assessments and to groups of individual assessments. When a pupil says, "I got a B on my book report," or "I got an A on my chemistry test," the pupil is talking about a grade on an individual assessment. Report card grades, on the other hand, represent a pupil's performance across all the individual subject area assessments that were completed during a term or grading period. Some people refer to the former process as "assigning grades" and to the latter as "assigning marks," but the basic processes are similar, so we shall use the term "grading" here. Grading will mean making a judgment about the quality of either a single performance or multiple performances made across time.

To judge the quality of a pupil's performance, it must be compared to something else. Thus, when a teacher grades, he or she is making a judgment about the quality of each pupil's performance by comparing it to some standard of good performance. Suppose that Jamal got a score of 95 on a test. His score *describes* his performance, 95 points. But does 95 mean excellent, average, or poor achievement? This is the grading question. In order to answer this question, one needs more than just Jamal's test score. For example, one might want to know how many items were on the test Jamal took, and how much each item counted. A score of 95 does not provide this information. It would undoubtedly make a difference in the way Jamal's performance were judged if he got 95 out of 200 items right as opposed to 95 out of 100 items right. Or, one might like to know how Jamal did in relation to the other pupils in the class. A score of 95 does not tell us this. It would make a difference to know whether Jamal's score was the highest or the lowest in the class. Finally, one might like to know whether Jamal's 95 represents an improvement or a decline compared to his previous test scores. A score of 95 does not tell us this.

GRADING: ITS RATIONALE AND DIFFICULTIES

The purpose of this chapter is to outline the questions teachers face when grading and to provide guidelines to help answer these questions. While the main focus is on the process of assigning report card grades in academic subjects, the principles discussed are also appropriate to grading single tests or performance assessments. A logical place to begin discussion is with the question, "Why grade?"

Why Grade?

The simplest and perhaps most compelling reason why classroom teachers grade their pupils is because they have to. Grading is one kind of official assessment that school teachers are required to carry out. Nearly all school systems demand that classroom teachers make periodic written judgments about their pupils' performance.

Grading is an official assessment required of teachers.

The form of these written judgments varies from one school system to another and from one grade level to another. Some school systems require teachers to record pupil performance in the form of letter grades (e.g., A, A−, B+, B, B−, C+, . . .); some in the form of achievement categories (e.g., excellent, good, fair, poor); some in the form of numerical grades (e.g., 90 to 100, 80 to 89, . . .); some in the form of pass-fail; some in the form of a checklist of specific skills or objectives that are graded individually; and some in the form of teachers' written descriptions of pupils' accomplishments. The most widely used systems are letter grades, which are the main grading system in upper elementary, middle, and high schools, and skill-based or objective-based ratings, which are the most prevalent in kindergarten and the primary grades (Robinson and Craver, 1989; Friedman and Frisbie, 1993).

Some school systems also require teachers to write comments about each pupil's performance on the report card, while others require teachers to grade performance in both academic subject areas and social adjustment areas. Generally, academic grades appear in a different section of the report card than comments or grades concerning social adjustment. There are many different varieties of grade reporting forms, and Figures 5.1, 5.2, and 5.3 show three examples. Regardless of the particular system or report form used, grades are always based on teacher judgments.

Regardless of the grading system or reporting form used, grades are always based on teacher judgments.

Figure 5.1 shows a report card for an early elementary school in which pupils are graded in academic and social adjustment areas using a grading system based on "commendable," "satisfactory (with options for + or −)," and "need for improvement." Figure 5.2 shows a high school report card that describes academic performance based on an A, A−, B+, B, B−, through F system. Figure 5.3 shows a kindergarten report card in which a grade is given to each item in a set of objectives pupils are expected to master.

The purpose of grades is to communicate information about a pupil's academic achievement. Within this general purpose are four more specific purposes: administrative, informational, motivational, and guidance (Hills, 1981; Simon and Bellanca, 1976). *Administratively,* schools need grades to determine such things as a pupil's rank in class, credits for graduation, and suitability for promotion to the next level. *Informationally,* grades are

The general purpose of grades is to communicate information about a pupil's academic achievement.

STOUGHTON PUBLIC SCHOOLS, STOUGHTON, MASSACHUSETTS
PUPIL PROGRESS REPORT
GRADES 1, 2 AND 3

Progress Report of _____ Grade _____ For Year _____

ACADEMIC GROWTH				Report For Term			
				I	II	III	IV
LANGUAGE ARTS (CHECK ONE)	ABOVE GR. LEVEL	AT GR. LEVEL	BELOW GR. LEVEL				
READING							
A. EFFORT							
B. LISTENING SKILLS							
C. ORAL READING							
D. SILENT COMPREHENSION							
E. PHONICS							
SPELLING							
HANDWRITING							
WRITTEN LANGUAGE SKILLS							
A. EFFORT							
B. MECHANICS							
C. CORRECT USAGE							
D. CREATIVE WRITING							
ARITHMETIC ☐ABOVE GRADE ☐AT GRADE ☐BELOW GRADE							
A. EFFORT							
B. UNDERSTANDS CONCEPTS							
C. IS MASTERING BASIC FACTS							
D. IS ACCURATE							
E. APPLIES REASONING IN PROBLEM SOLVING							
SOCIAL STUDIES (GRADE 3)							
A. EFFORT							
B. UNDERSTANDING BASIC CONCEPTS							
SCIENCE (GRADE 3)							
A. EFFORT							
B. UNDERSTANDS BASIC CONCEPTS							
MUSIC							
A. CONDUCT							
B. SHOWS APPRECIATION							
C. PARTICIPATES IN ACTIVITIES							
ART							
A. CONDUCT							
B. SHOWS APPRECIATION							
C. PARTICIPATES IN ACTIVITIES							
PHYSICAL EDUCATION							
A. CONDUCT							
B. MOTOR SKILLS							
C. PARTICIPATES IN ACTIVITIES							

FIGURE 5.1

Example of an Elementary School Report Card

Source: Pupil Progress Report from the Stoughton Public Schools System, Stoughton, MA. Reprinted by permission.

_ _ School_____ Teacher_____

	TERM 1	TERM 2	TERM 3	TERM 4	TOTAL		REPORT FOR TERM			
							I	II	III	IV
ATTENDANCE (NON-CUMULATIVE)										
PERSONAL GROWTH										

1. CONDUCT				
A. CLASSROOM BEHAVIOR				
B. GENERAL SCHOOL BEHAVIOR				
2. WORK HABITS				
A. LISTENS ATTENTIVELY				
B. DEMONSTRATES ORGANIZATION				
C. FOLLOWS DIRECTIONS				
D. USES TIME EFFICIENTLY				
E. WORKS INDEPENDENTLY				
F. COMPLETES HOME ASSIGNMENTS				

ITEMS NOT GRADED ARE NOT APPLICABLE AT TIME OF REPORT

COMMENTS

Assignment for September, 19_____

School_____ Grade _____ Room _____

      TEACHER'S SIGNATURE _____

FIGURE 5.1
(Continued).

FIGURE 5.2
**Example of a High
School Report Card**
SOURCE: Natick High School
Report Card Form, reprinted
by permission of Natick
Public Schools, Natick, MA.

STUDENT NAME			YEAR OF GRAD	STUDENT I.D.	TELEPHONE	HOME ROOM	SEMESTER 1 1989 - 1990	PREV. CREDITS
			1991					62.00

SEMESTER SCHOLARSHIP REPORT

NO.	COURSE		TEACHER	1ST GRADE	1ST MISSED	2ND GRADE	2ND MISSED	EXAM	FINAL GRADE	CREDITS EARNED
11	HEALTH	34	Mr. Fleagle	A	1	A-		B	A-	1.00
133	ENGLISH	30	Mr. Turcotte	B	2	B+		B	B+	2.50
221	AP EUR HIS	30	Mrs. Golden	B	1	B+		B	B	2.50
321	GEOMETRY	30	Ms. Franklin	B	2	C+	1	C+	B-	2.50
433	PHYSICS	31	Mr. Wind	B-		B	2	B-	B	3.00
737	INTRO LAW	34	Mr. Tarot	B+	1	A-		B+	A-	2.50
	MERITS			100		100				
									CREDITS TO DATE	76.00

ATTENDANCE	THIS GRADING PER.	TOTAL THIS YEAR
DAYS ABSENT	0	0
TIMES TARDY	0	0
TIMES DISMISSED	1	1

ATTENDANCE IS RECORDED AS OF 01-19-90

NATICK HIGH SCHOOL
15 WEST STREET
NATICK, MASS. 01760

GUIDANCE COUNSELOR
TELEPHONE

PARENT / STUDENT
PLEASE SEE REVERSE SIDE FOR EXPLANATION OF GRADES

KINDERGARTEN PROGRESS REPORT

Our Lady of Lourdes School
54 Brookside Avenue
Jamaica Plain, MA 02130
542-6136

Student's Name

Teacher's Name

School Year 19 - 19

ATTENDANCE

	D	M	J
Absent			
Tardy			

PHYSICAL DEVELOPMENT

READING READINESS	D	M	J
Recognizes own name			
Knows alphabet in sequence			
Recognizes upper case letters			
Recognizes lower case letters			
Associates sounds with letters			
Is able to blend sounds into words			
Works from left to right			
Shows interest in books/stories			

SMALL MUSCLE

	D	M	J
Dresses self			
Buttons			
Zips			
Laces			
Controls pencil well			
Can cut well			
Colors neatly			
Pastes neatly			

LARGE MUSCLE

	D	M	J
Runs and jumps well			
Can catch, bounce, and throw ball			
Shows partiality to left or right			

LANGUAGE DEVELOPMENT

ORAL

	D	M	J
Speaks clearly			
Expresses ideas and feelings well			
Shares ideas and feelings well			
Uses adequate vocabulary			
Speaks in complete sentences			
Tells story in sequence			

WRITTEN

	D	M	J
Can print full name			
Prints alphabet			

DEVELOPMENT IN ART AND MUSIC

	D	M	J
Is eager to explore art materials			
Is imaginative with art materials			
Identifies colors, shapes and sizes			
Shows enthusiasm for music			
Enjoys singing			

MATH READINESS

	D	M	J
Can count in order			
Recognizes numbers to 10			
Recognizes numbers above 10			
Writes numbers clearly			
Applies knowledge of numbers			
Identifies basic shapes			
Understands math items			
Visually discriminates among likenesses and differences			

SOCIAL DEVELOPMENT

	D	M	J
Accepts responsibility			
Respects others' property			
Respects others' feelings			
Respects authority			
Works well with others			
Plays well with others			
Listens when others talk			

WORK HABITS

	D	M	J
Observes rules and regulations			
Listens carefully			
Follows directions			
Has good attention span			
Completes activities promptly			
Works well independently			
Uses materials correctly			
Takes care of materials			
Cleans up after work period			
Finishes what has been started			
Values own work			
Is observant			

RELIGIOUS DEVELOPMENT

	D	M	J
Is learning to pray and talk to God			
Is learning about God and His creation			

PERSONAL

	D	M	J
Knows full name			
Knows address			
Knows phone number			
Knows age and birthday			

FIGURE 5.3
Kindergarten Report Form
SOURCE: Kindergarten Progress Report from Our Lady of Lourdes School, Jamaica Plain, MA. Reprinted by permission.

Administrative reasons for grading include determining a pupil's rank in class, credits for graduation, and readiness for promotion.

used to inform parents, pupils, and others about a pupil's academic performance. Grades represent the teacher's summary judgment about how well pupils have mastered the content and behaviors taught in a subject during a particular term or grading period. Because report card grades are given only four or five times a year, the information they convey is limited to summary judgments and rarely provide diagnostic information about pupil accomplishments and shortcomings. Teachers recognize this limitation (Hubelbank, 1994). However, it does not diminish the importance of grades for pupils and parents. Remember, grades are only one means of communicating with pupils and parents. Other methods such as parent conferences can provide more detailed information about school progress and will be described later in this chapter.

Grades are used to motivate pupils to study and to guide them toward appropriate courses, course levels, colleges, and special services.

Grades are also used to *motivate* pupils to study. A high grade can be a reward for studying and learning. This motivational aspect of grading is, however, a two-edged sword. Pupil motivation may be enhanced when grades are high, but it may be diminished when grades are lower than expected. Also, it is not desirable to have students study solely to get a good grade. Teachers should try to balance grading rewards with other kinds of rewards.

Lastly, grades are used for *guidance*. They help the pupil, parent, and counselor choose appropriate courses and course levels for the pupil. They help identify pupils who may be in need of special services, and they provide information to colleges about the pupil's academic performance in high school.

Thus, grades are used in schools for many reasons. And while there are periodic calls to abolish grades, it is difficult to envision schools in which judgments about pupils' performance would not be made by teachers and then communicated to various interested parties. The basis on which teacher judgments are made might change, the format in which the grades are reported might be altered, and the judgments might no longer be called "grades," but the basic process of teachers judging and communicating information about pupil performance, that is, "grading," would still be going on.

Because grades can affect students' chances in life, teachers are ethically bound to be as fair and objective as possible when grading pupils.

Grades of whatever form are potent symbols in our society, symbols that are taken very seriously by pupils, parents, and the public at large. Regardless of your personal feelings about the value and usefulness of grades, it is necessary to take the grading process seriously and to devise a grading system that: (1) is fair to your pupils and (2) conveys the message about pupil performance you wish to convey. The teacher has an ethical responsibility to be objective and fair in assigning grades and should never use grades to punish or reward pupils the teacher likes or dislikes.

The Difficulty of Grading

Grading is often a difficult task for teachers for four main reasons: (1) few teachers have had formal instruction in how to grade pupils (Gullickson,

1986; Schafer and Lissitz, 1987; Slavin, 1994); (2) school districts and principals provide little guidance to teachers regarding grading policies and expectations (Hubelbank, 1994); (3) teachers know that grades are taken seriously by parents and pupils and that the grades a pupil gets will be scrutinized and often challenged; and (4) there is a fundamental ambiguity in the teacher's classroom role (Brookhart, 1991; Lortie, 1975), in which the knowledge of pupil needs and characteristics teachers require to provide good instruction is difficult to ignore when the teacher is called upon to be a dispassionate, objective dispenser of grades.

Teachers inevitably face the dilemma of what constitutes fairness in grading. Must a teacher always be fair to the institution that expects dispassionate grading, or can fairness include consideration of a pupil's unique needs, circumstance, and problems? Which is the greater misuse of power: to ignore or to take into account individual pupil circumstances when grading? The special helping relationship that teachers have with their pupils makes it difficult for teachers to judge them on a totally objective basis (Brookhart, 1992; Hubelbank, 1994). This is especially so for grading, because the judgments are public, perceived to be very important, have real consequences for pupils, and can influence the pupil's educational, occupational, or home status.

The helping relationship that teachers have with their pupils makes it difficult to judge them on a completely objective basis.

The following remarks indicate some of the ambivalence teachers feel about grading.

> Report card time is always difficult for me. My pupils take grades seriously and talk about them with each other, even though I warn them not to. They're young (fourth graders), and some let their grades define their self-images, so grades can have a negative effect on some. Still, I guess it doesn't do a kid much good to let him think everything's great in his schoolwork when it really isn't . . . but putting it down on a report card makes it final and permanent. You know you can't make everyone happy when you grade and that some hopes will be dashed. One thing's for sure. I agonize over the grades I give.

> The first report card of the year is always the toughest because it sets up future expectations for the child and his or her parents.

> At the high school level where I teach, grades are given more "by the book" than I think they are in the elementary school. Here we don't get to know our students as well as elementary school teachers and so we can be more objective and give grades based almost exclusively on the students' academic performance. For many teachers at this level, the rank book average defines the grade a student gets, plain and simple. I have to admit that I do recognize differences in pupil interest, effort, and politeness that probably influence my grades a little bit.

These comments indicate that grading is a difficult, time-consuming process that demands considerable mental and emotional energy from teachers and that has important consequences for pupils. Grading is further complicated by the fact that there are no uniformly accepted strategies for assigning grades. Instead, each teacher must find his or her own answer to questions about the grading process. Table 5.1 summarizes both

There are no uniformly accepted strategies for assigning grades.

TABLE 5.1   THE PURPOSES AND DIFFICULTIES OF GRADING

Purposes	Difficulties
◆ **Informational.** Communicate pupils' subject matter achievement.	◆ Teacher's dual role: judgmental, disciplinarian relationship versus helping relationship.
◆ **Administrative.** Make decisions about graduation, grade promotion, class standing, etc.	◆ Preventing pupil's personal circumstances, characteristics, and needs from distorting judgment regarding academic achievement.
◆ **Motivational.** Raise pupils' academic efforts.	◆ Judgmental, subjective nature of grading; evidence always inconclusive.
◆ **Guidance.** Help choose appropriate courses, course levels, and services.	◆ Lack of formal training in grading.
	◆ Lack of universally accepted strategies for grading.

the purposes of grading and some of the more difficult considerations teachers face when assigning grades to their pupils.

GRADING AS JUDGMENT

The most important aspect of the grading process is its dependence on teacher judgments.

The single most important characteristic of the grading process is its dependence upon teacher judgments. Although there are general guidelines to help develop a classroom grading system, all such systems depend on teacher judgment because the teacher knows the pupils and their accomplishments better than anyone else. Consequently, in assigning grades, teachers are granted considerable discretion and autonomy; no one else can or should make grading judgments for a teacher.

Teacher judgments are dependent upon two characteristics: (1) information about the person being judged (e.g., test scores, book reports, performance assessments) and (2) a basis of comparison which can be used to translate that information into grading judgments (e.g., what level of performance is worth an A, a C, or an F). Since information provides the basis for judgment, judging is different from mere guessing. Guessing is what one does when there is no information or evidence to help make a judgment: "I have no information, so I'll just have to guess." To *judge* implies that one has some evidence to consider in making the judgment. Thus, a teacher gathers assessment evidence of various kinds to help make judgments and decisions about instruction and pupil learning. Without this evidence, the teacher's decisions would be guesses, not judgments.

But judgment also implies uncertainty, especially in the classroom setting. When there is complete certainty, there is no need for a teacher to judge. For example, when teachers state "John is a boy," "Mary's parents are divorced," or "Sigmund got the highest score on the math test," they are stating facts, not making judgments about pupils. Judgment, then, is somewhere between guessing and certainty. It is based upon evidence, but the evidence is rarely conclusive or complete, and this uncertainty requires that a teacher judge. Increasing amounts of information reduce, but rarely eliminate, the need for judgment. It is because assessment evidence is always incomplete that teachers must be concerned about the validity and reliability of judgments made from assessment evidence.

A judgment is neither a guess nor a certainty but is based upon evidence the teacher deems valid and reliable.

To summarize, the goal in grading is to obtain enough valid evidence about pupil accomplishments to make a grading judgment that is fair and can be supported. Since grades are important public judgments, they should be based upon mainly formal evidence such as tests and performance assessments. The concreteness of these types of information not only helps the teacher to be objective in awarding grades, they can also be used to help explain or defend a grade that is challenged. Bearing this in mind, there are three main teacher judgments that make up a **grading system:**

◆ Against what standard shall I compare my pupils' performance?

◆ What aspects of pupil performance shall I include in my grades?

◆ How should different kinds of evidence be weighted in assigning grades?

Few school districts have explicit grading policies that tell a teacher how to answer these questions. Most districts have particular grading formats teachers must use (A, B, C, . . .; good, satisfactory, poor, etc.), but teachers must work out for themselves specific details of their grading system such as, What level of performance is A work and what is D work? What is the difference between good and satisfactory performance? Should pupils be failed if they're trying? Even if a teacher does not consciously ask such questions when grading, he or she must implicitly answer them because grades cannot be assigned without confronting these questions.

STANDARDS OF COMPARISON

A grade is a judgment about the quality of a pupil's performance. It is impossible, however, to judge performance in the abstract. Recall the difficulty we had in judging how good Jamal's test score of 95 was when that was our only piece of information. We needed to seek additional information that would allow us to compare Jamal's performance to some standard of goodness or quality. Thus, without comparison, there can be no grading.

Many bases of comparisons can be used to assign grades to pupils (Hills, 1981; Frisbie and Waltman, 1992). Those most commonly used in classrooms compare a pupil's performance to:

♦ The performance of other pupils
♦ Predefined standards of good and poor performance
♦ The pupil's own ability level
♦ The pupil's prior performance (improvement)

A pupil's performance is most commonly compared to the performance of other pupils or predefined standards of good and poor performance.

The vast majority of teachers use one of the first two comparisons in assigning grades to their pupils (Terwilliger, 1971; Friedman and Frisbie, 1993). This is just as well since for technical and substantive reasons, the latter two types of comparison are not recommended.

Comparisons with Other Pupils

Norm-referenced grading is based upon a pupil's comparison with other pupils.

Assigning grades to a pupil based upon a comparison with other pupils in the class is referred to as **norm-referenced grading.** Other names for this type of grading are *relative grading* and *grading on the curve.* A high grade means a pupil did better than most of his or her classmates, while a low grade means the opposite. When a teacher says things like "Jim is smarter than Julie," "Rowanda works harder in social studies than Mike and Pat," and "Maria completes her math worksheets faster than anyone else in the class," the teacher is making norm-referenced comparisons. The quality of a pupil's performance is being determined by how that pupil compares to others in the class.

In this system, not all pupils can get the top grade no matter how well they perform. The system is designed to insure that there is a distribution of grades across the various grading categories. Notice that in the norm-referenced system, the grade contains no indication of how well a pupil did in terms of actually mastering what was taught. A pupil gets an A grade for being higher than his or her classmates. If a pupil answered only 40 out of 100 test questions correctly but was the highest scorer in the class, he or she would receive an A grade in a norm-referenced grading system, despite low mastery of what was tested. The opposite is true at the other end of the scoring range: a pupil may answer 97 out of 100 questions correctly (indicating high mastery) but still get a C, because so many other pupils in the class got 98's, 99's, and 100's. Compared to his classmates, his performance was in the middle of the group even though, in absolute terms, he performed very well.

A grading curve sets up quotas for each grade.

In practice, teachers set up a norm-referenced grading system by establishing a **grading curve.** This curve, which can vary from teacher to teacher and class to class, sets up quotas for each grade to be given. Below is one example of a grading curve.

A   top 20 percent of pupils
B   Next 30 percent of pupils
C   Next 30 percent of pupils
D   Next 10 percent of pupils
F   Last 10 percent of pupils

If this curve is to be applied to grading a chapter or unit test, the teacher would administer the test, score it, and arrange the pupils in order of their scores from highest to lowest. The highest-scoring 20 percent of the pupils (including ties) would get an A grade, the next 30 percent a B grade, the next 30 percent a C grade, and so on. If the same curve were to be applied to giving report card grades, the teacher would first have to summarize the varied information about pupil performance that has been gathered over the entire term. The summary score for each pupil would be arranged in order from highest to lowest, and the percentages in the curve would be applied to allocate grades.

There is no single best grading curve that should be used in every norm-referenced grading situation. Some teachers give mostly A's and B's, while others give mainly C's. Some teachers do not believe in giving pupils F's while others give many F's. If the curve gives too many high grades to mediocre pupils, pupils will not respect it. If it is too difficult to get an A for even bright, hard-working pupils, they will give up. In the end, one seeks a grading curve that is fair to the pupils and that represents academic standards that the teacher feels are appropriate and realistic for the pupils.

To be fair, use a grading curve that represents appropriate and realistic academic standards.

The comparison that is used to assign grades to pupils can influence the effort and attitude of the pupils. Norm-referenced standards, for example, tend to undermine the learning and effort of pupils who continually score near the bottom of the class, since they continually receive poor grades. Norm-referenced grading poses a lesser threat to the top pupils in the class (Crooks, 1988; Deutsch, 1979). Competitive, norm-referenced approaches can make a pupil's success or failure dependent on the performance of classmates and can also reduce pupil cooperation and interdependence, because success for one pupil reduces the chance of success for other pupils (Crooks, 1988).

Norm-referenced grading makes a pupil's grade dependent on the performance of classmates, which can reduce student cooperation.

Comparison to Predefined Standards

Instead of grading by comparison among pupils, the teacher can compare a pupil's performance to preestablished performance standards. These **performance standards** define the level of performance a pupil must attain to receive a particular grade. The test for a driver's license is a simple, pass-fail example of performance standards. In many states, the driver's test contains two parts, a written section covering knowledge of the rules of the road and a performance section in which the applicant must actually drive an automobile around local roads. (Notice how paper-and-

Grading that compares a pupil's achievement to pre-established performance standards rather than to other pupils' achievement is called criterion-referenced grading.

Criterion-referenced grading is the most commonly used grading system in schools.

pencil tests *and* performance assessment are combined in the driver's tests to make certain all important behaviors related to safe driving are assessed.)

The written portion of the driver's test must be passed before the performance portion is attempted, and the written part is usually made up of ten or twenty multiple-choice items. The test is administered to groups of applicants in much the same way paper-and-pencil tests are administered in schools. In most states, passing the test depends upon getting 70 percent of the items correct. In this case, 70 percent is the performance standard. Whether any single applicant passes or fails depends only on how he or she does compared to the performance standard of 70 percent. Passing has nothing whatsoever to do with how the other applicants do on the test because applicants' scores are not compared to one another. Note that in this system it is possible for all or none of the applicants to pass.

Grading that compares a pupil's achievement to a predefined performance standard is called **criterion-referenced,** or *absolute grading.* As in the driver's test, each pupil is graded on the basis of his or her own performance. Since pupils are not compared to one another and do not compete for a limited percentage of high grades, it is possible for all applicants to get high or low grades on a test. Criterion-referenced grading is the most commonly used grading system in schools.

Performance-Based Criteria

There are two types of performance standards that are used in criterion-referenced grading. One type spells out in detail the specific behaviors pupils must perform in order to receive a particular grade. For example, in some classrooms teachers utilize contract grading in which the pupil and teacher negotiate the kind and amount of work the pupil must satisfactorily complete in order to receive a particular grade. If the pupil meets the negotiated performance standard by the end of the semester, he or she receives the promised grade. Alternatively, a more narrow performance standard could be set up to grade each pupil who must give an oral speech. The teacher would observe the speech, concentrating on the specific behaviors listed in the performance standards. On the basis of comparing the observation to the following performance standard or rubric, the teacher would assign a grade to each pupil. Again, notice that each pupil's grade depends only upon how he or she performs in comparison to the standard, not in comparison to other pupils.

A   Pupil consistently faces audience; stands straight and maintains eye contact; projects voice well and clearly; pacing and tone variation appropriate; well-organized points logically and completely presented; brief summary at end.

B   Pupil usually faces audience, stands straight and makes eye contact; voice projection good, but pace and clarity vary during talk;

well organized but repetitive; occasional poor choice of words and incomplete summary.

C   Pupil fidgety; some eye contact and facial expression change; uneven voice projection, not heard by all in room, some words slurred; loosely organized, repetitive, contains many incomplete thoughts; poor summary.

D   Pupil body movements distracting, little eye contact or voice change; words slurred, speaks in monotone, does not project voice beyond first few rows, no consistent or logical pacing; rambling presentation, little organization with no differentiation between major and minor points; no summary.

Percentage-Based Criteria

The second, more common, type of criterion-referenced standard uses cutoff scores based on the percent of items answered correctly. In the case of report card grading, an overall percentage of mastery across many individual assessments is used. Perhaps the most widely used standard of this type is one that has the following cutoff percents:

A   90 to 100 percent of items correct
B   80 to 89 percent of items correct
C   70 to 79 percent of items correct
D   60 to 69 percent of items correct
F   less than 60 percent of items correct

Any pupil who scores within one of the above performance standards will receive the corresponding grade. There is no limit on the number of pupils who can receive a particular grade, and the teacher does not know what the distribution of grades will be until after the tests are scored and graded. Note that this is not the case in the norm-referenced approach.

In criterion-referenced grading, there is no limit to the number of pupils who can receive a particular grade.

Many teachers use different cutoff scores than these; some use 85 percent and higher as the cutoff for an A grade and readjust the cutoffs for the remaining grades accordingly. Others refuse to flunk a pupil unless he or she gets less than half (50 percent) of the items incorrect. Like the curve in norm-referenced grading, the grading standards that are used in criterion-referenced grading are based upon a teacher's judgment about what is suitable and fair for his or her class. Standards should be reasonable given the ability of the class and the nature of the subject matter, and they should be academically honest and challenging for the pupils.

MBO and OBE Programs

Some schools organize curriculum and instruction around sets of specific educational objectives pupils are expected to master in various subject areas. These objectives form the basis for instruction and assessment, with

Management by objectives and outcomes-based education are instructional approaches based on specific educational objectives students are expected to master.

pupils being graded on the number of objectives they have achieved. Common names for such instructional approaches are *management by objectives* (MBO) or *outcomes-based education* (OBE) (Educational Leadership, 1994). Report cards in these programs typically contain a list of each desired objective, and pupils are graded on each objective. Figure 5.3 on page 189 illustrates such a report card for kindergarten pupils.

Grading in MBO and OBE programs is criterion-referenced. Performance standards, generally based on the proportion of items or tasks pupils get correct on assessments of each objective, determine the grade. If the grade to be given has only two levels, say, mastery or nonmastery, the performance standard would specify a single cutoff score that would be used to differentiate pupils who mastered an objective from those who did not. For example, a performance standard might be, "Pupils will be judged to have mastered the objective if they get 80 percent of the items or tasks assessing the objective correct."

If the grade to be given has more than two levels, say, "commendable," "satisfactory," "limited," or "unsatisfactory" (see Figure 5.3), performance standards would have to be set up to differentiate among pupils who belong at each level. For example, "commendable" performance might be defined as getting 85 percent or more of the items or tasks used to assess an objective correct, "satisfactory" as getting 70 to 84 percent correct, "limited" as getting 55 to 69 percent correct, and "unsatisfactory" as getting less than 55 percent correct. Of course, the standards or criteria used to determine the grade may vary by school, teacher, and subject matter.

Interpreting and Adjusting Grades

A criterion-referenced grading system is intended to indicate how much a pupil has learned of the things that were taught. Grades based on invalid assessments or on assessments that fail to cover the full range of what pupils were taught will convey an incorrect message about pupil learning. Of course, valid instruments that fully assess what pupils have been taught should always be used, regardless of the grading approach. However, the content mastery focus of criterion-referenced grades makes it especially crucial that teachers using this grading system develop assessments that cover the full range of behaviors and skills taught.

Regardless of whether one employs a norm- or a criterion-referenced grading system, the grading curve or performance standards should be defined before assessment is carried out. Doing this leads teachers to think about expected performance and allows them to inform pupils of what will be needed to get high grades. When properly defined, a grading system tells pupils what constitutes high and low achievement. However, judgments are sometimes incorrect. Consequently, once established, performance standards and grading curves need not be set in stone. If a standard or curve turns out to be inappropriate or unfair for some reason, it can and should be changed before grades are assigned. If, for example, you found that many of the items on your test were not taught or were worded in a confusing manner, you might decide to discount these items when grades are assigned. In this case, the criterion-referenced standard should be changed to take into account untaught or poorly worded items.

If a grading standard or curve proves to be inappropriate or unfair, it should be changed before grades are assigned.

While changes in performance standards or grading curves should not be made frivolously, it is better to make occasional changes than to award grades that are unfair and incorrect. Usually, increased experience with a class helps a teacher arrive at a set of standards or a grading curve that is appropriate and fair.

Having made this point, it must also be emphasized that fairness to pupils does not mean selecting standards or curves to insure that everyone gets high grades. Lowering standards or a grading curve to guarantee high grades discourages pupil effort and seriousness and diminishes the validity of the grades. Fairness means fully assessing what pupils were taught, using assessment procedures appropriate to the grade level and type of instruction used, and establishing performance standards or grading curves that are realistic if pupils work hard. These are the teacher's responsibilities in integrating instruction, assessment, and grading. Table 5.2 compares the main features of norm- and criterion-referenced grading.

Fairness means assessing what pupils were taught, using appropriate assessment procedures, and establishing realistic performance standards or grading curves.

Comparison to a Pupil's Ability

Teachers frequently remark that "Ralph is not working up to his ability," "Maurice is not doing as well as he can," or "Rose continues to achieve much higher than I expected she would." When teachers make such

TABLE 5.2 COMPARISON OF NORM-REFERENCED AND CRITERION-REFERENCED GRADING

	Norm-Referenced	Criterion-Referenced
Comparison made	Pupil to other pupils	Pupil to predefined criteria
Method of comparison	Grading curve; percent of pupils who can get each grade	Standard of performance; scores pupils must achieve to get a given grade
What grade describes	Pupil's performance compared to others in the class	Pupil's percentage mastery of course objectives
Availability of a particular grade	Limited by grading curve	No limit on grade availability

statements, they are comparing a pupil's actual performance to the performance they expected based on their judgment of the pupil's ability. The terms *overachiever* and *underachiever* are used to describe pupils who do better or worse than judgments of their ability suggest they should. Many teachers assign grades by comparing a pupil's actual performance to their perception of the pupil's ability level (Hubelbank, 1994).

In this grading approach, pupils with high ability who do excellent work would receive high grades, as would pupils with low ability whom the teacher believed were achieving "up to their potential." Even though the actual performance of the low-ability pupils is well below that of the high-ability, high-achieving pupils, each group would receive the same grade if each was perceived to be achieving up to their ability. Conversely, pupils with high ability who were perceived by their teacher to be underachieving would receive lower grades than low-ability pupils who were achieving up to expectations. One of the main arguments that is advanced in defense of this grading approach is that it motivates pupils to do their best and get the most from their ability. Further, it punishes the lazy who do not work up to their perceived ability.

However, this approach to grading is not recommended for a number of reasons (Frisbie and Waltman; 1992; Kubiszyn and Borich, 1989; Terwilliger, 1971). First, it depends on the teacher having an accurate perception of each pupil's ability. In reality, teachers rarely know enough about their pupils to permit valid assessment of ability. Teachers do have a general sense of pupils' abilities from their sizing-up assessments and the pupils' classroom performance, but this information is too imprecise to use as a baseline for grading.

Second, teachers often have a difficult time separating their perception of a pupil's ability from other pupil characteristics such as self-assurance, motivation, or responsiveness. Even formal tests designed to measure ability are rarely precise enough to accurately predict a pupil's capacity for learning. Even for experts, it is all but impossible to make valid predictions about what a pupil of a certain general ability level is capable of achieving in any specific subject area.

Third, grades comparing performance against expectations are confusing to people outside the classroom. For example, a high-ability pupil who attained 80 percent mastery of the instruction might receive a C grade if perceived to be underachieving, while a low-ability pupil who attained 60 percent mastery might receive an A grade for exceeding expectations. An outsider viewing these two grades would probably think that the low-ability pupil mastered more of the course because that pupil got the higher grade. In short, there is little correlation between grades and student mastery of course content in ability-based grading systems.

All of these reasons argue strongly against the use of a grading system that compares actual to predicted achievement. However, some report cards do allow separate judgments about pupil achievement and ability.

Teachers should not assign grades by comparing a pupil's actual performance to their perception of the pupil's ability level.

Even formal tests designed to measure ability are rarely precise enough to accurately predict a pupil's capacity for learning.

The teacher can record a subject matter grade based on the pupil's actual achievement, and then, in a separate place on the report card, can indicate if the pupil is working up to expectations. Usually, the teacher writes comments or checks boxes to show whether the pupil "needs improvement," "is improving," or "is doing best" relative to his or her ability. Even in this approach, teachers must be cautious about putting too much faith in their estimates of pupils' abilities and potential.

Comparison to Pupil Improvement

Basing grades on the improvement a pupil has made over time creates problems similar to those encountered when comparing actual to predicted achievement. Improvement is determined by comparing a pupil's performance early and later in the term. Pupils who show the most progress or growth get the high grades, and those who show little progress or growth get the low grades. An obvious difficulty with this approach is that pupils who do well early in the term have little opportunity to improve and thus have little chance to get good grades. Low scorers at the start of the term have the best chance for improvement and, therefore, high grades. It is not surprising that students graded on improvement quickly realize that it is in their best interests to do poorly on the early tests. There is an incentive to play dumb so early performance will be low and improvement can be easily shown.

Also, like comparing actual to predicted performance, grading on the basis of improvement makes grades difficult to interpret. A pupil who improves from very low achievement to moderate achievement may get an A, while a pupil who had high achievement at the start and therefore improved little may get a B or a C, when, in fact, the latter pupil mastered considerably more of the subject matter than the pupil who got the A grade.

There is little correlation between grades and student mastery of course content in either ability-based or improvement-based grading systems.

Some teachers recognize this difficulty and propose the following solution: "Give the pupils who achieve highly throughout the term an A grade for their high performance, but also give A grades to those pupils who improve their performance a great deal." Certainly this suggestion overcomes the problem noted above. However, it creates a new problem. In essence, what these teachers are proposing to do is use two very different grading systems. The one for high-achieving pupils is based on content mastery while the one for low-achieving pupils is based on improvement. This approach provides rewards for both groups of pupils but confuses the meaning of the grades.

The only way that grades can convey a consistent, understandable message is to apply the same grading system to all pupils in the class. Thus, neither a grading system based on improvement nor a grading system based on different approaches for different groups of pupils is recommended.

The same grading system must be applied to all pupils in the class in order to convey a consistent and understandable message about classroom standards.

Grading in Cooperative Learning

Classrooms at all levels of education are increasingly emphasizing group-based or cooperative learning strategies. In cooperative learning, small groups of two to six pupils are presented with a task or problem situation that they must work together to solve. While the problem itself can be posed in virtually any subject area, the main purpose of cooperative learning is to have pupils learn to work together to arrive at a single, group-generated solution.

In cooperative learning, teachers are usually concerned with assessing two important outcomes: (1) the interactive, cooperative processes that go on within the group and (2) the quality of the group's solution and each member's contribution to and understanding of that solution. We saw in Chapter 4 how the process of assessing group cooperation could be observed and rated using checklists and rating scales (see Table 4.5). While assessing such group processes is important, assessment of subject matter learning is equally important. However, assessing the subject matter learning of individual group members is quite difficult because, in most cases, the group provides only a single, cooperatively reached solution or product. At issue is how one assigns individual pupil grades on the basis of a single group production.

The most common grading practice is to assign a single grade to a group's solution and to give that grade to each group member. The difficulty with such a strategy is that it assumes equal contributions and understanding on the part of each group member. Both the pupil who contributed and learned greatly and the pupil who contributed and learned minimally receive the same grade. On the other hand, to push too hard for individual pupil solutions and contributions destroys many of the benefits of cooperative problem solving. Thus, for many teachers, grading in cooperative learning situations creates problems not encountered in grading individual pupil performance.

There is no single acceptable solution to these problems. Many teachers see no difficulty in assuming equal contributions and learning by each group member and, hence, giving identical grades to all of them. Other teachers mingle assessment of the **group process** with assessment of the **group product,** relying on their observations and interactions with pupils to provide them with a sense of the contribution and comprehension of each group member. Teachers then adjust product grades according to their observation of individual pupil participation, contribution, and understanding. Still other teachers let the pupils self-assess their own contribution and understanding by grading themselves. This approach is less than ideal because pupils' self-assessments will often be based as much on their self-perceptions and confidence as on their actual contribution and learning.

Another strategy that has some advantages over the preceding ones combines group and individual grades. All members of the group get the same grade for their single, group-based solution or product. Subsequently, the teacher requires each pupil to individually answer or perform follow-up or application activities related to the group problem or task. The purpose of these follow-up activities is to determine how well each pupil understands and can apply the group solution in solving similar types of problems. This approach blends group participation and contribution with subject matter learning.

SELECTING PUPIL PERFORMANCES

Once the comparative basis for assigning grades is decided on, it is necessary to select the particular performances that will be considered in awarding the grades. If one is grading a single test or a project, there is obviously only one performance to be considered. If one is assigning report card grades, many formal and informal performances could be considered.

The quantity and the nature of the assessment information available to a teacher varies depending on the grade level and subject area. For example, assigning a term grade in spelling simply involves combining the results of each pupil's performance on the Friday spelling tests. In American history or social studies, however, a teacher may have information from quizzes, tests, homework, projects, reports, portfolios, and worksheets. High school math teachers have homework papers, quizzes, and test results to consider in assigning grades, while English teachers have tests, reports, homework, quizzes, portfolios, projects, and class discussion to consider. In addition to these formal assessments of achievement, teachers also have informal perceptions of pupils' effort, interest, motivation, helpfulness, and behavior. Each teacher must decide which of the available information sources will be used in determining report card grades. This decision is critical, because the performances that are included define what the grade really means. Note that it is not necessary or even desirable for teachers to include all available pupil information when assigning grades.

Each teacher must decide which of the many formal and informal information sources available will be used to determine a report card grade.

Academic Achievement

Subject matter grades are commonly interpreted as an indication of a pupil's mastery of the topics and behaviors that were taught in the course. Hence, formal indicators of pupils' achievement of course objectives should be a major component of subject matter grades. Conversely, effort, behavior, interest, motivation, and the like should not be a major part of subject matter grades. To give an A grade to a pupil who is academically

Subject matter grades should reflect a pupil's academic achievement rather than such things as motivation, cooperation, and attendance.

marginal but very industrious and congenial would be misleading to the pupil, the parents, and others who would likely interpret the grade as indicating high subject matter mastery. Pupils who work hard, are cooperative, and show greater motivation and interest than their classmates deserve to be rewarded, but subject matter grades are not the proper arena for such rewards. Finally, constitutional and case law related to pupil rights suggest that grades should not be heavily dependent upon behavior, interest, and attendance, and should not be used to punish pupils for behavior problems (Bartlett, 1987; Hills, 1991).

Formal, subject matter assessments such as teacher-made tests and homework provide the hard evidence needed to explain or defend a grade.

Formal, subject matter assessments such as teacher-made and textbook tests, papers, quizzes, homework, projects, worksheets, portfolios, and the like are the best types of evidence to use in assigning report card grades. They are suitable in two respects. First, they provide information about pupils' academic performance, which is what grades are intended to describe. Second, being tangible products of pupils' work, they can be used to defend or explain a grade if the need arises. It is defensible to say to a pupil or parent, "I gave a C grade because when I compared your test scores, projects, and homework assignments in this marking period to my grading standards, you performed at a C level." It is not defensible to say, "I gave a C grade because I had a strong sense that you were not working as hard as you could and because I have a negative general perception of your daily class performance."

Since formal assessments of pupil achievement ought to be accorded major weight in assigning grades, it is important to stress that the grades awarded will be only as good as the formal assessment information on which they are based. The meaningfulness of grades is dependent upon the meaningfulness of the assessments on which they are based. Grading as a process cannot be separated from the quality of the assessment information teachers collect prior to grading. Just as good instruction can be undermined by invalid assessment, so too can good grading be undermined by invalid achievement indicators. Irrelevant, invalid evidence about pupil achievement will produce irrelevant, invalid grades.

Pupils are given greater opportunity to demonstrate achievement when grades are based on several types of assessment information.

As the culminating step in the process of assessing pupils' academic achievement, grading ought to be based upon a varied assortment of sound evidence. A general rule of grading is to draw on several different types of information rather than a single type because this gives pupils more opportunity to show what they can do.

If subject matter grades were assigned by machines, it would be easy to base them solely upon formal assessments of pupil achievement. However, teachers are not machines and teachers know a great deal more about their pupils than any grading machine ever could. They know them as whole persons, not one-dimensional achievers. They understand the home background and different effects grades will have on particular pupils. Because of this, teachers rarely can be completely objective, dispassionate dispensers of report card grades, as the following excerpts illustrate:

Jerome works harder than any student in my class, but he cannot seem to overcome his lack of ability. No one tries harder yet his tests and projects are all failures. But I just can't in good conscience give Jerome a failing grade because he tries so hard and an F would destroy him.

Melissa had a terrible term. Her test scores dropped off, her attention during instruction was poor, and she failed to complete many homework assignments. The reason for these behaviors is in her home situation. Her father left the home, her mother had to find a job, and Melissa had to assume most of the household and babysitting responsibilities because she is the oldest child. How can I not take this into account when I grade her this term?

Joe is the ultimate itch: constant motion, inattention, socializing around the classroom at inappropriate times. He drives me crazy. However, his classwork is well done and on time. When I sit down to grade him, I have to refrain from saying "OK Joe, now I'm going to get you for being such a distraction." I have a hard time separating his academic performance from his classroom behavior.

Affective Considerations

One common instance in which pupil motivation, interest, effort, or behavior enter into grades is when they are used to give borderline pupils the benefit of the doubt. When a teacher awards a B+ to a pupil whose academic performance places her between a B and a B+ grade, but who is motivated, participates in class, and works diligently, the teacher is taking into account more than assessments of formal achievement. Teachers often nudge upwards the grades given to conscientious, participating pupils in order to keep them motivated. Strictly speaking, such adjustments distort the intended meaning of a grade, but most teachers do make them based upon their knowledge of particular pupil characteristics and needs. Grading is a human judgmental process, and it is virtually inevitable that such adjustments will occur (Brookhart, 1992).

Pupil effort and participation can be used to adjust a grade but should not be the main determiner of the grade.

Borderline adjustments such as those described above usually operate to the benefit of the pupil and the psychic comfort of the teacher. However, a teacher should guard against allowing effort, motivation, interest, behavior, or personality to become the dominant basis for grades. If this happens, grades will be distorted, providing little useful information about the pupil's academic achievement. Although few teachers can ignore nonacademic evidence like pupils' ability, effort, and improvement when they grade (Brookhart, 1992; Griswold and Griswold, 1992; Nava and Loyd, 1992), most correctly use such evidence as a basis for adjustments in pupils' grades, not as the central determiner of grades.

To summarize, we have seen that teachers must decide what standards of comparison they will use in assigning grades. This means deciding upon either a norm-referenced or a criterion-referenced standard. Once this decision has been made, the teacher must establish a grading curve in the norm-referenced approach or a set of performance standards in the criterion-referenced approach. Next, the teacher must determine what performances will be included in the grade. Since grades are mainly intended to convey information about a pupils' subject matter mastery, rather than their personal qualities, grades should be based primarily upon formal assessments of pupil achievement. Although teachers' subjective perceptions and insights inevitably influence the grading process to some extent, they should not be allowed to greatly distort the subject matter grade.

SUMMARIZING DIFFERENT TYPES OF ASSESSMENT

Report card grades summarize each pupil's performance on the many individual assessments gathered during the marking period.

Report card grades require teachers to summarize each pupil's performance on the many individual assessments gathered during the marking period. In some subject areas, summarization across a term is easy and straightforward. Suppose a teacher is getting ready to assign report card grades in spelling. The teacher would simply refer to her marking or grade book for the pupils' scores on each of the weekly spelling tests given during the grading period. It is very important that teachers maintain such grade books and that they be carefully guarded to insure confidentiality of pupil grades.

Suppose there were eleven tests for each pupil, each scored on the basis of 100 points. The teacher's task is to summarize the scores for each pupil and use the resulting number to assign a report card grade. This is a relatively easy task, since each test was scored on the basis of 100 total points and each test was equivalent in terms of importance. The teacher would sum each pupil's score on the eleven tests and find the mean or average score.

Let us assume that the teacher had decided to assign spelling grades using a criterion-referenced approach with the following performance standards: 100 to 90 is an A, 89 to 80 is a B, 79 to 70 is a C, and below 70 is a D. The teacher decided not to flunk any pupils in the first term, so D was the lowest grade she gave. She also decided not to award plusses and minuses but instead to use only A, B, C, and D as possible grades. It is important to recognize that not all teachers would have made these same decisions. Some might have used a norm-referenced grading system, selected different performance standards, and made adjustments based on effort and motivation. Since there is no best way to assign grades in all classrooms, we can discuss the topic only in terms of examples such as this one, which allows us to look at basic issues that should be considered in all grading. In this example, the teacher simply compares each pupil's average across the spelling tests to the performance standards and awards the corresponding letter grade.

This example provides a basic frame of reference for understanding the grading process. It shows how standards come into play in allocating grades, how formal assessment evidence is recorded in a marking book, and how individual scores can be summarized to provide an overall indication of pupil performance for report card purposes. However, most grading situations are not as simple as this example. Consider the more typical example of Ms. Fogarty's marking book for social studies, shown in Figure 5.4.

Notice two important differences between the information Ms. Fogarty has available to grade social studies and the information that was available in the spelling example. In spelling, the only formal assessments were the weekly spelling tests. In social studies, many different kinds of assessment information have been collected during the term. Four homework assignments, two quiz results, four unit test results, and two projects make up the information Ms. Fogarty can use to determine grades in social studies.

SOCIAL STUD.

TERM # 1

	HW #1	HW #2	HW #3	HW #4	quiz	quiz	test unit 1	test unit 2	test unit 3	test unit 4	proj. explor	proj. colon. Amer
Aston, J	✓	✓	✓	✓‑	85	90	80	85	50	80	B+	B
Babcock, W.	✓	✓	✓	✓‑	90	90	85	80	60	80	B	B
Cannata, T.	✓	✓‑	✓	✓	80	75	70	70	45	75	C-	C
Farmer, P.	✓+	✓+	✓+	✓	100	95	90	85	70	95	A-	A-
Foster, C	✓+	✓+	✓	✓	90	80	85	90	65	80	B	B+
Gonzales, E.	✓‑	✓‑	✓‑	✓‑	70	75	60	70	55	70	C	B-
Grodsky, F.	✓‑	✓‑	✓‑	✓‑	65	65	65	60	35	60	C	C
Martin, J.	✓	✓	✓	✓	80	90	70	85	65	85	C	B
Picardi, O.	✓	✓	✓	✓	75	80	85	75	65	80	B	B-
Ross, O.	✓+	✓	✓	✓	85	80	90	90	75	95	A	A-
Sachar, S.	✓‑	✓	✓	✓+	80	85	75	80	40	80	B+	B
Saja, J.	✓	✓	✓	✓	75	80	85	85	50	80	B	B+
Stamos, G.	✓	✓+	✓+	✓	70	60	75	85	50	70	B-	B
Whalem, W.	✓	✓	✓	✓	70	70	50	60	60	70	B-	B-
Yeh, T.	✓+	✓+	✓+	✓+	95	100	95	95	75	95	A	A-

FIGURE 5.4
Marking Book Assessments in Social Studies

In spelling, all test results were expressed numerically, on a scale of 0 to 100 in percents. In social studies, different grading formats are used for different activities: homework assignments are rated ($\sqrt{}$+, $\sqrt{}$, $\sqrt{}$−); quizzes and tests are recorded on a scale of 0 to 100 in percents; and the two projects are recorded as letter grades. Grading social studies will be a more complicated process than grading spelling.

The grading process involves (1) selecting a standard of comparison, (2) determining what kinds of evidence to include in the grade, and (3) determining how to weight each type of evidence.

Despite their differences, both grading processes start out with the same concerns. First, what standard of comparison will be used to award grades? Second, what specific performances will be included in the grade? Let us assume that in social studies, Ms. Fogarty wishes to use a criterion-referenced grading approach and that she wishes to use plusses and minuses in her grades. With this decision made, she must next determine which of the four different kinds of assessment information available to her will be included in the grade. She must not only decide which of these to include but how much each kind of information will count in determining the grades. For example, should a project count as much as a unit test? Should two quizzes count as much as one unit test or four homework assignments? These are questions all teachers face when they try to combine different kinds of assessment information into a single indicator. The following sections contain suggestions for answering such questions.

What Should Be Included in a Grade?

Figure 5.4 shows a marking book page with four different indicators of academic performance: homework, quizzes, unit tests, and projects. In addition to these formal indicators, Ms. Fogarty also has many informal, unrecorded perceptions of each pupil's effort, participation in class, interest, and behavior. Should all of these formal and informal kinds of information be included in the grades?

Some teachers view quizzes and homework to be more closely tied to the instructional process than to the grading process.

Almost all teachers would include the unit test and the project results in determining their pupils' grades. These are major, summative indicators of pupil achievement that should be reflected in the grade a pupil receives. Most teachers would also include quiz results and homework, although there would be less unanimity than for tests and projects. Some teachers regard quizzes and homework as practice activities that are more closely tied to instruction than to assessment. Other teachers view homework and quizzes as indicators of how well pupils have learned their daily lessons and thus include them as part of the pupil's grade. As with most grading issues, the final decision is the classroom teacher's.

Let us assume that Ms. Fogarty has decided to include three types of formal assessment information in her pupils' social studies grades: tests, projects, and quizzes. Let us also assume that she has decided not to include formal ratings of her pupils' effort, participation, interest, and behavior. Having decided what pupil performances will be included, she now must determine whether each kind of information will count equally or whether some kinds should be weighted more heavily than others.

Selecting Weights for Assessment Information

An immediate concern in summarizing pupil performance on different kinds of evidence is how each should be weighted. In general, teachers should give the more important types of pupil performance, such as tests, projects, and portfolios, more weight than short quizzes or homework assignments since they provide a more complete and integrated view of pupils' subject matter learning. In Ms. Fogarty's case, she looked over the information in her marking book, decided that unit tests and projects should count equally and that both should count more than quiz results. She was fairly certain that she had used valid tests that reflected the important aspects of her instruction and that the projects assigned required pupils to integrate their knowledge about the topic in the way she desired. Thus, she was confident in using tests and projects as the main components of her social studies grade. Finally, she decided that the two quizzes would count as much as one unit test.

Although many teachers do not count homework directly in determining grades, they often warn pupils that if more than three or four homework assignments are not turned in, their report card grade will be lowered. Used this way, homework is more an indicator of effort or cooperation than of subject matter mastery. Some teachers do not actually compute pupil homework averages but rely instead on an informal "sense" or "intuition" of how a pupil has performed. Although timesaving, this practice allows subjective factors such as the pupil's behavior or interest in the subject matter to influence the teacher's judgment. Neither lowering pupil grades for missed homework assignments nor determining grades on the basis of an informal "sense" of pupil performance is recommended.

Regardless of how a teacher weights each kind of assessment information, it is strongly suggested that the weightings be simple. It is better to weight some things twice as much as others than to weight some five times as much and others seven times as much. In most instances, the final grades arrived at using a simple weighting scheme will not differ greatly from those arrived at using a more complex weighting scheme.

Methods for weighting the various types of assessment information should be kept simple.

After deciding on her weightings for quizzes, unit tests, and projects, Ms. Fogarty identified seven pieces of information that she would combine to determine her pupils' report card grades in social studies. The seven pieces were:

♦ One overall assessment of quiz results
♦ Four scores from the unit tests
♦ Two project grades

In the final weightings, quiz results count one-seventh of the grade, unit tests count four-sevenths of the grade, and projects count two-sevenths of the grade. Ms. Fogarty next had to combine the available information according to the selected weights.

Combining Different Assessment Information

Figure 5.4 shows that pupil performance on different assessments often is represented in different ways. Somehow Ms. Fogarty must combine the selected scoring formats into a single summary score that includes performance on tests, projects, and quizzes. Some of the information shown in Figure 5.4 will have to be changed into another format, preferably a numerical one. This means that the project letter grades will have to be converted into numerical scores on a scale of 0 to 100 percent, so that they will correspond to the scores for the quizzes and unit tests.

Each type of assessment information should be expressed in terms of the same scale so that they can be combined into a composite score.

It is important that all performance indicators be expressed in terms of the same scale, so that they can be combined meaningfully. For example, suppose a teacher gave two tests, one with 50 items and one with 100 items and that the teacher wanted each test to count equally in determining a pupil's grade. Now suppose that two pupils, Mike and Sam, each got a perfect score on one of the tests and a zero score on the other: Sam getting his perfect score on the 50-item test and Mike getting his on the 100-item test. Since the tests are to count equally, one would think that Sam and Mike's grades should be the same regardless of the number of items on a test. However, if the teacher calculates the average performance for Sam and Mike using the *number* of items they got right across both tests, the result will be quite different averages [Sam's average = $(50 + 0)/2 = 25$; Mike's average = $(0 + 100)/2 = 50$]. Mike would get a higher grade than Sam, even though they each attained a perfect score on one test and a zero score on another and the tests were to count equally. Clearly, combining raw scores across both tests and finding their average does not give equal weight to each test.

The problem in the above example is that the teacher did not take into account the difference in the number of items on the two tests; the teacher did not put the two tests on the same scale before computing an average. If the teacher had changed the scores from number of items correct to *percentage* of items correct *before* averaging, Sam and Mike would have had the same overall performance [Sam = $(100 + 0)/2 = 50$; Mike = $(0 + 100)/2 = 50$]. Or if the teacher had expressed performance on both tests in terms of the 100-point test, the averages would have been the same, since Sam's perfect score on a 50-item test would be worth 100 points on a 100-point scale. Once again, if scores are not expressed in a common scale, pupil performance will be distorted and grades will not reflect actual achievement.

Returning to Ms. Fogarty's example, a way must be found to express project performance on a scale that corresponds to the 0 to 100 percent scale used for quizzes and unit tests. She decided that for project grades, the following scale would be used to give numerical scores to the projects: 95 = A, 92 = A–, 88 = B+, 85 = B, 82 = B–, 78 = C+, 75 = C, 72 = C–, 68 =

D+, 65 = D, 62 = D–, less than 60 = F. If, for example, a pupil got a B– on one of the projects, that pupil's numerical score on the project would be 82. When Ms. Fogarty applied these values to the projects, she ended up with the information shown in Table 5.3. It is important to note that Ms. Fogarty's is not the only way that the different scores could be put on the same scale, nor is it without limitations. It is, however, one way she could accomplish her task with a method she felt comfortable using. With this task completed, Ms. Fogarty has to confront one additional issue prior to computing grades.

Validity of Assessment Information

Before combining assessment information into a grade, the quality of that information must be considered. Grades will only be as meaningful as the information on which they are based. If the project grades were assigned subjectively, with no clear criteria in mind and with shifting teacher attention during scoring, they will not accurately reflect pupil achievement. If the tests were unfair to pupils or did not test a representative sample of what was taught, the scores pupils attained will not be valid indications of their achievement. In this regard, Ms. Fogarty ought to examine the results of Test 3, since they were much lower than the other tests. Do these scores indicate a problem with th3e test or a problem with the effort pupils put into preparing for the test? How should this result be handled in grading? These questions have to be answered before information can be combined and used to grade.

Grades are only as meaningful (valid) as the information upon which they are based.

TABLE 5.3   SOCIAL STUDIES ASSESSMENTS PLACED ON THE SAME SCALE

Social Studies, Term 1

	Quiz 1	Quiz 2	Test 1	Test 2	Test 3	Test 4	Proj. 1	Proj. 2
Aston, J.	85	90	80	85	50	80	85	85
Babcock, W.	90	90	85	80	60	80	85	85
Cannata, T.	80	75	70	70	45	70	72	70
Farmer, P.	100	95	90	85	70	95	92	92
Foster, C.	90	80	85	90	65	80	85	88
Gonzales, E.	70	75	60	70	55	70	75	82
Grodsky, F.	65	65	65	60	35	60	75	75
Martin, J.	80	90	70	85	65	85	75	85
Picardi, O.	75	80	85	75	65	80	85	82
Ross, O.	85	80	90	90	75	95	95	92
Sachar, S.	80	85	75	80	40	80	88	85
Saja, J.	75	80	85	85	50	80	85	88
Stamos, G.	70	60	75	85	50	70	82	85
Whalen, W.	70	70	50	60	60	70	82	82
Yeh, T.	100	95	95	95	75	95	95	92

Ms. Fogarty noticed the poor performance on Test 3 when she scored the test, and no doubt asked herself why the scores were so low. Normally, questions about the match between an assessment instrument and the things pupils were taught occur *before* an assessment instrument is used. Sometimes, however, mismatches are overlooked or do not become apparent until after an assessment is administered and scored. Typically, it is unexpectedly low scores that provoke teachers' concern and attention; rarely do unexpectedly high scores provoke the same reaction. The reason for this discrepancy in teacher reaction is that most teachers probably assume that unexpectedly low scores are the result of a faulty assessment instrument, while unexpectedly high scores are the result of their superior teaching.

Most teachers assume that unexpectedly low test scores are the result of a faulty assessment instrument, while unexpectedly high scores are the result of superior teaching.

Ms. Fogarty looked over the items in Test 3, which was a textbook test, and compared the items to the topics and skills she had taught in that unit. She found that one section of the unit that she had decided not to teach contributed a large number of test items that she had failed to remove. Thus, the match between the test and classroom instruction was not good. Pupils were being penalized because her instruction had failed to cover many concepts included in the test. Thus, to use these scores from Test 3 would provide a distorted picture of her pupils' actual achievement, and this, in turn, would reduce the validity of their grades.

To avoid this, Ms. Fogarty decided to change the pupils' scores on Test 3 to better reflect their achievement. She estimated that about 20 to 25 percent of the items on the test were from the section she had not taught. She checked and saw that most pupils had done poorly on these items so she decided to increase each pupil's Test 3 score by 20 percentage points. She correctly reasoned that the increased scores would provide a better indication of what pupils had learned *from the instruction provided* than would the original scores. After adjusting each pupil's Test 3 score, all of the assessment information in Table 5.3 will have been placed on a common scale that ranges from 0 to 100 and indicates the percentage of mastery by each pupil on each assessment.

If unexpectedly low scores on some part of a test indicate a mismatch with instruction, then grading adjustments should be made.

It is important to point out that Ms. Fogarty adjusted the low scores on Test 3 only after reexamining both the test and her instruction. She did not raise the scores to make the pupils feel better about themselves, to have them like her more, or for other, similar reasons. The test scores were raised so that they would provide a more valid indication of how well pupils learned from their instruction. It made her grades better reflect her pupils' subject matter mastery. Low assessment scores should not be raised simply because they are low or because the teacher is disappointed with them.

Computing Pupils' Overall Scores

Having decided on score equivalents for the project assessments and having adjusted scores on Test 3 to correct the partial mismatch between instruction and the test items, Ms. Fogarty is ready to compute her pupils' social studies grades. To do this, she must (1) give each kind of assessment information the weight she decided on; (2) sum the scores; and (3) divide by 7, which is the number of assessment items she is using to grade (1 overall quiz score, 4 test scores, and 2 project scores). This computation will provide an average social studies score for each pupil during the marking period. Table 5.4 shows the seven components to be included in each pupil's grade, their total, and their average. To make her task simpler, Ms. Fogarty decided that all fractions would be rounded off to the nearest whole number.

Strictly speaking, the actual weight that a particular assessment carries in determining a grade depends on the spread of scores on that assessment compared to the spread of scores on other assessments (Frisbie and Waltman, 1992). The greater the spread of scores on an assessment, the greater the influence that assessment will have on the final grade when averaged with other assessments. Fairly simple and straightforward techniques are available for equalizing the influence of assessments whose scores are widely spread (Oosterhof, 1987). However, this is not a major problem with most classroom assessments, which generally are given in a similar format to the same group of pupils, cover the topics taught in instruction, and are scored in the same way. Under these conditions, the spread of scores on different assessments will usually be close enough so that adjustments need not be made. Table 5.4 shows that the difference between the highest and lowest score on each of the seven assessments are 33 for the quiz score; 35, 35, 40, and 25 for the four tests; and 23 and 18 for the two projects. These

TABLE 5.4   COMPUTATION OF PUPILS' SOCIAL STUDIES GRADES

Social Studies, Term 1

	Quizzes	Test 1	Test 2	Test 3	Test 4	Proj. 1	Proj. 2	Total Score	Average
Aston, J.	88	80	85	70	80	88	85	576	82
Babcock, W.	90	85	80	80	80	85	85	585	84
Cannata, T.	78	70	70	65	70	72	70	495	71
Farmer, P.	98	90	85	90	95	92	92	642	92
Foster, C.	85	85	90	85	80	85	88	598	85
Gonzales, E.	73	60	70	75	70	75	82	505	72
Grodsky, F.	65	65	60	55	60	75	75	455	65
Martin, J.	85	70	85	85	85	75	85	570	81
Picardi, O.	78	85	75	85	80	85	82	570	81
Ross, O.	83	90	90	95	95	95	92	640	91
Sachar, S.	83	75	80	60	80	88	85	551	79
Saja, J.	78	85	85	70	80	85	88	565	81
Stamos, G.	65	75	85	70	70	82	85	532	76
Whalen, W.	70	50	60	80	70	82	82	494	71
Yeh, T.	98	95	95	95	95	95	92	665	95

ranges are similar enough to permit the seven components to be added and averaged to determine an overall pupil score.

Table 5.4 shows the final average of each pupil after each piece of assessment information was weighted in the way chosen. Consider J. Aston's scores in Table 5.4. This pupil received a quiz score of 88, based upon the average of two quizzes rounded off to a whole number. The four test scores are as shown in Table 5.3, except that 20 points have been added to Test 3 as Ms. Fogarty decided. The two project grades are expressed in terms of the numerical equivalents Ms. Fogarty selected. Adding these scores gives a total score of 576, which, when divided by 7 (for the seven pieces of information that were combined), gives an average performance of 82. The average for each pupil provides an indication of the proportion of social studies objectives each pupil achieved during the marking period. Notice that this interpretation is only appropriate if Ms. Fogarty's various assessments are scored in terms of *percentage* mastery and if they are fair and representative samples of the things that were taught. Ms. Fogarty now can apply her performance standards to award pupils grades.

Combining all assessments into a numerical average estimates the proportion of objectives each pupil achieved during the period.

ASSIGNING GRADES

A Criterion-Referenced Example

Ms. Fogarty decided to assign grades based upon a criterion-referenced approach because she felt that this approach gave each pupil a chance to get a good grade if he or she mastered what was taught. The performance standards Ms. Fogarty adopted for her social study grades were:

A = 94 or higher	C− = 70 to 73
A− = 90 to 93	D+ = 67 to 69
B+ = 87 to 89	D = 64 to 66
B = 84 to 86	D− = 60 to 63
B− = 80 to 83	F = less than 60
C+ = 77 to 79	
C = 74 to 76	

This is a widely used criterion-referenced grading standard.

Looking at the overall semester averages as shown in Table 5.4, Ms. Fogarty can apply her performance standards to award grades. It is at this juncture that she is likely to consider pupils' nonacademic characteristics. For example, she may say to herself, "This child has worked so hard this term despite an unsettled home situation that it's amazing she was able to focus on her schoolwork at all," or "There is so little positive reinforcement in this kid's life right now that a failing grade would absolutely crush him, even though his performance has been very poor." In short, Ms. Fogarty, like most teachers, is aware of her responsibility to grade pupils primarily on their academic performance but allows herself some room for small individual adjustments. Opinions will always differ about making such grading adjustments, as the following excerpts show:

> I grade strictly by the numbers. I calculate each pupil's average and assign grades based strictly on that average. A 79.4 average is not an 80 average, and thus will get a C+. This is the only way I can be fair to all pupils.

> I calculate the averages based on tests and assignments just like the books say to. But when it comes time to assign the grade, I know I'm not grading an average, I'm grading a kid I know and spend time with every day. I know how the kid has behaved, how much effort has been put into my class, and what effect a high or low grade will have on him or her. I know about the pressure the kid gets from parents and what reaction they will have to a particular grade. If I didn't know about these things, grading would be much easier.

When Ms. Fogarty applied her performance standards to her class averages, her grades were as follows:

Name	Average	Grade	Name	Average	Grade
Aston, J.	82	B−	Picardi, O.	81	B−
Babcock, W.	84	B	Ross, O.	91	A−
Cannata, T.	71	C−	Sachar, S.	79	C+
Farmer, P.	92	A−	Saja, J.	81	B−
Foster, C.	85	B	Stamos, G.	76	C
Gonzales, E.	72	C−	Whalen, W.	71	C−
Grodsky, F.	65	D	Yeh, T.	95	A
Martin, J.	81	B−			

Notice that S. Sachar and G. Stamos are within one point of the performance standard for the next higher grade. It is for pupils who are close to reaching the next higher grade that teachers' judgments about nonacademic characteristics usually enter into grading, although Ms. Fogarty chose not to raise either pupil's grade.

To summarize, Ms. Fogarty had to make many decisions to arrive at these grades. She had to decide whether to use a norm-referenced or a criterion-referenced grading approach. Having selected the criterion-referenced approach, she had to decide on performance standards for awarding

Teachers' judgments about nonacademic characteristics often enter into grading when the student is close to reaching the next higher grade level.

TABLE 5.5   STEPS IN THE GRADING PROCESS

- ◆ Select a standard of comparison (norm or criterion).
- ◆ Select types of performances (tests, quizzes, projects, etc.).
- ◆ Determine weights for selected performances.
- ◆ Review selected performances and adjust scores if necessary.
- ◆ Put selected performances on a common scale.
- ◆ Summarize scores.
- ◆ Calculate grades and decide if individual pupil adjustments are warranted.

grades. Next she had to decide upon the kinds of assessment information that would be included in her grades and how to weight each one. Since some of the information she wished to include was expressed as percentage scores out of 100 and others were expressed as project grades, Ms. Fogarty had to decide how to put the project grades on the same scale as the test scores. Then she had to decide whether to adjust any scores because of faulty instruments. Finally, she had to decide whether to base her grades solely on the pupil's average academic performance or to alter them slightly because of affective or personal characteristics. Different teachers with different classes and in different schools would likely have made different decisions than Ms. Fogarty, but they all would have had to confront the same issues. Table 5.5 summarizes the steps in the grading process.

A Norm-Referenced Example

In norm-referenced grading, a teacher decides in advance the percentage of pupils receiving each grade.

To complete this example, consider how Ms. Fogarty would have assigned grades if she had chosen a norm-referenced grading approach. In this case, she would have decided in advance upon a grading curve that identified the percentage of pupils whom she wanted to receive each grade. Suppose she used a norm-referenced curve that gave the top 20 percent of the pupils an A, the next 20 percent a B, the next 40 percent a C, and the last 20 percent a D.

To assign grades using this norm-referenced curve, Ms. Fogarty must first arrange the pupils from highest to lowest in terms of their average score over the marking period. Since a norm-referenced approach is based on how a pupil's performance compares to that of the rest of the class, the best way to compare performance is to rank pupils from highest to lowest in terms of their overall average as shown in Table 5.4. This ordering for Ms. Fogarty's class is shown below:

Name	Score	Name	Score
Yeh, T.	95	Saja, J.	81
Farmer, P.	92	Sachar, S.	79
Ross, O.	91	Stamos, G.	76
Foster, C.	85	Gonzales, E.	72
Babcock, W.	84	Cannata, T.	71
Aston, J.	82	Whalen, W.	71
Martin, J.	81	Grodsky, F.	65
Picardi, O.	81		

Since there are 15 pupils in the class, 20 percent of the class is three pupils. Thus, T. Yeh, P. Farmer, and O. Ross, the three highest scoring pupils, will receive A grades. The next 20 percent of her pupils will receive B grades. Thus, C. Foster, W. Babcock, and J. Aston, will get B grades. The next 40 percent of the class (six pupils) will get C grades. Finally, the last 20 percent of the class, T. Cannata, W. Whalen, and F. Grodsky, will receive D grades. In assigning grades by the norm-referenced approach it is important to bear in mind that two pupils who attain the same score must receive the same grade, regardless of the curve being used. Notice the differences in the grade distributions under the norm-referenced and the criterion-referenced approaches. Remember that these differences are mainly the result of decisions made about the grading curve or performance standards that are used.

In norm-referenced grading, two pupils who achieve the same score must receive the same grade, regardless of the curve being used.

OTHER METHODS OF REPORTING PUPIL PROGRESS

Grades, whether on individual classroom assignments or on report cards, are the most common way that pupils and their parents are kept informed of how things are going in the classroom. But grades are limited in the information they convey: They are given infrequently; they provide little *specific* information about how a pupil is performing; and they rarely include information about the teacher's perceptions of a pupil's effort, motivation, cooperation, and classroom demeanor. Moreover, since report card grades usually reflect pupil performance on a variety of assessment tasks, it is quite possible for two pupils to receive the same grade but to have performed very differently on the assessments used to determine the grade. Because of these limitations, other approaches for reporting pupils' school progress also are needed and used by teachers. Table 5.6 lists the

Grades are the most common device by which students and parents are kept informed about how things are going in the classroom.

To have a complete and specific picture of their child's school performance, parents must be informed beyond the report card.

> ### TABLE 5.6   OPTIONS FOR PARENT-TEACHER COMMUNICATION
>
> - ♦ Report cards
> - ♦ Weekly or monthly progress reports
> - ♦ Parents' nights
> - ♦ School visitation days
> - ♦ Parent-teacher conferences
> - ♦ Phone calls
> - ♦ Letters
> - ♦ Class or school newsletter
> - ♦ Papers and work products

many ways teachers can communicate and interact with parents. Each of these forms of communication can provide important supplementary information that rounds out the picture of a pupil's life at school.

Parent-Teacher Conferences

Unlike grades, parent-teacher conferences provide flexible, two-way communication.

Parent-teacher conferences allow flexible, two-way communication, unlike the one-way communication that grades provide. The nature of the communication differs as well. Conferences permit discussion, elaboration, and explanation of pupil performance. The teacher can get information from the parents about their concerns and perceptions of their child's school experience. Information can also be obtained about special problems the pupil is having, from physical and emotional problems to problems of classroom adjustment. Parents can inform the teacher of their concerns, and they can ask questions about the pupil's classroom behavior and about the curriculum being followed. Teachers who are in nursery school or at the last grade of elementary school or middle school will often be asked by parents to recommend the type of school, teacher, or academic program that is most suitable for their child. Certainly a parent-teacher conference addresses a broader range of issues and concerns than a report card grade does.

It is natural for teachers to feel somewhat uneasy at the prospect of a conference with parents. The teacher will want to be respected by the parents, will not want a confrontational experience, and may have to tell parents some unpleasant things about their child. Because the teacher will have certain things he or she wants the parents to know and because there is always an element of uncertainty about the way the conference will go, it is recommended that the teacher have an agenda of the things he or she wants to cover. For example, most teachers will want to provide a description of the pupil's academic and social classroom performance. The teacher will also want to ask the parents questions such as "Does Robert act this way at home?"; "What does he say about the work load in school?" Certainly the teacher will want to give parents the opportunity to ask questions. Finally, the teacher, in conjunction with the parents, will often want to plan a course of action to help the pupil.

Planning is necessary to accomplish such agendas. The teacher will want to gather samples of the pupil's work, perhaps in a portfolio, and identify (with examples) particular behavioral or attitudinal issues that should be raised. If there is a major existing or potential problem, the teacher ought to look over the pupil's permanent record file in the school office to see whether the problem surfaced in other grades. All this needs to be done before the conference.

Finally, the teacher will want to locate a comfortable, private spot to hold the conference. Usually this means before or after school in the teacher's classroom, when pupils are not present. If this is the case, provide suitable, adult-sized chairs for the parents. The author is a veteran of many elementary school conferences in which the teacher sat comfortably behind his or her desk and the author was scrunched down in a primary-sized pupil chair, knees near his chin, trying to act dignified and carry on a productive conference. Conferences work better when they are private and undisturbed and when all parties are comfortably situated.

The following tips can help the actual parent-teacher conference proceed successfully (Gronlund, 1974; Sax, 1980). Set a proper tone. This means making parents feel welcome, maintaining a positive attitude, and remembering that a pupil is not "their" concern or "your" concern, but a mutual concern. If possible, find out what parents want to know about before the conference so that you can prepare for their questions. Don't do all the talking; be a good listener and use the conference to find out about parents' perceptions and concerns. Talk in terms parents will understand; avoid educational jargon that often confuses rather than clarifies. Concrete examples, perhaps from pupil portfolios, help when explaining things to parents. Be frank with parents, but convey both the pupil's strengths and weaknesses. Don't hold back unpleasant information because you think the parents will become confrontational. The aim of parent-teacher conferences is to understand and help the pupil. It is your responsibility to raise issues with parents that will help the pupil, even though discussion of those issues might be unpleasant. If you don't know the answer to a question, don't bluff. Say you don't know and try to find an answer following the conference.

Further, don't talk about other pupils or colleagues by name or by implication. Don't belittle colleagues or the principal in front of parents, no matter what your feelings. Don't say things like, "Last year's teacher did not prepare Rosalie well in math" or "Teachers get so little support for their ideas from the principal." Regardless of whether the statements are true, it is not professional to discuss such issues with parents. Do not compare a child to other pupils by name or show parents other pupils' work,

Conferences should be private, undisturbed, and well planned.

Teachers must maintain their professional demeanor during parent conferences.

test scores, or grades. Teachers are professionals and they have an obligation to act professionally. This means being truthful with parents, not demeaning colleagues in front of parents, concentrating discussion only on the parents' child, and not discussing information from the conference with other teachers. These guidelines are appropriate for all forms of parent-teacher interaction.

If a course of remedial action for the pupil seems appropriate, plan the action jointly with the parents. Make both parties responsible for implementing the plan: "I will try to do these things with Charles in class, and you will try to do these other things with him at home." Finally, summarize the conference before the parents leave. Review the main points and any decisions or courses of action that have been agreed upon.

Parent-teacher conferences can be very useful to both teachers and parents if planned and conducted successfully. They allow the teacher to supplement his or her information about the pupil and the parents to obtain a broader understanding of their child's school performance. The main drawback to parent-teacher conferences is that they are time-consuming, although many school districts are beginning to set aside a day or two in the school calendar specifically for parent conferencing. Table 5.7 summarizes the above guidelines for holding an effective parent-teacher conference.

TABLE 5.7   GUIDELINES FOR PARENT-TEACHER CONFERENCES

1. Plan in advance of the conference by gathering samples of pupil's work and identifying issues to be discussed with parents; find out what parents want to know before the conference, if possible.

2. Identify a private, comfortable place for the conference.

3. Set a proper tone by:
   a. Remembering that the pupil is of mutual concern to you and the parents
   b. Listening to the parents' perspectives and concerns
   c. Avoiding educational jargon and giving concrete examples
   d. Being frank with parents when conveying pupil's strengths and weaknesses

4. If you don't know the answer to a question, say so and find out; don't try to bluff parents.

5. Don't talk about or belittle other colleagues or pupils by name or implication; don't compare one pupil to another by name.

6. If a remedial action is agreed to, plan the action jointly with parents, and make each party responsible for part of the plan.

7. Orally review and summarize decisions and planned actions at the end of the conference.

Other Reporting Methods

Other, less commonly used methods of conveying information about a pupil's school performance are letters or phone calls to parents and pupil-teacher conferences. Letters and phone calls to parents are used mainly to inform parents of a special problem that has occurred and, as such, are used quite infrequently by teachers. Regular written or phone communication between a teacher and a parent is very rare and occurs only if the parent specifically requests frequent progress reports and the teacher agrees to provide them. Certainly from a time efficiency viewpoint, phone calls are better than writing letters to parents. If you do write to parents, it is extremely important that your letter be free of spelling and grammatical errors. Few things can create a poorer impression in a parent's mind than a misspelled, grammatically incorrect letter from their child's teacher.

CHAPTER SUMMARY

- ◆ The process of judging the quality of a pupil's performance is called grading. The single most important characteristic of the grading process is its dependence on teacher judgment, which is always subjective to some degree.
- ◆ Grading is a difficult task for teachers because they have had little formal instruction in grading, they have to make judgments based on incomplete evidence, they have conflicting classroom roles, they must not allow pupils' personal characteristics and circumstances to distort subject matter judgments, and there is no single, universally accepted grading strategy.
- ◆ In grading, the teacher's prime aims are to be fair to all pupils and reflect pupils' subject matter learning.
- ◆ The main purpose of report card grades is to communicate information about pupil achievement. Grades have administrative, informational, motivational, and guidance functions.
- ◆ All grades represent a comparison of pupil performance to some standard of excellence or quality.
- ◆ Norm-referenced grades compare a pupil's performance to that of other pupils in the class. Pupils with the highest scores get the highest grades as defined and rationed by the grading curve.
- ◆ Criterion-referenced grades compare a pupil's performance to a predefined standard of mastery. There is no limit on the number of pupils who can receive a particular grade.
- ◆ Basing grades on comparisons of a pupil's performance to the pupil's ability or record of improvement is not recommended.
- ◆ After selecting the comparative basis for grading, the teacher next must decide what pupil performances will be considered in awarding grades. For subject

matter grades it is recommended that pupil performances that demonstrate subject matter mastery be included in the grade. Effort, motivation, participation, and behavior should not be major parts of subject grades.

♦ Grading requires teachers to summarize many different types of information into a single score. More important types of pupil performance such as tests and projects should be weighted most heavily in arriving at a grade.

♦ In order to summarize various types of information, each one must be expressed in the same way and on the same scale, usually a percentage scale.

♦ Before combining information into a grade, the quality of each piece of selected assessment information should be reviewed and adjustments made if invalid assessments are found. Grades will only be as valid as the assessment information on which they are based.

♦ Grading information should be expanded and supplemented by other means of parent-teacher communication such as conferences, parents' nights, progress reports, and papers and projects sent home.

QUESTIONS FOR DISCUSSION

1. What are the purposes of giving grades to pupils? How well do different grading formats meet these purposes?

2. What are a teacher's responsibilities to pupils when grades are assigned on a paper, test, or project? What additional responsibilities to pupils do teachers have when they assign report card grades?

3. Is the task of assigning report card grades the same for elementary and high school teachers? How might the process of assigning grades differ at the two levels?

4. How can the information on report cards be made more informative for parents and pupils?

5. What are possible ways, both good and bad, that grades can impact on pupils? What can be done to lessen the detrimental impact of grades?

REFLECTION EXERCISES

1. Suppose you were asked to develop the ideal report card for a school. What would the report card look like? What would be its major strengths and major weaknesses?

2. It was argued in this chapter that many teachers dislike report card grading and find it difficult to do. List as many reasons as you can to explain why this is so.

3. (Do this exercise after the grading activity on the next page is completed.) What are the strengths and weaknesses of the grading system you have developed?

TABLE 5.8   GRADING ACTIVITY

Students	Test 1	Test 2	Test 3	Test 4	Project
Malcolm	40	60	55	100	A–
Gretchen	90	95	45	85	A
Charles	70	65	20	30	C
Thomas	85	80	50	85	B–
Jack	70	70	15	65	D
Susan	45	75	45	100	C
Maya	75	80	45	75	B–
Maria	70	75	30	70	A
Oscar	80	90	45	85	C
Angelina	30	40	10	40	D–
James	60	60	15	45	D

ACTIVITY

Table 5.8 contains information that a teacher had accumulated about her students during a marking period. Use this information to assign a report card grade to each student. Answer the following questions as you work through the activity.

1. Will you use a norm-referenced or a criterion-referenced grading approach? Why?

2. Will you include all the information in the table in determining a grade or only some of the information? What will you include and not include?

3. Will all the pieces of information you have decided to include count equally, or will some things count more than others?

4. How will you take into account the fact that students' performance on different pieces of information is represented differently (e.g., percentages, letter grades, excellent-good-poor, high-middle-low)?

5. What, if anything, will you do about Test 3?

6. How will you summarize the different pieces of information into a single score or rating?

7. What will be your grading curve (norm-referenced) or performance standards (criterion-referenced) for awarding grades?

8. What grade would each student receive?

9. In what ways is this exercise artificial? That is, would there be a difference between the way you graded these students and the way a teacher who had actually taught them for the marking period would grade them?

10. If you graded the students in a norm-referenced way, go back and regrade using a criterion-referenced approach. If you graded the students in a criterion-referenced approach, go back and regrade using a norm-referenced approach.

11. Complete Reflection Exercise 3.

TABLE 5.8   GRADING ACTIVITY *(Cont.)*

Class Participation	General Effort	Quizzes and Homework	Behavior	Teacher's Ability (Estimate)
Good	G	G	G	M
Excellent	Ex	Ex	Ex	H
Excellent	G	P	P	M
Poor	P	G	P	H
Good	Ex	P	Ex	L
Excellent	Ex	G	G	M
Good	G	G	G	M
Excellent	G	G	G	M
Poor	P	P	P	M
Poor	Ex	P	Ex	L
Poor	P	P	P	H

REVIEW QUESTIONS

1. What are grades and why are they important? Why do schools give grades?

2. What questions must a teacher answer in order to carry out the grading process? What teacher judgments must be made in the grading process? Why is there no single best way to assign grades to students?

3. In what way is all grading based on comparison? What are common methods of comparison used in grading and how do they differ? What is the difference between norm- and criterion-referenced grading? Which method would you use and why?

4. What are advantages and disadvantages of different grading methods?

5. Why should grades be determined mostly by the academic performances of students rather than by other information a teacher has about them?

6. What information about the grading process should a teacher provide to students?

REFERENCES

Bartlett, L. (1987). Academic evaluation and student discipline don't mix: A critical review. *Journal of Law and Education, 16*(4), 155-165.

Brookhart, S. M. (1991). Grading practices and validity. *Educational Measurement: Issues and Practice, 10*(1), 35-36.

Brookhart, S. M. (1992). *Teachers' grading practices: Meaning and values.* Paper presented at the Annual Meeting of the American Educational Research Association, San Francisco, April.

Crooks, T. J. (1988). The impact of classroom evaluation practices on students. *Review of Educational Research, 58*(4), 438-481.

Deutsch, M. (1979). Education and distributive justice: Some reflections on grading systems. *American Psychologist, 34,* 391-401.

Educational Leadership (1994). *51*(6).

Friedman, S. J., and Frisbie, D. A. (1993). *The validity of report cards as indicators of student performance.* Paper presented at the Annual Meeting of the National Council on Measurement in Education, Atlanta, GA, April.

Frisbie, D. A., and Waltman, K. K. (1992). Developing a personal grading plan. *Educational Measurement: Issues and Practice, 11*(3) 35-42.

Griswold, P. A., and Griswold, M. M. (1992). *The grading contingency: Graders' beliefs and expectations and the assessment ingredients.* Paper presented at the Annual Meeting of the American Educational Research Association, San Francisco, CA, April.

Gronlund, N. E. (1974). *Improving marking and reporting in classroom instruction.* New York: Macmillan.

Gullickson, A. R. (1986). Teacher education and teacher-perceived needs in educational measurement and evaluation. *Journal of Educational Measurement, 23*(8), 347-354.

Hills, J. R. (1981). *Measurement and evaluation in the classroom.* Columbus, OH: Charles E. Merrill.

_____ **(1991).** Apathy concerning grading and testing. *Phi Delta Kappan, 72*(7), 540-545.

Hubelbank, J. H. (1994). *Meaning of elementary school teachers' grades.* Unpublished doctoral dissertation, Boston College, Chestnut Hill, MA.

Kubiszyn, T., and Borich, G. (1989). Marks and marking systems. In L. Anderson (Ed.), *The effective teacher* (pp. 365-369). New York: Random House.

Lortie, D. C. (1975). *Schoolteacher.* Chicago: University of Chicago Press.

Nava, F. J., and Loyd, B. (1992). *The effect of student characteristics on the grading process.* Paper presented at the Annual Meeting of the National Council on Measurement in Education, San Francisco, CA, April.

Oosterhof, A. C. (1987). Obtaining intended weights when combining students' scores. *Educational Measurement: Issues and Practice, 6*(4), 29-37.

Robinson, G. E., and Craver, J. M. (1989). *Assessing and grading student achievement.* (ERS report). Arlington, VA: Educational Research Service.

Sax, G. (1980). *Principles of educational and psychological measurement and evaluation.* Belmont, CA: Wadsworth.

Schafer, W. D., and Lissitz, R. W. (1987). Measurement training for school personnel: Recommendations and reality. *Journal of Teacher Education, 38*(3), 57-63.

Simon, S. B., and Bellanca, J. A. (1976). *Degrading the grading myths: Primer of alternatives to grades and marks.* Washington, DC: Association for Supervision and Curriculum Development.

Slavin, R. E. (1994). *Educational Psychology, 4/E.* Boston: Allyn and Bacon.

Terwilliger, J. S. (1971). *Assigning grades to students.* Glenview, IL: Scott Foresman.

CHAPTER 6

STANDARDIZED ACHIEVEMENT TESTS

TEACHERS' PERCEPTIONS OF STANDARDIZED TESTS

COMMERCIAL ACHIEVEMENT TESTS
Test Construction

ADMINISTERING COMMERCIAL ACHIEVEMENT TESTS

INTERPRETING COMMERCIAL ACHIEVEMENT TEST SCORES
Percentile Rank Scores
Stanine Scores
Grade Equivalent Scores
Three Examples of Test Interpretation

THE VALIDITY OF COMMERCIAL ACHIEVEMENT TESTS
Content Coverage
Test Norms
Test Administration
Interpreting Commercial Test Results

STATE MANDATED ACHIEVEMENT TESTS
Group-Based, State-Mandated Tests
Individual-Based, State-Mandated Tests
An Example of State-Mandated Assessment

CHAPTER SUMMARY

T he types of classroom assessment discussed so far are ones that are initiated and controlled by the classroom teacher. The teacher decides whom to assess, when to assess, what to assess, how to assess, how to score and grade, and how to use the results. These teacher-produced assessments are fundamental ingredients in the teaching-learning process.

However, two types of external, standardized assessments are also administered in most classrooms. A **standardized assessment instrument** is one that: (1) is designed to be used in many different classrooms and schools and (2) is administered, scored, and interpreted in the same way no matter when or where it is administered. These assessments, which rarely are under the direct control of the classroom teacher, include commercially published national achievement tests and state-mandated achievement tests.

Commercially published, national, standardized achievement tests are constructed and sold to school systems by private testing companies. Among the most widely used (Cannell, 1988) of these tests are the: California Achievement Tests, Comprehensive Tests of Basic Skills, Iowa Tests of Basic Skills, Metropolitan Achievement Tests, Sequential Tests of Educational Progress, SRA Achievement Series, and Stanford Achievement Tests.

Most school systems administer at least one commercial test each year to pupils in most grades. Decisions about the use of commercial tests are made either by committees in individual school districts or by state boards of education (Cannell, 1988). Their three main purposes are: (1) to compare the performance of local pupils to that of similar pupils from across the nation, (2) to provide developmental information about pupil performance over time, and (3) to identify areas of pupil strength and weakness.

State-mandated achievement tests are a more recent phenomenon and, as their name suggests, are mandated by a state legislature or board of education for use within that state (Airasian, 1987; 1993). Pupils' performance is compared to statewide performance standards to determine whether pupils will be allowed to graduate, be promoted to the next grade, or be assigned to remedial instruction. Other state-mandated tests are used to assess school-wide achievement and to certify teachers.

Commercial and state-mandated achievement tests are similar in that both are standardized, are intended for use across many different classrooms, assess content that is not selected by the classroom teacher, and are administered infrequently during the school year. They also differ from each other in many ways. Commercial achievement tests are given at the discretion of the local school system, whereas local systems are mandated to give the statewide achievement tests. Their purposes also differ. National commercial achievement tests are usually intended to compare the performance of pupils in a particular classroom, school, or district to the performance of similar pupils nationwide. State-mandated tests are intended to determine whether an individual pupil or a group of pupils has achieved a minimum level of competence in basic skill

Since standardized tests are designed to be used across many different classrooms and schools, they should be administered, scored, and interpreted the same way no matter where or when given.

Commercial achievement tests are usually given each year. They provide information about pupil performance over time and identify areas of pupil strength and weakness.

Commercial achievement tests compare the performance of local pupils to that of similar pupils from across the nation.

State-mandated tests indicate the level of pupil or group mastery of basic skills deemed important by state educational authorities.

objectives defined by state educational authorities. Table 6.1 compares teacher-made, commercially published, and state-mandated achievement tests.

Table 6.1 shows that teacher-made tests focus more on instructional objectives specific to a particular classroom than do commercial or state-mandated tests, which focus on objectives that are common to most classrooms. The type of test item found on teacher-made tests varies at the teacher's discretion, while most commercial tests are composed largely of multiple-choice items, although recently these tests have begun to include performance-based exercises. Teacher-made tests provide information about the number or percentage of items a pupil gets right; commercial tests provide information about how a pupil compares to his or her peers

TABLE 6.1 COMPARISON OF TEACHER-MADE, COMMERCIAL, AND STATE-MANDATED ACHIEVEMENT TESTS

	Teacher-Made	**Commercial**	**State-Mandated**
Content and/or objectives	Specific to class instruction; picked or developed by the teacher; narrow range of content tested, usually one unit or chapter of instruction in a subject	Topics commonly taught in many schools across the nation; broad range of content covering a year of instruction in a subject	Topics commonly taught or desired to be taught in schools of a state or district; broad range of content covered in a subject area, often covering many years of instruction in a subject
Item construction	Written or selected by the classroom teacher	Professional item writers	Professional item writers
Item type	Various types used	Mainly multiple-choice	Multiple-choice and performance
Item selection	Teacher picks or writes items as needed for test	Many items written and then screened and tried out on pupils before few best items chosen for test	Many items written and then screened; best items chosen for test
Scoring	Teacher	Machine	Machine and scorers
Scores reported	Number correct, percent correct	Percentile rank, stanine, grade-equivalent scores	Usually pass-fail for individuals; percent or proportion of mastery for groups
Interpreting scores	Norm- or criterion-referenced, depending on classroom teacher's preference	Norm-referenced and developmental	Criterion-referenced

the Iowa Tests of Basic Skills battery for the fifth grade is made up of the following thirteen subject tests, or, as they are commonly called, **subtests:** vocabulary, reading comprehension, spelling, capitalization, punctuation, usage and expression, maps and diagrams, reference materials, math concepts and estimation, math problem solving and data interpretation, math computation, social studies, and science. A pupil gets a separate score on each subtest. The entire battery consists of 458 items that take over five hours to complete. The main advantages of a test battery are (1) that its broad content coverage in many subject areas provides a general picture of a pupil's school performance and (2) that a pupil's score on one subtest can be compared to his or her score on other subtests.

A test battery provides a general picture of a pupil's school performance and compares performance across subject areas.

Test Construction

Since the information obtained from a commercial achievement test differs from that obtained from a teacher-made or textbook test, it should not be surprising to learn that the commercial test is constructed differently from the teacher-made or textbook achievement test (Millman and Greene, 1989). A well-constructed, commercial achievement test has three characteristics: (1) it is carefully constructed, with item tryouts, analysis, and revision occurring before the final version of the test is completed; (2) there are written directions and procedures for administering and scoring the test; and (3) score interpretation is based on the test having been administered to a carefully selected sample of pupils from across the nation. The performance of this national sample or **norm group** is what local pupils are compared to when they take the test. Figure 6.1 compares the steps in constructing a teacher-made achievement test with the steps in constructing a commercial achievement test.

Choosing Objectives

Teacher-made and national achievement tests both start with the educational objectives to be tested. In the teacher-made test, the objectives the classroom teacher has emphasized during his or her instruction are assessed. The commercial test constructor, on the other hand, seeks to assess only objectives that are commonly taught in all classrooms at a particular grade level. These objectives are found by examining widely used textbooks and state curriculum guidelines. Those topics and skills that are *common* across textbooks and guidelines are selected for inclusion in the test. This means that some objectives a particular classroom teacher emphasizes may not be assessed by a commercial achievement test.

Commercial tests try to assess objectives that are taught nationally in classrooms at a particular grade level.

Writing and Reviewing Items

Once the objectives to be assessed are identified, the commercial test publisher, like the classroom teacher, must construct or select test items.

CONSTRUCTING ACHIEVEMENT TESTS

TEACHER-MADE

State educational objectives

↓

Write test items (total number needed)

↓

Administer test

COMMERCIAL

State educational objectives

↓

Write test items (three times number needed)

↓

Try out test items on a national sample

↓

Select items for final version

↓

Administer final version to a national sample of pupils

↓

Develop test norms

↓

Sell test for use in schools

FIGURE 6.1
Steps in Constructing Teacher-Made and Commercial Achievement Tests

Unlike the classroom teacher, who writes just as many items as are needed for a test, the commercial test publisher writes two or three times more items than will be needed on the final test.

> To provide a large pool of items for final test selection, one and one-half to two times as many items as would be needed were developed. A staff of professional item writers, most of them experienced teachers, researched and wrote items and passages to be tried out. (CTB/McGraw-Hill, 1985, p. 5)

The items, which are primarily multiple-choice, go through several cycles of review and revision before being accepted for use. Curriculum specialists study the items to be sure that they assess the intended objectives. Test construction specialists review them to be sure they are well written, without ambiguity or clues. Other groups review the items to determine whether they are biased in favor of particular pupil groups. At the end of this stage of test construction, a large group of items that have been screened by many groups are available to the test publisher.

> Each item and subtest was reviewed and edited for content, style, and appropriateness for measuring the stated objective, as well as for ethnic, cultural, racial, and sex bias. (The Psychological Corporation, 1984, p. 1-1)

Commercial test items are reviewed and edited for content, style, and validity, as well as for ethnic, cultural, racial, and sex bias.

Item Tryout

All the items written are tried out and the more valid and reliable ones are selected for the final version of the test. Since no test constructor, whether a classroom teacher or a commercial test publisher, knows how well an item will work until it actually is tried out on a group of pupils, the commercial test publisher tries out the items on a sample of pupils similar to those for whom the final test is intended. The communities chosen for these tryouts represent different sizes, geographical locations, and socio-economic levels (e.g., income and education levels). The trial test forms look like the final test form and are administered by classroom teachers, so that the administrative situation during the tryout will be as similar as possible to the way that the final, published tests will be administered.

There are two reasons why the standardized test constructor tries out test items before finalizing the test. First, the test constructor wants to make sure that all the items are clearly written and understood by pupils. By examining pupil responses after the tryout, unclear items can be identified, revised, or discarded. Second, test items that will ensure a spread of scores among the pupils who take the test must be selected. After the tryout, the statistical properties of each item are analyzed to ensure that the final test contains items that will differentiate among test takers and permit the norm-referenced comparisons that are desired in commercial achievement tests.

Two important indices for judging test items are difficulty and discrimination. The **difficulty** of a test item indicates the proportion of test takers who answered the item correctly. Thus, a difficulty of 90 means that 90 percent of the pupils answered the item correctly, while an item with a difficulty of 15 was answered correctly by only 15 percent of the test takers. The **discrimination** of an item indicates how well pupils who scored high on the test as a whole scored on a particular item. An item that discriminates well between test takers is one that high test scorers get correct, but low test scorers get incorrect. That is, the item discriminates between pupils in the same way as the test as a whole.

The test constructor's purpose is to differentiate among pupils according to their levels of learning. The test constructor is not likely to select items for the final version of the test that all pupils got right or wrong in the tryout because such items do not help differentiate high achievers from low achievers. To accomplish the desired differentiation among pupils, the test must be comprised mainly of items that about half the pupils get correct and half get incorrect and that discriminate among pupils in the same way as the test as a whole. Only then will the test differentiate pupils across the possible scoring range and permit the desired norm-referenced comparisons among test takers. The item tryout provides the information needed to select items for the final test version.

The preceding steps accomplish three important aims: (1) They identify test objectives that reflect what most teachers across the nation are teaching; (2) they produce test items that assess these objectives; and (3)

After tests are tried out, commercial test items are statistically analyzed to ensure that they will provide the spread among scores that are needed on norm-referenced tests.

Item difficulty indicates the proportion of test takers who answered the item correctly.

Item discrimination compares overall test scores to scores on a particular item.

To differentiate among students, commercial tests contain many items that approximately one half of the test takers get right and one half get wrong.

they identify a final group of items that will produce the desired norm-referenced comparisons among test takers. The final version of the test, including the selected test items, directions for administration, separate answer sheets, and established time limits, must then be "normed."

Norming the Test

In order to provide information that allows comparison of an individual pupil's performance to that of a national sample of similar pupils, the final version of the test must be given to a sample of pupils from across the country. This process is called "norming the test." **Norms** describe how a national sample of pupils who took the test actually performed on it.

Suppose that a commercial test publisher wishes to norm the final version of an achievement test for fifth graders. To do this, the publisher needs to obtain information about how fifth graders across the country perform on the test. The publisher would (1) select a representative sample of fifth graders from across the country, (2) administer the test to this sample, (3) score the test, and (4) use the scores of the sample to represent the performance of all fifth graders across the country. Assuming the sample of fifth graders was well chosen, the scores made by the sample would be a good indication of how all fifth graders would perform on the test.

Obviously, the representativeness of the sample determines how much confidence a teacher can have in the comparisons made between individual pupils and the "national average" (Phillips and Finn, 1988). The development of norms is a critical aspect of constructing these tests. Commercial test publishers recognize this fact and strive to select samples that are representative of the group for whom a test is intended.

> A test is standardized nationally by administering it under the same conditions to a national sample of students. The students tested become a norm or comparison group against which future individual scores can be compared. . . . The sample should be carefully selected to be representative of the national population with respect to ability and achievement. The sample should be large enough to represent the many diverse elements in the population. (Riverside Publishing Company, 1986, p. 11)

Four criteria are used to judge the adequacy of standardized test norms: sample size, representativeness, recentness, and description of procedures (Popham, 1990). In general, a large sample of pupils in the norm group is preferable to a small sample; other things being equal, we would prefer a norming sample of 10,000 fifth graders to one of 1,000 fifth graders. But size alone does not guarantee representativeness. If the 10,000 pupils in the norming sample were all from private schools in the same state, the sample would not provide a good representation of the performance of pupils nationwide. There must be evidence that the norming sample is representative of the national group for whom the test is intended.

Test norms describe how a national sample of students who are representative of the general population perform on the test.

If we assume a norming sample is representative of the general population, a large sample is preferred to a small one.

School curricula change over time. New topics are added and others are dropped. Thus, it is important that commercial norm-referenced tests be renormed about every seven to nine years in order to keep up with these changes. If today's curriculum is different from the one followed when a standardized test was first normed, it is unfair to compare today's pupils to a norm group that was taught a different curriculum.

The final criterion for judging the adequacy of standardized test norms is the clarity of the procedures used to produce the norms. The more clear and detailed the description of the procedures followed in test construction, the better the test user can judge the appropriateness of the test for his or her needs. To describe their procedures, publishers provide different kinds of manuals to accompany their tests. A technical manual provides information about the construction of the test, including objective selection, item writing and review, item tryout, and norming. A teacher or class guide provides a description of the areas tested as well as guidelines for interpreting and using the results of the test. These manuals ought to be accessible to classroom teachers to help them understand and use the test results. Another source of information about published tests is the *Mental Measurement Yearbooks,* which provide reviews of published tests written by experts in the field of assessment.

Commercial test manuals provide information about test construction and interpretation.

ADMINISTERING COMMERCIAL ACHIEVEMENT TESTS

Once a test is normed, it is ready to be sold to local school systems. School systems usually base their selection of a particular test on the judgment of a district administrator or a joint administrator-teacher committee. Once the testing program is selected, other decisions have to be made. In what grades will pupils be tested? Will all subtests of the achievement battery be administered? What types of score reports are needed? Should pupils be tested at the start of the school year or at the end of the year? Different school systems answer these questions differently. Whatever the ultimate decisions, it is usually the classroom teacher who is given the task of administering the tests.

A standardized test is meant to be administered to all pupils under the same conditions whenever and wherever it is given. The reason for standardizing administrative conditions is to allow valid comparisons between local scores and those of the national norm group. If a pupil takes the test under conditions different than the national norm group, then comparisons of the pupil's performance to the norm group will be misleading. It wouldn't be fair to compare the performance of a pupil who was given forty minutes to complete a test to others who were given only thirty minutes. It wouldn't be fair to compare a pupil who received coaching during testing to pupils who did not. Thus, every national commercial achievement test comes with very specific and detailed directions to follow during test administration.

The directions spell out in great detail how a teacher should prepare for testing, how the room should be set up, what to do while the pupils are taking the test, how to distribute the tests and answer sheets, and how to time the tests. In addition, the directions suggest ways to prepare pupils for taking the test. Finally, the directions provide a script for the teacher to read when administering the test.

Commercial tests must always be administered under the same conditions in order for there to be valid comparisons between local scores and those of the national norm group.

Every teacher who administers a commercial standardized test is expected to use its accompanying script and not deviate from it. If the conditions of administration vary from the directions provided by the test publisher, comparisons with the norming sample and interpretations of pupils' performances may be invalid.

INTERPRETING COMMERCIAL ACHIEVEMENT TEST SCORES

Four to eight weeks after administration, test results are returned to the school. It is important to remember that the tests usually are norm-referenced and compare a pupil's performance to those of a reference group of pupils. The most common comparisons are of a pupil against a national sample of pupils in the same grade or of a pupil against his or her own performance in different subtest areas. However, these are not the only comparisons that can be made from a commercial achievement test.

A school system also might wish to compare its pupils to a narrower sample than pupils in the same grade nationwide. For example, suppose your school district is an urban one that serves a large, multiracial, multiethnic population. What you might really like to know is how pupils in your district compare to a national sample drawn from similar school districts. Most commercial test publishers can provide such a comparison.

Or, suppose your school district is in an affluent suburban area. Past experience has shown that when pupils in your district are compared to a representative national sample, they generally do very well. What you would really like to know is how pupils in your district do in comparison to similar pupils in other affluent suburban districts. Once again, commercial test publishers can usually provide such a comparison.

Sometimes school districts are interested in comparing pupil performance within that district. Test publishers can provide this information. Norms that compare pupils in a single school district are called **local norms.** Although national norms are the most commonly reported and used, most commercial test publishers can provide more specific standardized test norms according to geographic location, type of community (rural, suburban, urban), type of school (public, private), and particular school system. Note that a pupil's test performance may appear quite different depending on the choice of norm group he or she is compared with: a representative national sample, a sample of pupils in urban schools, a sample of pupils in suburban schools, or a sample of pupils from his or her own school district.

A pupil's test score may appear quite different depending on the norm group he or she is compared to.

Commercial achievement tests provide the classroom teacher with many different kinds of scores. In interpreting these tests, the number of items a pupil got correct, called the **raw score,** is not useful in itself. The teacher needs to know how that raw score compares to the chosen norm group, and special types of scores provide this information. Since there are so many types of scores available, discussion here will be confined to the three most common types: percentile rank, stanine, and grade equivalent score. If there is a question about the meaning and interpretation of scores not discussed here, the teacher or class guide manual that accompanies a test will contain the desired explanation.

The raw score, which is the number of items a student answered correctly, does not provide a basis for comparing commercial test scores.

Percentile Rank Scores

Probably the most commonly used score is the percentile rank. **Percentile ranks** range from 1 to 99 and indicate what percentage of the norm group the pupil scored above. If Tina, a seventh grader, had a percentile rank of 91 on a standardized science test, we can say that she scored higher on the test than 91 percent of the national sample of seventh-grade pupils who made up the norm group. If Josh had a percentile rank of 23 in reading, we can say that he scored higher on the reading test than 23 percent of the pupils in the norm group. Percentiles do not refer to the percentage of items a pupil answered correctly; they refer to the percentage of pupils in the norm group who scored *below* a given pupil.

The most commonly used score is the percentile rank, which indicates what percentage of the norm group a student scored above.

The composition of the norm group defines the comparison that can be made. Thus, if Tina had a percentile rank of 91 based upon local norms, Tina's score would be interpreted to mean that she did better than 91 percent of the seventh graders in her own school district. This does not necessarily mean that she would have a percentile rank of 91 if compared to seventh graders nationally. A pupil's percentile rank can vary, depending on the group he or she is compared to.

One of the main advantages of commercial achievement test batteries is that they are normed on a single group. This allows the teacher to compare a pupil's performance across the many subtests and to identify areas of relative strength and weakness. Thus, a teacher can make statements about how a given pupil performs in math as compared to science, reading, vocabulary, and other tested areas.

Stanine Scores

The stanine is a second type of standardized test score. **Stanines** are a nine-point scale with a stanine of 1 representing the lowest performance and a stanine of 9 the highest. These nine numbers are the only possible stanine scores a pupil can receive. Like a percentile rank, stanines are designed to indicate a pupil's performance in comparison to a larger norming sample. Table 6.2 shows the approximate relationship between percentile ranks and stanines.

Stanines are a 9-point scale with 1 representing the lowest performance category and 9 the highest.

Although there is comparability between stanine scores and percentile rank scores, most teachers use stanines to represent general achievement categories, with stanine scores of 1, 2, and 3 considered below average, 4, 5, and 6 considered average, and 7, 8, and 9 considered above average. While stanines are not as precise as percentile ranks, they are easy to work with and interpret, which is a major reason for their popularity with teachers and test publishers. As with the percentile rank, a pupil's stanine score in one subject can be compared to his or her stanine performance in another subject on the same test battery to identify strong and weak areas of the pupil's achievement.

Grade Equivalent Scores

While stanines and percentile ranks provide information about a pupil's standing compared to the norm group in a particular grade level, other types of standardized test scores seek to identify a pupil's development across grade levels. They are intended to compare pupil performance to a series of reference groups that vary developmentally. The most common

TABLE 6.2 APPROXIMATE PERCENTILE RANKS CORRESPONDING TO STANINE SCORES

Stanine Score	Approximate Percentile Rank
9	98
8	93
7	84
6	68
5	50
4	32
3	16
2	7
1	2

A grade equivalent score is an estimate of a pupil's developmental level but is not indicative of the grade in which a pupil should be placed.

"developmental" scale is the **grade equivalent score,** which is intended to represent pupils' achievement in terms of a scale based upon grade and month in school. A grade equivalent score of 7.5 stands for seventh grade, fifth month of school. A grade equivalent score of 11.0 stands for the beginning of the eleventh grade. On some tests, the decimal point is omitted in grade equivalent scores, in which case a grade equivalent score of 43 stands for fourth grade, third month and a score of 108 stands for tenth grade, eighth month.

Grade equivalent scores are easily misinterpreted. A scoring scale that is organized in terms of grade and month in school is so familiar to most test users that it can seduce them into making incorrect interpretations regarding their pupils. Consider Audrey, who took a standardized achievement test battery at the start of the fifth grade. When her teacher received the results he saw that Audrey's grade equivalent score in mathematics was 7.5. What does this score indicate about Audrey's mathematics achievement?

If we were to ask 100 teachers what Audrey's grade equivalent score in math meant, the great majority of them would say that Audrey does as well in mathematics as a seventh grader in the fifth month of school or that she can succeed in a seventh-grade mathematics curriculum or that she is working at a seventh-grade level in mathematics. In fact, except under very rare conditions, each of these interpretations is incorrect or unsubstantiated.

The grade equivalent provides an estimate of a pupil's developmental level, but it is not a prescription for the grade in which a pupil should be placed. Remember, Audrey took a *fifth*-grade mathematics test, which contained mathematics objectives commonly taught in the fifth grade. Audrey did not take a seventh-grade mathematics test, so we have no way of knowing how Audrey would do on seventh-grade math material. Certainly she wouldn't have had the benefit of what is normally taught in the sixth grade. All we know is how Audrey performed on a fifth-grade test, and this tells us nothing about how she might perform on higher-grade-level tests. If a common test had been given to both fifth- and seventh-grade pupils, we might be able to say how Audrey performed in comparison to seventh graders, but this is rarely done.

If all of the preceding interpretations are inappropriate, what is the correct interpretation of Audrey's grade equivalent score of 7.5? The most appropriate interpretation is that compared to other fifth graders, Audrey is well above the national average in *fifth*-grade mathematics. Her score was higher than expected of the average fifth grader who took the test at the start of the fifth grade. Developmentally, she is ahead of the "typical" fifth grader in mathematics achievement.

Another use of the grade equivalent score is to assess a pupil's academic development over time. That is, the change in a grade equivalent score over time is used as an indication of whether the pupil is making "normal progress" in his or her learning. For example, if a pupil's grade equivalent score is 8.2 when tested in the eighth grade, one might expect the pupil's grade equivalent to be around 9.2 if tested at the same time and *with the same test* in the ninth grade. However, teachers must be careful when assessing pupils' growth across different grades because development is an irregular process, which may jump ahead greatly at certain times but remain static at others. Thus, small deviations from "normal" growth should not be interpreted as a problem. Table 6.3 compares the characteristics of percentile rank, stanine, and grade equivalent scores.

Three Examples of Test Interpretation

Although many types of standardized test scores can be provided by test publishers, the percentile rank, stanine, and grade equivalent are the most used. Given the preceding discussion, we are now ready to examine some specific examples of how commercial achievement tests are reported to classroom teachers.

Standardized commercial tests usually report percentile rank, stanine, and grade equivalent scores.

Example 1: Pupil Performance Report

Figure 6.2 shows Brian Elliott's test results on the Metropolitan Achievement Test battery. The extreme top of the report tells us that Brian was administered both the Metropolitan Achievement Test and the Otis Lennon School Ability Test, which is a test of general ability, not of

TABLE 6.3 COMPARISON OF THREE COMMON STANDARDIZED TEST SCORES

	Percentile Rank	Stanine	Grade Equivalent Score
Format of score	Percentage	Whole number	Grade and month in school
Possible scores	1 to 99 in whole numbers	1 to 9 in whole numbers	Prekindergarten to 12.9 in monthly increments
Interpretation	Percent of pupils a given pupil did better than	1 to 3 below average; 4 to 6 average; 7 to 9 above average	Above average, average, below average compared to pupils in the same grade
Special issues	Small differences often overinterpreted	General index of pupil achievement	Frequently misinterpreted and misunderstood

MAT METROPOLITAN ACHIEVEMENT TESTS
SEVENTH EDITION WITH OTIS-LENNON SCHOOL ABILITY TEST, SIXTH EDITION

INDIVIDUAL REPORT
FOR
Brian Elliott

TEACHER: SMITH	MAT/	OLSAT
SCHOOL: LAKESIDE ELEMENTARY GRADE: 04	1992 NORMS: SPRING	
DISTRICT: NEWTOWN	NATIONAL	NATIONAL
TEST DATE: 05/93	LEVEL: ELEM 2	E
	FORM: S	2

AGE 09 YRS 10 MOS

TESTS	NO. OF ITEMS	RAW SCORE	SCALED SCORE	NATL PR-S	NATL NCE	GRADE EQUIV	ACC RANGE
Total Reading	85	66	632	68-6	59.9	5.9	MIDDLE
Vocabulary	30	27	667	90-8	77.0	8.4	HIGH
Reading Comp.	55	39	618	53-5	51.6	5.0	MIDDLE
Total Mathematics	64	43	602	55-5	52.6	5.1	MIDDLE
Concepts & Problem Solving	40	29	617	68-6	59.9	6.0	MIDDLE
Procedures	24	14	579	37-4	43.0	4.3	LOW
Language	54	33	609	51-5	50.5	4.8	MIDDLE
Prewriting	15	10	606	47-5	48.4	4.7	MIDDLE
Composing	15	8	602	43-5	46.3	4.5	LOW
Editing	24	15	614	56-5	53.2	5.3	LOW
Science	35	25	628	65-6	58.1	5.9	MIDDLE
Social Studies	35	25	630	69-6	60.4	6.0	MIDDLE
Research Skills	36	29	635	73-6	62.9	6.5	MIDDLE
Thinking Skills	83	56	615	61-6	55.9	5.7	LOW
Basic Battery	203	142	617	60-6	55.3	5.4	MIDDLE
Complete Battery	273	192	619	62-6	56.4	5.5	MIDDLE

NATIONAL GRADE PERCENTILE BANDS
1 10 30 50 70 90 99

(markers A, B, C)

OTIS-LENNON SCHOOL ABILITY TEST	RAW SCORE	SAI	AGE PR-S	AGE NCE	SCALED SCORE	NATL GRADE PR-S	NATL GRADE NCE
Total	49	112	77-7	65.6	632	81-7	68.5
Verbal	25	114	81-7	68.5	637	85-7	71.8
Nonverbal	24	109	71-6	61.7	627	76-6	64.9

FIGURE 6.2
Standardized Test Report for an Individual Pupil

achievement in specific school subjects. The top of the form tells us also that Brian's teacher is Ms. or Mr. Smith, his school is the Lakeside Elementary School, and that the Lakeside school is in the Newtown school system.

The top middle portion of the form tells us that Brian is in the fourth grade and that he took the Metropolitan in May, 1993. This is near the end of the school year, which has an important bearing on the national norming group against whom Brian's performance is compared. Suppose that Brian took the test in October, at the beginning of the school year. How would his performance in October probably compare to his performance in May? In October, Brian was just starting the fourth grade and had not had much instruction on fourth-grade objectives. By May, Brian had nine months of instruction on fourth-grade objectives, so it is likely that he would test better at that time than if he took the test in October. The time of year when a pupil takes a standardized achievement test makes a considerable difference in his or her performance level; the more instruction on the test objectives the pupil has had, the higher his or her scores should be.

Constructors of commercial achievement tests recognize this fact and take it into account when they norm their tests. Most standardized test constructors norm their tests in both the fall and the spring, so that pupils who are tested in the fall can be compared to the fall norming group and pupils who take the test in the spring can be compared to the spring norming group. At the top of the report form under "Norms" is the entry "Spring," which means that Brian's scores were compared to a national sample of fourth graders who were tested in the spring.

Because pupils tested in the spring have received more instruction than those tested in the fall, commercial tests contain both fall and spring norms.

Finally, the top of the form describes the **level** and **form** of the test Brian took. This information usually is not critical to interpreting the test results. The level of a test describes the grade level for which the test is intended. On the Metropolitan Achievement Test the level called "Elem 2" is intended for the fourth grade. The form of the test refers to the version of the test administered. Often standardized test constructors will produce two interchangeable versions of a test to allow schools that wish to test more than once a year to use a different but equivalent version of the test each time.

Below this general information are Brian's actual test results. First, marked by the circled "A," is a list of all the subtests that make up the Metropolitan Achievement Test battery and the number of items in each. These subtests start with Total Reading and end with Thinking Skills. Each of these subtests assesses pupils' performance in a distinct curriculum area. Subtest results can be grouped to provide additional scores. Thus, the Total Reading score is made up of the combined performance on the Vocabulary and Reading Comprehension subtests. What three subtests are combined to make the Total Language score? The Basic Battery Total includes all subtests except Science and Social Studies, while the Complete

Subtests assess pupils' performance in a specific curriculum area.

Battery Total includes these two subtests. Finally, below the Metropolitan scores, are the scores on the Otis Lennon School Ability Test.

What kind of information is provided about Brian's performance on the Metropolitan subtests? Scores included in the section marked with a circled "B" are: raw scores, scaled scores (a developmental score used to measure year-to-year growth in pupil performance), national percentile ranks and national stanines (NATL PR-S), national normal curve equivalents (NATL NCE, a score similar to the percentile rank), grade equivalent scores, and an achievement-ability comparison. The raw score tells how many items Brian got correct on each subtest. He got twenty-seven of the thirty items on the Vocabulary subtest and twenty-nine of the forty items on the Concepts and Problem Solving subtest correct. Because subtests contain different numbers of test items, raw scores are not useful for interpreting a pupil's performance or comparing performance on different subtests. Also, since scaled scores are difficult to interpret and normal curve equivalents replaceable by percentile ranks in most cases, we shall not describe them here. More detailed information about these and other standardized test scores can be found in the interpretive guides for teachers that are available for most commercial achievement tests.

The score column labeled "NATL PR-S" shows Brian's national percentile rank and corresponding stanine score on each subtest. How should Brian's performance of 56-5 on the Editing subtest be interpreted? Brian's percentile rank of 56 means that he scored higher than 56 percent of the fourth-grade national norm group on the Editing subtest. His stanine score of 5 places him in the middle of the stanine scores and indicates that his performance is average for fourth graders nationwide. How would you interpret Brian's national percentile rank and stanine on the Vocabulary test?

Compare Brian's performance in Reading Comprehension and Composing. In terms of percentile rank, Brian did better in Reading Comprehension (53rd percentile rank) than in Composing (43rd percentile rank), but in terms of stanines, Brian's performance on the two subtests was the same (stanine 5). The apparent difference in the percentile rank and stanine scores illustrates two points. First, the stanine score provides a more general indication of performance than the percentile rank. Second, and more important, fairly large differences in percentile ranks, especially near the middle of the percentile rank scale, are not different when expressed as stanines.

Fairly large differences in percentile rank, especially near the middle of the percentile rank, may produce no difference when scores are expressed as stanines.

Many teachers and parents forget that all test scores contain error. No test score, not even one from a commercial standardized test, can be assumed to provide an exact, error-free assessment of a pupil's performance. Unfortunately, people who ignore this fact mistakenly treat small differences in percentile ranks (up to 8 or so percentile ranks) as indicating a meaningful difference in performance. The stanine score, though more inclusive than the percentile rank, reminds us that although Brian's percentile ranks differed on the two subtests, his performance did not differ when expressed in terms of stanines. Sometimes answering only one or two more items correctly can change a pupil's score by eight to ten percentile ranks, yet not alter a pupil's stanine score. This fact should act as a caution for Brian's teacher not to read too much into the percentile rank differences in these two areas.

Note that standardized test batteries such as Brian took are not only useful for comparing a pupil's performance to that of similar pupils nationwide, they also are useful for identifying a given pupil's areas of strength and weakness. Thus, Brian's teacher can see that although Brian is average in most subtests (stanines of 4, 5, or 6), he is weaker in Math Procedures (37-4) than he is in Vocabulary (90-8). The use of standardized tests to identify areas of pupils' strengths and weaknesses is more important from an instructional viewpoint than is information about how pupils' rank compared to a national sample of pupils in the same grade.

Brian is a fourth grader who took the Metropolitan Achievement Test in the ninth month of the school year. If he had performed the same as the average of fourth graders from across the country who took the test in May, his grade equivalent scores on each subtest would have been 4.9, since that is the score given to average performance for fourth graders who take the test in May. Examination of Brian's grade equivalent scores in Figure 6.2 shows that in most areas his score is at the fourth-, fifth-, or sixth-grade level. Compared to the national sample of fourth graders who took the test, Brian is average to a bit above average in comparison to the national norm group. He got more answers correct on the fourth-grade tests than did the average fourth grader in the norm sample. This is basically the same information as provided by Brian's percentile ranks and stanines. As with percentile ranks, small differences in grade equivalent scores (4 to 6 months) should not be overinterpreted or used as the primary basis for decision making about pupils.

The "Achievement-Ability Comparison" shown in Figure 6.2 is provided by many test publishers when the school testing program includes both a standardized achievement test and a standardized ability test. In essence, the comparison tries to provide information about how a pupil performs on the achievement test compared to a national sample of pupils who have a similar ability level. The issues associated with interpreting and using the ability-achievement comparison meaningfully are similar to those raised in the discussion of grading pupils based on their ability in Chapter 5: (1) There are problems in assessing ability; (2) the error in each test used in the comparison compounds the imprecision of the information; (3) the information is difficult to translate into meaningful, instructionally-related practices; and (4) the information may label a pupil or influence a teacher's expectations for the pupil. For these reasons, achievement-ability comparisons are and can be misleading and should be used with extreme caution.

In the area marked with a circled "C," Figure 6.2 shows the National Percentile Bands for Brian's performance on each subtest. Presenting

Brian's performance in this way is useful, not only because it provides a graphic contrast to numerical scores, but because it reminds the test user about the error in all test scores. In essence, the **percentile bands** indicate that "No score is error-free, so it is wrong to treat a score as if it were precise and infallible. It is best to think of a score not as a single number but as a range of numbers, any one of which could be the pupil's true performance on an error-free test." Thus, because of the imprecision of the test, it is more appropriate to say that Brian's performance on the Total Reading subtest is somewhere between about the 62nd and 80th percentile rank, than it is to say it is exactly and precisely at the 68th percentile. His performance on the Math Procedures subtest is best interpreted to be between a percentile rank of about 22 and 45, than exactly 37. Thinking of performance in terms of a range of scores prevents overinterpretation of test results based on small score differences. Even if percentile bands are not provided as a reminder of the error in test scores, it is important to think of all types of test scores as representing a range of performance, not a single point.

Percentile bands are provided on standardized tests as a reminder that no test scores are error-free.

What does all of this information tell about how Brian performs in his fourth-grade classroom? In itself, it tells very little. However, in conjunction with the teacher's own classroom observations and assessments, commercial achievement test results can be useful. Commercial achievement tests usually provide information about (1) how a pupil compares to a national sample of pupils in the same grade, (2) the pupil's areas of relative strength and weakness in important subject areas, and (3) the pupil's development level. The tests do not tell how the pupil does in the day-to-day confines of his or her own classroom. If Brian is in a class of low achievers, he may perform very well in class, much better than would be expected on the basis of his standardized test scores. If he is in a class of high achievers, he may perform much lower than his standardized test scores would suggest. In either case, commercial achievement tests scores should *not* be interpreted without also considering information about the pupil's daily classroom performance.

Commercial achievement tests do not always tell how well students perform within their own classroom.

In addition to the information shown in Figure 6.2, commercial test publishers often provide information on pupils' performance on specific topics and skills that make up each subtest. For example, the Vocabulary subtest of the Metropolitan is made up of test items covering synonyms, antonyms, and multiple-meaning words. The Science subtest contains items covering life science, physical science, earth science, science process skills, and research skills. Commercial test publishers can provide information about each pupil's performance on each of the more specific skill areas that make up a subtest. Similar information about the performance of the class as a whole can also be obtained. Performance in each specific skill area is usually reported as being below average, average, or above average in comparison to the national norm group. The classroom teacher can use this information to identify more specific areas where a pupil or the class as a whole has difficulty.

One caution should be noted in using this skill-level information. In most cases, any single skill will be assessed by a small number of items, so teachers should not undertake substantial curriculum review or change on the basis of a few test items. A small number of items cannot be relied upon to provide reliable enough information for curriculum planning or decision making. Rather, teachers should follow up the commercial test information with additional information collected on their own.

Example 2: Class Performance Report

Figure 6.3 shows the overall class performance for Mr. or Ms. Ness's fourth grade on the Iowa Tests of Basic Skills. The subtests of the Iowa are listed across the top of the figure, beginning with Vocabulary and ending with Math Computation. The scores reported are the average scale or standard score (SS), the average grade equivalent score, the average normal curve equivalent, and the average national percentile rank. This information can provide the teacher with a general picture of the performance of the class as a whole.

Class performance reports help teachers identify subject areas in which their class is doing well and those in which they need additional work.

The percentile ranks indicate the average of the class as a whole on each of the subtests of the Iowa in comparison to a national sample of fourth-grade pupils. The composite score, which describes class performance across all the subtests in the battery, is a percentiles rank of 82, indicating that the typical pupil in the class did better than 82 percent of similar students across the nation. Overall, on the various subtests, the average percentile ranks and average grade equivalents indicate that the class is somewhat above the national average in most areas. However, note that the figure also shows that compared to most other subject areas, the class is relatively weak in Vocabulary. This is something the teacher may wish to investigate further.

Example 3: Summary Report for Parents

Figure 6.4 shows a report that is sent home to parents after testing with the California Achievement Test to help them understand their child's performance. All commercial achievement test publishers have similar forms. The section of the figure marked with a boxed "A" provides parents with a general introduction to the the test and its purposes. The section marked "B" shows Ken Allen's percentile ranks on the Total Reading, Total Language, and Total Math tests, as well as his performance on the Total Battery. Note the areas labeled "below average," "average," and "above average" to give parents a general indication of how Ken did compared to his national fifth-grade peers.

The right third of the figure ("C," "D," and "E") provides more detailed information about Ken's performance. The four boxes contain, respectively, percentile ranks for the subtests that made up the Total Reading, Total Language, Total Math, and remaining battery subtests. Thus, for

Iowa Tests of Basic Skills

Service 9:
Report of Class Averages

Class/Group:	NESS
Building:	WEBER
Building Code:	304
System:	DALEN COMMUNITY
Norms:	SPRING 1992
Order No.	000-A33-76044-00-001

Grade:	4
Form:	K
Test Date:	03/93
Page:	40

	READING			LANGUAGE					MATHEMATICS			
	VOCAB-ULARY	COMPRE-HENSION	TOTAL	SPELL-ING	CAPITAL-IZATION	PUNC-TUATION	USAGE/EXPRESS	TOTAL	CON-CEPTS/ESTIM.	PROBS/DATA INTERP.	TOTAL	CORE TOTAL
N	24	24	24	24	24	24	24	24	24	24	24	24
SS	203.0	224.3	213.6	214.5	255.7	249.2	227.8	296.9	214.5	216.4	215.5	221.9
GE OF AVG SS	5.0	6.5	5.8	5.9	9.3	8.7	6.9	7.6	6.1	6.0	6.0	6.4
NCE	54.2	67.1	62.5	62.8	78.7	76.6	65.4	75.4	65.5	61.8	63.8	68.8
PR OF AVG SS: NATL STUDENT NORMS	58	78	72	74	91	88	77	88	77	72	74	81

AVERAGES ITBS:

N TESTED = 27

	SOCIAL STUD-IES	SCI-ENCE	SOURCES OF INFO.			COM-POSITE	MATH COMPU-TATION
			MAPS & DIA-GRAMS	REF. MATLS	TOTAL		
N	24	24	24	24	24	24	24
SS	221.3	228.5	219.0	227.0	223.0	223.0	213.9
GE	6.2	6.9	6.1	6.8	6.3	6.4	5.9
NCE	66.4	69.2	61.8	71.2	67.1	69.8	66.0
PR	78	81	74	84	79	82	78

SS—Standard Score, GE=Grade Equivalent, NCE=Normal Curve Equivalent, NPR=Natl%ile Rank

THE RIVERSIDE PUBLISHING COMPANY
a Houghton Mifflin Company

FIGURE 6.3

Standardized Test Report for a Class

(SOURCE: *ITBS Interpretive Guide for Teachers and Counselors (Levels 9-14).* The Riverside Publishing Company, 1993, p. 73. Copyright © 1993 by The University of Iowa. All rights reserved. No part of this work may be reproduced or transmitted in any form or by any means, electronic or mechanical, including photocopying and recording, or by any information storage or retrieval system without the prior written permission of The Riverside Publishing Company unless such copying is expressly permitted by federal copyright law. Address inquiries to Test Division Permissions, The Riverside Publishing Company, 8420 Bryn Mawr Avenue, Chicago, IL 60631.)

CAT/5 Home Report

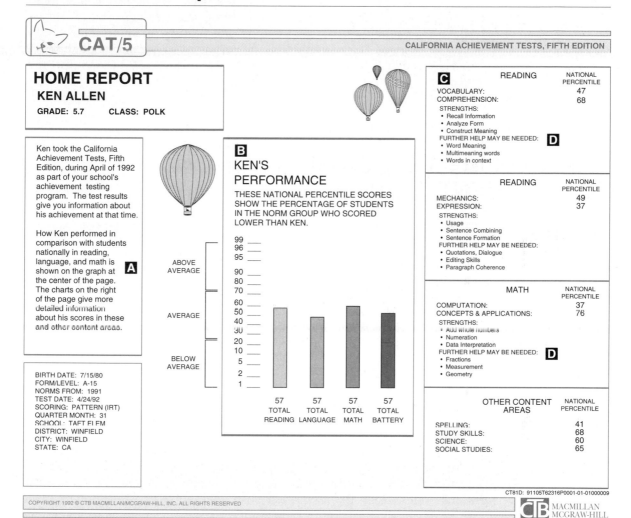

FIGURE 6.4

Parent Report Form
(SOURCE: Reproduced from the *California Achievement Tests, 5th Edition,* by permission of the publisher, CTB/McGraw-Hill, a division of McGraw-Hill School Publishing Company. Copyright © 1992 by McGraw-Hill School Publishing Company. All rights reserved.

example, Ken's percentile ranks in Vocabulary and Comprehension, the two subtests that make up Total Reading, were 47 and 68. The boxes also show areas of Ken's strength and weakness on the skills that make up the Reading, Language, and Math tests. This information is similar to the skill-level information described during the discussion of Figure 6.2. Teachers should be prepared to answer parents' questions about the information contained in such home reports.

Commercial test publishers can provide scores and information additional to that described in the preceding sections, but Figures 6.2 through

Teachers should be prepared to answer parents' questions about standardized test results.

6.4 show the basic types of information that are returned to classroom teachers and parents as part of a school district's commercial achievement testing program. Each test publisher presents the results in slightly different formats, but the basic information and its interpretation do not vary much from publisher to publisher. The variety of forms and pupil analyses that are available from a commercial test publisher can be found in the teacher or class information manual that accompanies the test.

THE VALIDITY OF COMMERCIAL ACHIEVEMENT TESTS

A great deal of time, expertise, and expense are put into the construction of commercial achievement tests. The most widely used tests are technically strong, with well-written items, an attractive format, statistically sophisticated norms, and reliable, consistent pupil scores. More care, concern, and expertise are put into producing a standardized achievement test than are typically put into constructing a teacher-made or textbook test.

It is still appropriate, however, to raise the question of whether a commercial achievement test provides the information needed to make valid decisions about pupil achievement. Teacher-made and textbook achievement tests are judged mainly in terms of whether they provide a fair assessment of how well pupils have learned the things they were taught. Standardized achievement tests are judged on this basis too but also on other bases as well. Regardless of the test, if it does not provide the desired information about pupil achievement it is not valid and therefore not useful for decision making. For commercial achievement tests, four factors influence validity: (1) the appropriateness of the content and objectives tested; (2) the representativeness of the norming sample; (3) the conditions under which the test is administered; and (4) misinterpretations of test results. This section examines these issues and their potential effect on the validity of commercial achievement tests.

Content Coverage

Commercial tests are designed to assess the core objectives that most classroom teachers at that grade level cover in their instruction.

Commercial tests are not constructed to assess every classroom teacher's unique instructional objectives. Rather they are designed to assess the core objectives that *most* classroom teachers cover in their instruction. By selecting a common set of objectives, test constructors seek to insure that most pupils will have had exposure to what is tested. Studies have shown considerable variation in the amount of time teachers devote to these core topics in their instruction, with many topics receiving only 5 to 10 minutes of instructional time (Porter, Floden, Freeman, Schmidt, and Schwille, 1986). Other studies have shown that all commercial achievement tests do not assess the same objectives in a subject area: the "core" content such tests seek to assess varies with the test (Floden, Porter, Schmidt, and Freeman, 1980; Freeman, Kuhs, Knappen, and Porter, 1982). This means that some of the topics taught in a given classroom will not be included on commercial tests.

While most classroom teachers will find the objectives tested on commercial achievement tests included in their own instruction, few teachers will find all of the topics they teach included in commercial tests. Teachers whose classroom instruction deviates greatly from the text or who consistently introduce unusual materials and concepts, often find that the topics covered by the commercial tests are different from those they have been teaching. The time of year when testing takes place and the teacher's sequencing of topics also influence pupils' opportunities to learn the content being assessed.

A commercial test cannot be valid for a particular class if it does not match the instruction given in that class.

Finally, virtually all commercial achievement tests rely heavily on multiple-choice test items. Restricting items to the multiple-choice format means that some topics or objectives may be tested differently than they were taught or tested in the classroom. For example, to assess spelling, most teachers give a weekly spelling test in which pupils have to spell each word correctly when it is said aloud by the teacher. In commercial achievement tests, spelling is assessed by presenting pupils with four or five words and asking them to identify the one that is spelled incorrectly. This is not the way pupils are taught spelling. All of the above factors can reduce the match between the content of a commercial achievement test and the content of classroom instruction.

It is the responsibility of each local school district to determine if the content of a commercial achievement test is appropriate for pupils in that system or classroom. If, after inspecting the test items and the publisher's description of what is tested, the test content appears to be different from what pupils were taught, judgments about pupils' achievement may not be valid and should be made with caution.

Each school or district must decide if the content of a commercial achievement test matches its own objectives.

Test Norms

Commercial test publishers strive to obtain norming samples that are representative of national groups of pupils. However, there are some important factors that can undermine the appropriateness of test norms and thereby test validity: (1) Norms go out of date; (2) the curriculum in a subject area changes; (3) textbooks are revised and new instructional materials appear; and (4) the same test is often administered in a school district over a number of years so teachers and pupils become familiar with its content and items (Drahozal and Frisbie, 1988; Lenke and Keene, 1988; Phillips and Finn, 1988). Inappropriate or out-of-date test norms reduce

When commercial test norms don't match the characteristics of the local students, valid decisions cannot be made from the test results.

the validity of comparisons and decisions made from commercial achieve-ment tests. While there is no hard-and-fast period within which test norms should be revised, seven to nine years is a generally accepted time period used by the publishers of the most widely used commercial tests. Obvi-ously, the older the test norms, the less representative they will be of instructional content and national pupil performance. Specific informa-tion about test-norming procedures and the age of the norms should be provided in the publisher's test manual.

Test Administration

Deviating from test administration directions reduces the validity of test results.

It was emphasized earlier that valid interpretations of pupils' commercial test performance depend on pupils taking the test under the conditions recommended by the test publisher. Deviations from the test administra-tion directions, such as allowing pupils more time than specified, helping pupils while they are taking the test, coaching pupils before the test on the specific items they will be asked, and generally not following the direc-tions provided, all reduce the validity of the the test results and the deci-sions based on those results.

Interpreting Commercial Test Results

There are two common problems in interpreting commercial test scores: misinterpretation and overinterpretation. Because the types of scores that are used to describe pupil performance on commercial achievement tests are different from those teachers commonly use, the likelihood of misin-terpretation is heightened. The most common misinterpretations involve the percentile rank, which is mistaken for the percentage of items a pupil answered correctly, and the grade equivalent score, which is mistakenly thought to indicate the curriculum level at which a pupil is performing in a subject area. Percentile ranks indicate the percentage of pupils in the norm group that a pupil scored above. Grade equivalent scores indicate how well a pupil did on grade-level objectives compared to other pupils in his or her grade.

The main problem in interpreting commercial test scores is overinterpretation.

The main problem in interpreting commercial test scores is *over*inter-pretation, not misinterpretation. Because these tests are constructed by professionals, tried out on nationwide samples of pupils, and provide numerical indices that describe a pupil's performance compared to pupils nationwide, there is a widespread belief that they give precise and accu-rate descriptions of pupils' achievement. Certainly parents and the public at large put more faith in commercial test results than in teacher-made assessments gathered over time in the day-to-day classroom setting (Airasian, 1988b). While the information provided by the forty or so multiple-choice items found in a typical commercial subtest is useful, it can never match the information a teacher accumulates through daily instruction and assessment of pupils.

> . . . test scores represent achievement in basic skills areas at only one particular time and must be reviewed together with the student's actual classroom work and other factors. Parents [and others: author] should also understand that the test measures the basic content skills that are most common to curricula throughout the country. It cannot possibly measure, nor should it attempt to measure, the full curriculum of a particular classroom, school, or district. (CTB/McGraw-Hill, 1986b, p. 100)

Even when there are no problems with test content, norms, and administration, commercial test scores still are overinterpreted. For example, it is common for teachers and parents to treat small test score differences as if they were significant and indicated real performance differences. A percentile rank difference of 6 to 8 points or a two- to five-month grade equivalent difference between pupils rarely indicates important differences in their achievement or development. There is sufficient error in any test score, whether commercial or teacher-made, to make small scoring differences unreliable indicators of real differences between pupils. Commercial test constructors try to defeat overinterpretation of small score differences by warning against them in their test manuals and by presenting scores as percentile or stanine bands (see Figure 6.2), but they are not always successful. In short, teachers should guard against treating small score differences as if they were meaningful.

Overinterpretation also occurs when teachers put too much faith in achievement-ability comparisons. These comparisons provide at best a general indication of how a pupil compares to other pupils of similar ability. Before a teacher acts on test information of this type, he or she should reflect on personal knowledge about the pupil's work habits, personality, and achievement gained by daily exposure to the pupil in the classroom.

Finally, the smaller the number of items that make up a test score, the less reliable its results and the less trustworthy its score. Normally, the subtest scores on commercial test batteries are quite reliable and consistent. However, when a subtest is further broken down into specific topics, skills, or objectives, and separate scores given for each, caution about reading too much into the scores must be exercised. Often such topic, skill, or objective level information is used to provide diagnostic information about a pupil's strengths and weaknesses. While such information may provide a basis for further exploration of pupil performance, it should be reviewed critically because of the very few items on which it is typically based.

While commercial achievement tests can give teachers useful assessment information that they cannot gather for themselves, such information should be used in conjunction with information gathered from

Information gained from commercial tests may not be as revealing as information gathered through daily instruction and assessment by the classroom teacher.

Teachers should guard against treating small score differences in standardized test scores as if they were reliable indicators of real differences between pupils.

Information from commercial achievement tests usually corroborates a teacher's perceptions of pupils.

teacher assessments. For the most part, the information from commercial tests will corroborate perceptions the teacher has already formed about pupils. When the two types of evidence do not corroborate each other, the teacher should look again at his or her perceptions to be sure the pupil is not being misjudged.

STATE-MANDATED ACHIEVEMENT TESTS

The use of **state-mandated tests** has been common in the United States for about ten years. Sometimes called "competency tests," "minimum competency tests," or "high-stakes tests," they are a response to perceptions that today's pupils are performing considerably worse in school than pupils in prior years. To rectify this problem, legislatures and boards of education in many states have mandated the administration of two types of tests: those intended to assess the performance of individuals (Airasian, 1993) and those intended to assess the performance of schools or school districts (Guskey, 1994).

State-mandated tests are used to assess the performance of individuals, schools, and school districts.

Individually focused tests are used to make decisions about individual pupils or teachers. In many states, performance on these tests is used to determine whether a pupil will receive a high school diploma, be promoted to the next grade, or be placed in a class for remedial education. Many states also mandate the use of such tests to certify or recertify classroom teachers.

Group-focused tests are used to summarize and assess pupils' achievement on specific skills or objectives at the school or district level. These tests are commonly referred to as "statewide assessments" or "basic skills assessments" and describe performance of a school or district as a whole, not of individual pupils. These tests are used to allocate funds to school districts, rate school quality, and reform or decertify poorly performing schools. Both types of state-mandated tests assess mainly achievement in basic reading and math skills, although recent years have seen content areas expand to include writing, speaking, and other performance-oriented areas (Mitchell, 1992; Office of Technology Assessment, 1992).

Group-Based, State-Mandated Tests

The primary aim of group-based mandated tests is to provide information about how a school or school district is achieving on important objectives and skills. The particular objectives or skills tested are determined by statewide curriculum committees made up of teachers, administrators, parents, business people, and other concerned citizens. The task of these committees is to identify important objectives and skills that pupils should learn. The list of objectives and skills need not be confined to ones that are presently taught in schools.

Because school and districtwide testing is intended to provide information about group performance, it is not necessary for every pupil in a school or district to answer every test question. The amount of information gathered can be maximized while the amount of testing time is minimized by having each pupil answer only some of the questions. Moreover, it is not necessary to test every grade, so in most cases, the assessments focus on only a few grades in any one year.

School or districtwide testing can be done using samples of students who take only part of the test.

Suppose a curriculum committee identified twenty science objectives that it felt seventh graders ought to know. Suppose also that 10 test items were written to assess each of the twenty objectives, thus producing a total of 200 science items. Rather than giving each pupil a 200-item test, the items could be divided into four tests of 50 items each. All four tests would then be administered at random in each school or district, but each pupil would be required to take only one of the tests. Summing the results of all four tests across all pupils would give a good estimate of school or district performance on all twenty science objectives. Note, however, that if the purpose of testing is to make separate decisions about *individual* pupils, it would be necessary for all pupils to take the same test.

After the tests are given, the results are summarized to describe the percentage of pupils in the school or district who mastered each objective or the set of objectives as a whole. Scoring on most state-mandated tests, whether intended to assess individuals or groups, is criterion-referenced. That is, mastery is defined as correctly answering a certain percentage of its items. For example, if a statewide standard defines mastery as a score of 70 percent or above, pupils who correctly answer 70 percent of the test items or 70 percent of the objectives tested would have mastered the test content. Pupils not meeting these performance standards would be recorded as "nonmasters." Some state testing programs categorize pupils into three or more categories, for example, mastery, near-mastery, and nonmastery.

By examining the percentage of pupils in the district who attain mastery, one can determine how well pupils across the district are doing on the objectives tested. When the results of school or districtwide testing are reported, one often hears teachers and administrators making comments such as these: "Our pupils did all right in adding and subtracting, but not as well in problem solving," "Over 80 percent of our third graders mastered objectives in punctuation and spelling, but only 30 percent mastered the capitalization objective," "The district had high levels of mastery on objectives dealing with science definitions, the scientific method, and general facts, but much lower levels of mastery on estimation and metric system objectives."

Results of group-based, state-mandated tests provide information that a school or district can use to examine its curriculum.

The results of such tests provide information that a school or district can use to examine its curriculum. It can see how pupils in certain grades performed on targeted curriculum objectives. It can compare its curriculum to the objectives on the state test and then decide if its curriculum ought to be revised. Test results do not *dictate* changes in a curriculum, but they do provide information that schools and districts can weigh when deciding whether or not to revise their instructional emphases.

State-mandated testing increases pressure on schools to align their curricula with state curriculum objectives.

State-mandated testing is increasing the pressure on schools, districts, and teachers to revise their curricula to better match the state tests (Canner et al., 1991; Smith and Rottenberg, 1991). Two factors account for this. First, there often are important consequences resulting from test performance, ranging from the award of bonuses or merit pay to teachers to the closing of poorly performing schools. Second, school or district performance on state tests is usually made public, typically in newspapers. Parents and school administrators follow school and district scores with the same intensity that they follow baseball pennant races and the Dow Jones Average. This interest produces pressure on schools and districts to "look good" relative to other schools and districts. In Massachusetts, for example, state-mandated test results are reported not only on a district-by-district basis but also in smaller groupings composed of districts of similar size, location, and socioeconomic status. A district's results are reported along with the results of similar districts in its group.

Parents pressure administrators who then pressure teachers to respond to low performance, usually by rearranging the curriculum to spend more time on tested topics. This pressure is magnified when comparisons are also made among the individual schools within a given school district. A general rule that describes the impact of assessment on instruction is: Whenever the results of an assessment have important consequences for pupils, teachers, or school districts, the assessment will be taken seriously and there will be pressure to incorporate the tested objectives into the school curriculum.

Classroom teachers have little say about the construction, scoring, and interpretation of state-mandated tests. Teachers are told when to test and whom to test. Results do not come back to the teacher directly but only indirectly through newspaper reports or school staff meetings. Teachers are, however, asked to implement curriculum changes that have been identified from pupils' performance on the tests. It is little wonder that teachers often complain that such testing creates pressure to focus instruction on the particular objectives contained in the test. Should teachers succumb to such pressures? Each teacher must make this decision for himself or herself after asking such questions as what is in the best interests of my pupils, what will be the consequences in terms of community support for my school, and what are appropriate and inappropriate ways to prepare my pupils for such assessments?

Individual-Based, State-Mandated Tests

Individual-based, mandated assessments are used to make educational decisions about individual pupils and teachers. As mentioned, performance on mandated tests is used in many states to determine whether a pupil will receive a high school diploma, be promoted to the next grade, or placed in remedial education. State-mandated tests also are used to certify, recertify, and evaluate classroom teachers. Before the advent of these tests, many of these decisions were made by the classroom teacher or local school administrator. State-mandated tests were instituted in part to replace local-level responsibility for such decisions with statewide standards. Initially, individually-oriented, state-mandated tests assessed pupils' and teachers' *minimum* competency on basic reading and mathematics objectives. More recently, however, they have begun to incorporate more performance-based objectives (e.g., writing, speaking, and problem solving) and a broader array of school courses (Tittle, 1991; Mitchell, 1992; Office of Technology Assessment, 1992).

The purpose of individually oriented, state-mandated tests is to identify pupils who are not minimally competent in basic academic skills.

The construction of individual-centered tests is similar to that of school or districtwide mandated tests except for two features. First, unlike school or districtwide testing, all pupils or teachers take the same test. Second, on tests designed to make decisions about individuals, a single test score is selected to indicate acceptable or passing test performance. This criterion-referenced performance standard, or "cut score," differentiates pupils who pass the tests from those who do not. The same score is used for all individuals who take the test. Suppose a state-mandated test uses a cut score of 70 percent to determine whether a pupil should be promoted to the next grade. Any pupil who scores 70 percent or higher on the statewide test will be eligible for promotion, and any pupil who scores below 70 percent will not. Generally, classroom teachers and local school administrators have little or no voice in the decision. However, pupils who do not reach the cut score on the initial test administration usually are given additional opportunities to take the test.

Individually oriented state tests usually provide a single test score, called a "cut score," which indicates acceptable test performance.

There are two aspects of individual-centered tests that have particular relevance to classroom teachers. The first involves pressures to devote substantial amounts of instructional time to the objectives tested (Madaus and Kellaghan, 1992). These pressures may be even more acute for pupil-centered tests than for the group-based tests discussed above (Airasian, 1988a). The fact that the tests are used to make important decisions about individual pupils can put a teacher in the difficult position of having to decide whether it is better or worse to "teach the test." Teaching the test may narrow or refocus the desired classroom curriculum, but not teaching it may put one's pupils in jeopardy of failing the test. Each teacher must face the dilemma of how much he or she will let tests dictate the classroom curriculum. Obviously, the more consequential the tests are for pupils, the more pressure there is to focus one's instruction on test content.

Each teacher must face the dilemma of how much he or she will let tests dictate their classroom curriculum.

The more important the test consequences are for students, the more temptation there is for teachers to "teach the test."

The second teacher-related issue concerns the use of cut scores in decision making. To standardize decisions, a single cut score is applied uniformly to all pupils who take the mandated test. If, for example, the cut score on a high school graduation test is 70 percent and a particular pupil gets 69 percent of the items correct, the pupil does not pass the test and is denied a high school diploma until he or she can pass it.

Although the cut score is always a constant, any assessment score will contain some error and imprecision. When a pupil scores 69 percent on a mandated test and is denied promotion because he or she did not reach the 70-percent criterion, the assumption made is that the test score provides a precise indication of a pupil's achievement. It is assumed that the test can make a meaningful discrimination between a pupil who scores 69 percent and one who scores 70 percent. In fact, no test can make meaningful distinctions between such small score differences. Thus, decisions about pupils who are very near the cut-off score should be made cautiously since this is the score range where most errors of classification are made.

An Example of State-Mandated Assessment

One of the most highly developed and pervasive state-mandated testing programs has been proposed in North Carolina (North Carolina Department of Public Education, 1992). While the program is not yet fully implemented, it provides an example of how states are using testing to assess pupils and improve schools. One unique aspect of the North Carolina program is that it is based upon the Standard Course of Study, a state-adopted curriculum that defines what pupils are to know and do in every school subject at every grade level. All tests will be constructed to closely match this state curriculum. The assessment features of the North Carolina program are outlined below. Note that in addition to the tests mandated by the state, local school districts may also administer commercial and teacher-made achievement test batteries to their pupils.

- ♦ *Grades 1 and 2.* Assessment in the first two grades will be by portfolios of pupils' work. The samples of pupil work can be reviewed by parents and teachers to determine pupil progress towards the designated goals.
- ♦ *Grades 3 through 8.* Three different mandated assessments are administered in these grades:
    1. The North Carolina End-of-Grade (EOG) Tests will be administered at the end of each school year to assess mastery of grade-level knowledge and skills. Pupils will be tested annually in five subject areas: reading, writing, mathematics, science, and social studies.

2. Minimum Skills Diagnostic Tests (MSDTs) will be given at the end of the year in grades 3, 6, and 8 to pupils who score below the state-designated passing score on the End-of-Grade Tests and who show other forms of difficulty with school work. The primary purpose of the Minimum Skills Diagnostic Tests is to identify a pupil's strengths and weaknesses so proper instruction and remediation can be planned. The MSDT is administered in reading, mathematics, and language.

3. North Carolina Competency Tests (NCCTs) are administered to pupils in grade 8 in the subjects of reading, mathematics, and writing. Pupils in grade 8 who score below the cutoff score for the tests will be retested every year until they reach the minimum passing score in all three subjects. Obtaining a passing score on all three tests is necessary to receive a high school diploma.

◆ *Grades 9 through 12.* Two types of mandated assessment are carried out at these grades.

1. North Carolina Competency Tests (NCCT) are administered yearly to those pupils who failed to attain the minimum passing score in reading, mathematics, and writing in grade 8.

2. North Carolina End-of-Course (EOC) Tests are administered at the end of each course in the following subject areas: algebra I and II, geometry, biology, physical science, physics, chemistry, U.S. history, economic/legal/political systems, and English I and II. Tests in other courses are planned in the future.

Features of the North Carolina assessment program that are common in many other state-mandated assessment programs are:

◆ A sizable amount of testing is mandated.

◆ Part of the assessment includes performance/portfolio-based information.

◆ Decisions about performance are made by comparing a pupil's score to a predetermined, statewide passing score.

◆ The tests result in important decisions that influence pupils' lives.

◆ Because poor performance on the assessment can affect pupils' opportunities, teachers must decide how much emphasis they will devote to preparing pupils for the tests.

◆ Combining performance across pupils provides information that can be used for district, school, or teacher accountability.

The North Carolina state assessment program is more extensive than in most other states. This is mainly because very few other states have specific end-of-course or end-of-grade tests to determine pupil and school-wide progress. Moreover, the North Carolina program is one of the few that specifically links a statewide curriculum to its assessment program. However, this may become a future direction for many other states. In other respects, however, from the format of the tests to their criterion-referenced scoring to their impact on pupils and teachers, the North Carolina assessments are like those in other states.

To summarize, state-mandated achievement tests are of two types: those that assess the achievement of individuals and those that assess the achievement of groups. Because state authorities assume responsibility for constructing, scoring, and using the results of its mandated tests, classroom teachers have little involvement in the assessment process. There is no sense of ownership for the classroom teacher, either in the testing process or its results. One of the main purposes of state-mandated tests is to take some decision-making responsibility out of the hands of the classroom teacher and local school administrator and to standardize the basis for decision making across a state. In states where the tests are used, they have succeeded in doing this.

One purpose of state-mandated tests is to take some decision-making responsibility out of the hands of classroom teachers and local school administrators.

In terms of results, most teachers have a good sense of how pupils will perform on competency tests from their daily interactions with them in the classroom. There are few surprises in the results of the tests for most classroom teachers. The main way in which mandated tests impact on classroom teachers is by producing pressure to teach the objectives assessed by the tests.

CHAPTER SUMMARY

♦ Two important types of standardized achievement tests are (1) commercial, norm-referenced tests and (2) state-mandated, criterion-referenced tests. Commercial, norm-referenced tests provide information about how a pupil's achievement compares to that of similar pupils nationwide. State-mandated tests usually provide criterion-referenced information about a pupil's or school's performance in relation to statewide achievement standards.

♦ Standardized assessment instruments must be administered, scored, and interpreted in the same way no matter where or when they are used. Otherwise, valid interpretations of their scores are difficult.

♦ Although teachers have little voice in the selection and scoring of either type of standardized test, pressures are often exerted on them to ensure that their pupils do well on such tests.

♦ Commercial, norm-referenced tests are constructed and scored differently than teacher-made classroom assessments. The steps in construction are: (1) identifying objectives that are common to most classrooms at a given grade level, (2) trying out many items to find ones that will spread out the scores of test takers for the final version of the test, (3) administering the final version to a large, national norm group of pupils, and (4) using the performance of the norm group as a basis for comparing the performance of pupils who subsequently take the test.

♦ Four criteria are used to judge the adequacy of commercial standardized test norms: sample size, representativeness, recency, and description of procedures.

◆ Commercial, standardized achievement tests usually come in the form of a test battery containing subtests in a variety of subject matter areas. Scores are provided for each subtest and a composite score is provided for the overall test. A pupil's or classes' scores can be compared across subtests of a test battery to identify areas of relative strength and weakness.

◆ In order to make valid interpretations from a commercial achievement test, its directions must be strictly followed.

◆ Special comparative and developmental scores are used to represent pupil performance on commercial achievement tests. The most commonly used scores are: (1) the percentile rank, which indicates the percentage of similar pupils nationwide a given pupil scored above; (2) the stanine, which uses the scores 1 to 9 to indicate whether a pupil is below average (stanines 1, 2, or 3), average (stanines 4, 5, and 6), or above average (stanines 7, 8, and 9) compared to similar pupils nationwide; and (3) grade equivalent score, which is a developmental score that indicates whether a pupil is above, below, or at the level of similar pupils in his or her grade.

◆ A pupil's test performance may appear quite different depending on the norm group he or she is being compared to: national, state, local, high or low achieving, etc.

◆ Caution should be exerted when interpreting small differences in norm-referenced test scores, especially percentile ranks and grade equivalent scores. Since all tests have some degree of error in them, it is best to think of a score not as a single number, but as a range of numbers, any one of which might indicate the pupil's true performance. Small differences in test scores are not usually significant.

◆ Interpretation and use of commercial, norm-referenced achievement tests should be guided by a number of concerns: how well the tested content matches classroom instruction, how the information agrees or disagrees with the teacher's own perceptions of pupils, the recency of the test norms, the extent to which administrative directions were followed, and the understanding that no score is exact or infallible.

◆ Commercial achievement tests provide useful comparative and developmental information that teachers cannot get for themselves. However, teachers should always use such information in conjunction with their own assessments when making decisions about pupils. Usually, the two types of information corroborate each other.

◆ State-mandated tests are intended to provide information about the achievement of individuals or groups. Group tests assess curriculum mastery across pupils, while individual tests focus on the performance of each pupil. Group tests are used to make decisions about merit pay and the quality of a school's or district's instructional program. Individual tests are used to make decisions about whether a pupil will graduate from high school, be promoted to the next grade, or placed in a remedial class. They are also used to make decisions about teacher certification and evaluation. Both student and teacher tests are scored in terms of statewide, criterion-referenced standards.

◆ Because the results of state-mandated tests are important and are usually made public, they can create pressures that influence what teachers teach. Teachers inevitably must weigh the extent to which they will focus their instruction around test content.

QUESTIONS FOR DISCUSSION

1. Are standardized tests fair to all students? Why or why not? What student characteristics might influence how one does on a standardized test? Would these same characteristics influence how one performs on a teacher-made test? Why?

2. What can a teacher do to help make students less anxious about taking standardized tests? Would the same actions help students when they take teacher-made tests?

3. If you could select only one scoring format from a norm-referenced standardized test to explain to parents, which would you choose? Why? What limitations would your choice have?

4. What factors should influence the use of standardized test results by classroom teachers?

5. What are the differences in the information provided by a norm-referenced and a criterion-referenced standardized test?

6. What are some of the reasons why many states have adopted state-mandated standardized testing programs for all schools in the state?

REFLECTION EXERCISES

1. Why do students, parents, and school administrators put so much emphasis on standardized test results?

2. How might a state-mandated testing program such as that in North Carolina influence classroom instruction for the better and for the worse?

3. Make a list of the words and thoughts that come to mind when you think about all the standardized tests you have taken. What does your list tell you about your perceptions and feelings about standardized tests?

4. How influential have standardized tests been in your life? Do you think your life would have been much different if you had never taken a standardized test?

ACTIVITY

Read the standardized test report for Nicole Kovitz, a fourth-grade student (Figure 6.5). Your task is to write a *one-page letter to Nicole's parent explaining the results of her standardized test performance.* The following suggestions should guide your letter.

1. Nicole's parent will receive a copy of the test report sheet.

2. Nicole's parent is not a standardized testing expert and basically will want to know how his or her daughter performed.

3. You should start with some information about the test and its purpose.

4. You should describe the information in the test report sheet.

Iowa Tests of Basic Skills

Student:	KOVITZ, NICOLE	Level:	10
I.D. No.:		Form:	K
Class/Group:	NESS	Grade:	4
Building:	WEBER	Test Date:	03/93
Bldg. Code:	304	Norms:	SPRING 1992
System:	DALEN COMMUNITY	Page:	359
Order No.:	000-A33-76044-00-001		

SS = Standard Score
GE = Grade Equivalent
NS = Nat'l Sta9
NCE = Normal Curve Equivalent
NPR = Nat'l %ile Rank
N Att. = Number Attempted

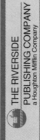

THE RIVERSIDE PUBLISHING COMPANY
a Houghton Mifflin Company

Tests	SS	GE	NS	NCE	NPR	National Percentile Rank
Vocabulary	187	4.0	4	40	31	
Reading	208	5.4	6	57	63	
Reading Total	198	4.6	5	50	49	
Spelling	222	6.5	7	70	82	
Capitalization	215	5.9	6	60	69	
Punctuation	222	6.5	6	63	74	
Usage & Expression	189	4.0	4	43	37	
Language Total	212	5.6	6	59	66	
Math Concepts & Estimation	207	5.3	6	59	66	
Math Probs & Data Interp.	200	4.8	5	51	53	
Math Total	204	5.2	5	55	59	
Core Total	205	5.1	5	54	58	
Social Studies	227	6.8	7	70	83	
Science	193	4.2	5	46	42	
Maps & Diagrams	174	3.0	3	30	17	
Reference Materials	251	8.9	9	88	96	
Sources of Info. Total	212	5.6	6	60	68	
Composite	208	5.3	6	57	62	
Math Computation	210	5.6	6	63	72	

FIGURE 6.5

Standardized Test Report for an Individual

5. You should interpret the information about Nicole's performance.

6. What are Nicole's overall strengths and weaknesses? How can the parent see these on the test report form?

7. Describe Nicole's overall performance to the parent.

8. Indicate what the parent should do if she or he has questions.

Your letter will be judged on the accuracy of the information about Nicole's performance you convey to the parent *and* the extent to which you make the information understandable by the parent. You do not have to convey every bit of information in the test report. You must identify what is the most important information and convey that in a way that a parent could understand. A letter full of technical terms will not do. Remember, the parent can always arrange to visit you in school if more information is desired.

REVIEW QUESTIONS

1. What is a standardized test? What information can a standardized test provide a teacher that a teacher-made or textbook test cannot? What is a test battery? What are subtests? How does the construction of a standardized achievement test differ from that of a teacher-made achievement test? Why are there these differences?

2. What are test norms? What information do they provide a teacher about a pupil's performance? How are the following norms interpreted: percentile rank, stanine, and grade equivalent score? How do test norms differ from raw scores? Why are norms used instead of raw scores?

3. What are Fall and Spring Norms? Why do standardized tests provide them?

4. What factors should teachers consider when they try to interpret their pupils' standardized test scores? That is, what factors influence the results of standardized tests and thus should be thought about when interpreting scores?

5. What are the differences in construction and use of district-focused and individual pupil-focused state-mandated tests?

REFERENCES

Airasian, P. W. (1987) State mandated testing and educational reform: Context and consequences. *American Journal of Education, 95*(3), 393-412.

_____ **(1988a).** Measurement driven instruction: A closer look. *Educational Measurement: Issues and Practice, 7*(winter), 6-11.

_____ **(1988b).** Symbolic validation: The case of state-mandated, high-stakes testing. *Educational Evaluation and Policy Analysis, 10*(4), 301-313.

_____ **(1993).** Policy-driven assessment or assessment-driven policy? *Measurement and Evaluation in Guidance and Counseling, 26*(April), 22-30.

Cannell, J. J. (1988). Nationally normed elementary achievement testing in America's public schools: How all 50 states are above the national average. *Educational Measurement: Issues and Practices, 7*(2), 5-9.

Canner, J., Fisher, T., Fremer, J., Haladyna, T., Hall, J., Mehrens, W., Perl-man, C., Roeber, E., Sandifer, P. (1991). *Regaining trust: Enhancing the credi-bility of school testing programs. A report from a National Council on Measurement in Education Task Force.* Mimeo, April 1991.

CTB/McGraw-Hill (1985). *California achievement tests forms E and F: Technical bulletin 1.* Monterey, CA: CTB/McGraw-Hill.

———— **(1986a).** *California achievement tests forms E and F: Test coordinator's hand-book.* Monterey, CA: CTB/McGraw-Hill.

———— **(1986b).** *California achievement tests forms E and F: Class management guide.* Monterey, CA: CTB/McGraw-Hill.

Drahozal, E. C., and Frisbie, D. A. (1988). Riverside comments on the Friends of Education Report. *Educational Measurement: Issues and Practice, 7*(2), 12-16.

Floden, R. E., Porter, A. C., Schmidt, W. H., and Freeman, D. J. (1980). Don't they all measure the same thing? Consequences of selecting standardized tests. In E. Baker and. E. Quelmalz (Eds.), *Educational testing and evaluation: Design, analysis, and policy* (pp. 109-120). Beverly Hills, CA: Sage.

Freeman, D. J., Kuhs, T. M., Knappen, L., and Porter, A. C. (1982). A closer look at standardized tests. *Arithmetic Teacher, 29*(7), 50-54.

Gusky, T. R. (1994). *High stakes performance assessment.* Thousand Oaks, CA: Corwin Press.

Lenke, J. M., and Keene, J. M. (1988). A response to John J. Cannell. *Educa-tional Measurement: Issues and Practice, 7*(2), 16-18.

Madaus, G. F., and Kellaghan, T. (1992). Curriculum evaluation and assess-ment. In P. W. Jackson (Ed.), *Handbook of research on curriculum* (pp. 119-154). New York: Macmillan.

Millman, J., and Greene, J. (1989). The specification and development of tests of achievement and ability. In R. Linn (Ed.), *Educational Measurement* (pp. 335-365). New York: American Council on Education and Macmillan.

Mitchell, R. (1992). *Testing for learning.* New York: Free Press.

North Carolina Department of Public Instruction (1992). Quick reference for parents and teachers: Testing at various grade levels. *Parent Involvement,* September-October, 1992.

Office of Technology Assessment, U.S. Congress (1992). *Testing in American schools—asking the right questions.* Washington, DC: U.S. Government Printing Office.

Phillips, G. W., and Finn, C. E. (1988). The Lake Wobegone effect: A skeleton in the testing closet. *Educational Measurement: Issues and Practice, 7*(2), 10-12.

Popham, W. J. (1990). *Modern educational measurement.* Englewood Cliffs, NJ: Prentice Hall.

Porter, A. C., Floden, R. E., Freeman, D. J., Schmidt, W. H., and Schwille, J. R. (1986). *Content determinants* (129). Institute for Research on Teaching, Michigan State University.

The Psychological Corporation (1984). *Stanford achievement test technical review manual.* New York: Psychological Corp.

Riverside Publishing Co. (1986). *Iowa tests of basic skills: Preliminary technical summary.* Chicago: Riverside.

Smith, M. L., and Rottenberg, C. (1991). Unintended consequences of exter-nal testing in elementary schools. *Educational Measurement: Issues and Practice, 10*(4), 7-11.

Tittle, C. K. (1991). Changing models of teacher and student assessment. *Educa-tional Psychologist, 26*(2), 157-165.

GLOSSARY

Ability What one has learned over a period of time from both school and nonschool sources; one's general capability for performing tasks.

Achievement What one has learned from formal instruction, usually in school.

Affective behaviors Behaviors related to feelings, emotions, values, attitudes, interests, and personality; nonintellective behaviors.

Analytic scoring Essay scoring method in which separate scores are given for specific aspects of the essay (e.g., organization, factual accuracy, spelling).

Anecdotal record A short, written report of an individual's behavior in a specific situation or circumstance.

Aptitude One's capability for performing a particular task or skill; usually involves a narrower skill than ability (e.g., mathematics aptitude or foreign language aptitude).

Assessment The process of collecting, synthesizing, and interpreting information to aid classroom decision making; includes information gathered about pupils, instruction, and classroom climate.

Assessment error Inconsistencies in scores, ratings, or observations that result from systematic factors such as faulty test items and a poor testing environment as well as from nonsystematic, uncontrollable factors such as guessing success and physical or emotional state at the time of assessment; all assessments have some degree of error.

Behavioral objective *See* Educational objective.

Bias A situation in which assessment information produces results which give one group an advantage or disadvantage over other groups because of problems in the content, procedures, or interpretation of the assessment information; a distortion or misrepresentation of performance.

Checklist A written list of performance criteria associated with a particular activity or product in which an observer marks the pupil's performance on each criterion using a scale that has only two choices.

Cognitive behaviors Behaviors related to intellective processes like thinking, reasoning, memorizing, problem solving, analyzing, and applying.

Cooperative learning Groups of pupils working together to perform a task or solve a problem.

Criterion-referenced Determining the quality of a pupil's performance by comparing it to preestablished standards of mastery.

Curriculum The skills, performances, attitudes, and values pupils are expected to learn from schooling; includes statements of desired pupil outcomes, descriptions of materials, and the planned sequence that will be used to help pupils attain the outcomes.

Diagnose Identify specific strengths and weaknesses in pupils' past and present learning.

Difficulty index The proportion of pupils who answered a test item correctly.

Discrimination index The extent to which pupils who get a particular test item correct are also likely to get a high score on the entire test.

Distractor A wrong choice in a selection test item.

Educate To change the behavior of pupils; to teach pupils to do things they could not previously do.

Education The process designed to change pupil's behaviors in particular ways.

Educational objective A statement that describes a pupil accomplishment that will result from instruction; the statement describes the behavior the pupil will learn to perform and the content on which it will be performed.

Evaluation Judging the quality or goodness of a performance or a course of action.

Formative assessment Assessment carried out for the purpose of improving learning or teaching while it is still going on; assessment for improvement, not grading.

Grade   The symbol or number used by a teacher to represent a pupil's achievement in a subject area.

Grade-equivalent score   A standardized test score that describes a pupil's performance on a scale based upon grade in school and month in grade; most commonly misinterpreted score; indicates pupil's level of performance relative to pupils in his/her own grade.

Grading curve   The proportion of pupils who can receive each grade in a norm-referenced grading system.

Grading system   The process by which a teacher arrives at the symbol or number that is used to represent a pupil's achievement in a subject area.

Group assessment   Assessing many pupils at the same time.

Higher level processes   Intellectual processes that are more complicated than simple memorization; e.g., problem solving, interpretation, analysis, and comprehension.

Holistic scoring   Essay scoring method in which a single score is given to represent the overall quality of the essay across all dimensions.

Individual assessment   Assessing one pupil at a time.

Instruction   The methods and processes by which pupils' behaviors are changed.

Instructional assessment   Collection, synthesis, and interpretation of information needed to make decisions about planning or carrying out instruction.

Instructional objective   *See* Educational objective.

Interpretive exercise   Test situation that contains a chart, passage, poem, or other material that the pupil must interpret in order to answer the questions posed.

Item   A single question or problem of an assessment instrument.

Key   A list of correct answers for a test.

Local norms   Test norms that describe a pupil's performance in comparison to pupils in his/her class, school, or city.

Logical error   The use of invalid or irrelevant assessment information to judge a pupil's characteristics or performance.

Lower level processes   Intellectual processes that involve only memorization (e.g., reciting number facts, writing spelling words, stating a poem from memory).

Measurement   The process of quantifying or assigning numbers or categories to performance according to rules and standards.

Norm group   The group of pupils who were tested to produce the norms for a test.

Norm-referenced   Determining the quality of a pupil's performance by comparing it to the performance of other pupils.

Norms   A set of scores that describes the performance of a specific group of pupils, usually a national sample at a particular grade level, on a task or test; these scores are used to interpret scores of other pupils who perform the same task or take the same test.

Objective scoring   Different scorers or raters will independently arrive at the same scores or rating for a pupil's performance.

Observation   Watching or listening to pupils performing an activity or producing a product.

Observer prejudgment   The use of prior information or beliefs that leads a teacher to label a pupil prematurely.

Official assessments   Assessments teachers are required to carry out to fulfill their official, bureaucratic decision-making responsibilities, such as grading, grouping, placing, and promoting pupils.

Options   Choices available to select from in a multiple-choice test item.

Peer review   Pupils discuss and rate each other's work based on clear performance criteria.

Percentile band   The range of percentile ranks in which a pupil would be expected to fall on repeated testing; a way to indicate the error in scores to avoid overinterpretation of results.

Percentile rank   A standardized test score that describes the percentage of pupils a given pupil scored higher than; 89th percentile rank means that a pupil scored higher than 89 percent of the pupils in the norm group.

Performance assessment   Observing and judging a pupil's skill in actually carrying out a physical activity (e.g., giving a speech) or producing a product (e.g., building a birdhouse).

Performance criteria   The observable aspects of

a performance or product that are observed and judged in performance assessment.

Performance standards The levels of achievement pupils must reach to receive particular grades in a criterion-referenced grading system (e.g., higher than 90 receives an A, between 80 and 90 receives a B, etc.).

Portfolio A well-defined collection of pupil products or performances that shows pupil achievement of particular skills over time.

Practical knowledge The beliefs, prior experiences, and strategies that enable a teacher to carry out classroom duties and activities.

Psychomotor behaviors Behaviors related to the performance of physical and manipulative activities such as holding a pencil, buttoning buttons, serving a tennis ball, playing the piano, and cutting with scissors.

Rating scale A written list of performance criteria associated with a particular activity or product in which an observer marks the pupil's performance on each criterion in terms of its quality using a scale that has more than two choices.

Raw score The number of items or total score a pupil obtained on an assessment.

Reliability How consistent the results of an assessment procedure are; if an assessment is reliable, it will yield nearly the same performance information about a pupil on retesting.

Scoring rubric A rating scale based upon written descriptions of varied levels of achievement in a performance assessment situation.

Self-assessment Making a pupil responsible for judging and critiquing his or her own performance or product according to clear performance criteria.

Selection item Test item in which the pupil responds by selecting the answer from choices given; multiple-choice, true-false, and matching items.

Self-fulfilling prophecy Process in which teachers form perceptions about pupil characteristics, treat pupils as if the perceptions are correct, and pupils respond as if they actually have the characteristics, even though they might not have originally had them; an expectation becomes a reality.

Sizing-up assessments Assessments used by teachers in the first weeks of school to get to know pupils so that they can be organized into a classroom society with rules, communication, and control.

Specific determiner Words that give clues to true-false items: all, always, never, none (choose false); some, sometimes, may (choose true).

Standardized An assessment approach designed to be administered, scored, and interpreted in the same way no matter when and where it is administered.

Stanine A standardized test score that describes pupil performance on a nine-point scale ranging from 1 to 9; scores of 1, 2, and 3 are often interpreted as being below average; 4, 5, and 6 as being average; and 7, 8, and 9 as being above average.

State-mandated test Test required of all pupils at certain grade levels in a state; intended to assess individual pupil competence or school-level performance.

Stem The part of a multiple-choice item that states the question to be answered.

Subjective scoring Different scorers or raters will not agree on a pupil's score or rating; independent scorers produce different scores or ratings for a pupil.

Subtest A set of items administered and scored as a separate portion of a longer, more comprehensive test.

Summative assessment Assessment carried out at the end of instruction to determine pupil learning and assign grades; different from formative assessment, which is intended to improve a process while it is still going on.

Supply item Test item in which the pupil responds by writing or constructing his/her own answer; short answer, completion, essay.

Taxonomy A classification system.

Test A formal, systematic procedure for obtaining a sample of pupils' behavior; the results of a test are used to make generalizations about how pupils would have performed on similar but untested behaviors.

Test battery A group of subtests, each assessing a different subject area but all normed on the same sample; designed to be administered to the same group of test takers.

Test form Identifies the grade level(s) for which a test is intended.

Test norms *See* Norms.

Test wiseness   The ability of a test taker to identify flaws in items that give away the correct answers; skill at taking tests and outwitting poor item writers.

Validity   The extent to which assessment information is appropriate for making the desired decision about pupils, instruction, or classroom climate; the degree to which assessment information permits correct interpretations of the desired kind; the most important characteristic of assessment information.

NAME INDEX

Adams, R., 67, 76
Airasian, P. W., 8, 22, 26, 32, 38, 76, 77, 82, 83, 127, 228, 252, 255, 257, 264
Almi, M., 172, 179
Anderson, L. M., 37, 76
Annis, L. F., 93, 127

Baker, E., 173, 179
Barger, S. A., 38, 78
Bartlett, L., 204, 224
Bellanca, J. A., 185, 225
Berliner, D. C., 84, 128
Biddle, B., 67, 76
Bixby, J., 132, 179
Bloom, B. S., 9, 19, 11, 26, 27, 76
Borich, G. D., 146, 179, 200, 225
Brandt, R., 48, 76
Briggs, L. J., 48, 77
Brookhart, S. M., 191, 195, 224
Brophy, J. E., 5, 26, 37, 38, 76, 77
Bullough, R. V., 37, 63, 76
Bushway, A., 117, 128

Cannell, J. J., 228, 264
Canner, J., 92, 128, 231, 256, 265
Carey, L. M., 146, 179
Cartwright, C. A., 44, 77, 146, 148, 179
Cartwright, G. P., 44, 77, 146, 148, 179
Chambers, B., 102, 128
Clandinin, D. J., 38, 60
Clark, C. M., 22, 26, 32, 33, 49, 63, 77
Craver, J. M., 185, 225
Crooks, T. J., 82, 102, 128, 195, 225
Crow, N. A., 37, 63, 76
CTB/McGraw-Hill, 233, 253, 265

Deutsch, M., 195, 225
Downey, M., 37, 77
Doyle, W., 49, 62, 77

Drahozal, E. C., 251, 265
Driscoll, A., 33, 77
Dunbar, S., 173, 179

Ebel, R. E., 93, 116, 128, 146, 179
Eby, J. W., 48, 77
Educational Leadership, 48, 77, 198, 225
Eisner, E. W., 30, 48, 77
Elliot, D. L., 48, 78
Elliott, E., 118, 128
Englehart, M. D., 9, 26, 76
Evertson, C. M., 37, 76, 77

Farr, R., 48, 77
Feiman-Nemser, S., 32, 37, 77
Fenstermacher, G. D., 22, 26
Finn, C. E., 235, 251, 265
Fisher, T., 92, 128, 265
Fitzpatrick, R., 132, 179
Fleming, M., 102, 128
Floden, R. E., 32, 37, 77, 251, 265
Freeman, D. J., 251, 265
Freiberg, H. J., 33, 77
Fremer, J., 92, 128, 265
Friedman, S. J., 185, 194, 225
Frisbie, D. A., 21, 26, 93, 97, 116, 128, 146, 179, 185, 200, 213, 225, 251, 265
Furst, E. J., 9, 26, 31, 76, 77

Gagne, R. M., 48, 77
Gall, M., 69, 77
Gardner, H., 132, 179
Genishi, C., 172, 179
Glen, J., 132, 179
Good, T. L., 5, 26, 37, 38, 76, 77
Gordon, M., 40, 77
Greene, J., 232, 265
Griswold, M. M., 205, 225

Griswold, P. A., 205, 225
Gronlund, N. E., 21, 26, 146, 148, 173,
    179, 219, 225
Guerin, G. R., 44, 77, 137, 179
Gullickson, A. R., 190, 225
Guskey, T., 254, 265

Haladyna, T. M., 92, 128, 265
Hall, J., 92, 128, 265
Hannah, L. S., 11, 27
Harrow, A. J., 11, 27
Hawkes, T. H., 38, 77
Herbert, E. A., 165, 171, 179
Hill, W. H., 9, 26, 76
Hills, J. R., 94, 128, 185, 194, 204, 225
Hubelbank, J. H., 190, 191, 200, 225
Hunter, M., 48, 77

Jackson, P. W., 5, 27, 38, 77
Jenkins, B., 38, 77
Johnson, D., 48, 77
Johnson, R., 48, 77

Keene, J. M., 251, 265
Kellaghan, T., 38, 76, 77, 257, 265
Knappen, L., 251, 265
Knowles, J. G., 37, 63, 76
Krathwohl, D. R., 9, 11, 26, 27, 76
Kubiszyn, T., 200, 225
Kuhs, T. M., 251, 265

Lahaderne, H., 38, 77
Leinhardt, G., 49, 77
Lenke, J. M., 251, 265
Lewis, R. B., 137, 179
Lieberman, A., 32, 78
Linn, R., 21, 26, 146, 148, 173, 179
Lissitz, R. W., 191, 225
Lortie, D. C., 64, 78, 191, 225
Loyd, B., 205, 225

McLoughlin, J. A., 137, 179
Madaus, G. F., 38, 76, 77, 257, 265
Maier, A. S., 44, 77, 137, 179
Marso, R. N., 102, 128

Marston, D. B., 121, 128
Masia, B. B., 11, 27
Mehrens, W. A., 92, 128, 265
Merrill, M. A., 15, 27
Messick, S., 19, 27
Michaels, J. V., 11, 27
Millman, J., 94, 128, 232, 265
Mitchell, R., 162, 179, 254, 257, 265
Morgan, N., 69, 78
Morrison, E. J., 132, 179

Nash, W. R., 117, 128
Nava, F. J., 205, 225
Nisbett, R. E., 40, 44, 78
North Carolina Department of Public
    Education, 258, 259

Office of Technology Assessment, 135,
    162, 179, 254, 258, 266
O'Neil, J., 162, 179
Oosterhof, A. C., 213, 225

Pauk, W., 94, 128
Pedulla, J. J., 38, 76
Perkinson, H., 30, 78
Perlman, C., 92, 128, 265
Peterson, P. L., 32, 38, 63, 78
Phillips, G. W., 235, 251, 265
Pigge, F. L., 102, 128
Popham, W. J., 30, 31, 235, 265
Porter, A. C., 251, 265
Psychological Corporation, The, 233,
    265

Quellmalz, E. S., 10, 27

Rist, R., 5, 27, 67, 78
Riverside Publishing Co., 235, 265
Robinson, G. E., 185, 225
Roeber, E., 92, 128, 265
Ross, L., 40, 44, 78
Rottenberg, C., 231, 256, 265

Salvia, J., 137, 179
Sandifer, P., 92, 128, 265

Sarnacki, R. E., 94, 128
Sax, G., 146, 179, 219, 225
Saxton, J., 69, 78
Schafer, W. D., 191, 225
Schmidt, W. H., 251, 265
Schwille, J. R., 251, 265
Scriven, M., 22, 27, 82, 128
Shavelson, R. J., 33, 78
Simon, S. B., 185, 225
Slavin, R. E., 52, 78, 117, 128, 191, 225
Smith, M. L., 231, 256, 265
Solas, J., 37, 78
Soltis, J., 22, 27
Starch, D., 118, 128
Stern, P., 33, 78
Stiggins, R. J., 139, 179
Stodolsky, S. S., 48, 78
Strike, K., 22, 27

Terman, L. M., 15, 27
Terwilliger, J. S., 194, 200, 225
Tindal, G. A., 121, 128
Tittle, C. K., 257, 265
Tulley, M. A., 48, 77
Tyler, R. W., 30, 31, 78

Wagner, W. W., 48, 77
Waltman, K. K., 194, 200, 213, 225
Wechsler, D., 15, 16, 27
Wiggins, G., 132, 136, 179
Willis, S., 36, 78
Wolf, D. P., 132, 162, 179
Woodward, A., 48, 78

Yinger, R. J., 33, 49, 77
Ysseldyke, J. E., 137, 179

Ability, 30, 199
Absolute grading (*see* Criterion-
    referenced comparison)
Achievement-ability comparison, 245
Achievement battery (*see* Test battery)
Achievement tests (*see* Assessment;
    Classroom tests; Standardized
    achievement tests; State-mandated
    achievement tests)
Administering assessments, 115–118,
    236–237
Affective behaviors, 10–11, 205
Alternative assessment (*see*
    Performance assessment)
American College Testing Program
    (ACT), 14
Analytic score, 121, 147
Anecdotal record:
  defined, 148
  difficulty of use, 149
  example, 148–149
Anxiety (*see* Test anxiety)
Aptitude, 30
    (*See also* American College Testing
    Program; Scholastic Aptitude Test)
Assessment:
  in classroom decision making, 2–3
  defined, 4–5
  in grading, 184–185, 190, 193
  during instruction, 62–65
  interpretation principles, 42–45, 172–
    174, 241–250, 252–253, 255, 257–258
  of performance, 135–139, 158–170
  in planning instruction, 46–49, 58
  preparing pupils for, 92–95, 171
  purposes, 5–8
  standardized tests, 228–236
  at start of school, 33–39
  state-mandated tests, 254–258
  types, 8–9

Assessment (*cont.*):
  (*See also* Classroom tests; Delivering
    instruction; Official assessment;
    Sizing-up assessment; Standardized
    achievement tests; State-mandated
    achievement tests)
Assigning grades (*see* Grading pupils)

Battery (*see* Test battery)
Behavior change (*see* Educate;
    Educational objectives)
Behavioral objective (*see* Educational
    objectives)
Bias:
  consequences of, 40, 233
  cultural, 40, 233
  gender, 40, 233
  observer, 40, 172
  in performance assessment, 172–174
  race, 40, 233
Bluffing, 98–99

California Achievement Tests, 14, 228, 247
Carry over effect, 122
    (*See also* Scoring tests)
Cheating, 116–117
Checklists:
  advantages and disadvantages, 150
  defined, 149
  examples, 141, 149, 159
  scoring, 150–151
Classroom decisions, 1–7
Classroom social system, 33–34
Classroom tests:
  administering, 115–118
  assembling, 114–115
  common errors in, 88, 91, 113
  defined, 82–83

Classroom tests (cont.):
  directions for, 114
  evaluating, 90–91
  as formal assessments, 82
  improving, 113
  item arrangement in, 114–115
  item types, 87–88, 95–102
  item writing, 102–114
  length, 88–89
  preparing pupils for, 92–95
  purpose, 84
  relation to instruction, 85–86, 102–103
  reliability of, 115
  reviewing for pupils, 93
  scheduling, 94–95
  scoring, 118–122
  steps in developing, 85–91, 102–114
  teaching to, 92
  textbook tests, 89–91
  trivializing objectives, 102–103
  validity, 86, 91, 103, 115, 172–174
  (See also Assessment; Official assessment; Test items)
Cognitive behaviors, 9–10, 71
Commercial achievement test (see Standardized achievement tests)
Completion item (see Short-answer item)
Comprehensive Tests of Basic Skills, 228
Concept acquisition, 135–136
Cooperative learning, 136, 141, 202–203
Criterion-referenced comparison, 194–199, 214–216, 257–258
Curriculum defined, 30
Curriculum guides, 47–48, 54–58, 258
Curriculum objective (see Educational objectives)
Cut score, 257–258

Delivering instruction:
  assessing, 64–65
  examples of, 63–64
  good vs. effective instruction, 84
  improving, 68–69
  monitoring, 62–64
  oral questions, 68–72
  vs. planning instruction, 61–62
  questioning, 69–72
  reliability problems, 67

Delivering instruction (cont.):
  teacher as actor in, 68
  teachers' tasks during, 62
  teachers' thoughts during, 63–64
  validity problems, 66–67
Derived scores (see Norms)
Descriptive rating scale, 154–155
Diagnosis, 6
Difficulty (see Item difficulty)
Distractor (see Options)
Distributing scores, 234–235

Editing test items, 113
Educate, 30
Educational ends, 49–60, 84
  (See also Educational objectives)
Educational means, 60, 84
  (See also Delivering instruction; Lesson plans)
Educational objectives:
  assessing textbook objectives, 58
  cautions in using, 54
  examples of, 51–53
  extended, 52
  higher-level, 53
  model for stating, 51
  number needed, 53
  purposes, 49, 51
  relation to pupil achievement, 49
  in standardized achievement tests, 232
  stating, 50–53
  textbook, 58–59
  (See also Lesson plans)
Equivalent form (see Test form)
Error bands (see Percentile bands; Reliability)
Errors of classification, 40–41, 258
Essay items:
  advantages and disadvantages, 98
  bluffing, 98–99
  construction of, 109–110
  examples of, 98, 160
  outcomes assessed, 98
  as performance assessment, 133–134
  scoring, 119–122
Ethical issues in assessment:
  cheating, 116–117
  effects on pupils, 22–23, 40–41

Ethical issues in assessment *(cont.)*:
  in interpreting assessments, 40–41,
    48, 66–67, 172–173, 252–253
  obtaining valid information, 22–24,
    37–38, 40–41, 91, 211–212
  in parent-teacher conferences,
    218–219
  in planning instruction, 46, 55–56
  respecting privacy, 23–25
  in test preparation, 92
Evaluation:
  defined, 4–5
  of educational objectives, 51–52, 58
  of informal observations, 40–43
  of instructional resources, 47–48
  of pupil characteristics, 40–42, 46
  of standardized achievement tests,
    234–236
  of teacher characteristics, 46–47
  of textbook lesson plans, 58
  of textbook tests, 58
External testing programs, 228–229
  (See also Standardized achievement
    tests; State-mandated achievement
    tests)

Fill in the blank item *(see* Short-answer
  items)
Formal vs. informal assessment, 84
Formative assessment, 82–83

Goal *(see* Educational objectives)
Grade, 184
  (See also Grading pupils)
Grade equivalent score, 239–241
Grading curve *(see* Norm-referenced
  comparison)
Grading pupils:
  adjustments in, 198–199, 211–212
  affective considerations in, 205–206
  ambiguity, teacher's role in, 190–192
  combining assessment information,
    210–211
  as comparison, 184, 193–202, 214–217
  computing, 212–214
  in cooperative learning, 202–203
  defending, 193
  defined, 184, 193

Grading pupils *(cont.)*:
  difficulty of, 190–192, 204–205
  ethical aspects of, 199
  examples, 186–189
  fairness in, 199
  importance of, 190
  legal issues, 204
  limitations of, 217–218
  in management by objectives (MBO),
    197–198
  nonrecommended methods, 199–202
  in outcomes-based education, 197–198
  parent/pupil reactions to, 190
  purposes of, 184, 185, 190, 192
  role of judgment in, 191–193
  selection of pupil performances for,
    203–206, 208
  standards of comparison, 192–203
  subject matter differences, 206–208
  teacher responsibility in, 184, 191
  validity issues, 211–212
  weighting pupil performances,
    209–210
Grading systems, 193–194
Graphic rating scale, 153
Group-administered assessment, 16–17,
  228
Guessing, 96, 97, 99

Higher-level behavior, 10, 53, 99–100,
  135
Holistic score, 121, 147
  (See also Essay items)

Individual ability test, 16
Individually administered assessments,
  15–16
Informal assessment:
  characteristics of, 37–39
  in delivering instruction, 62–65
  vs. formal assessment, 135
  improving, 42–45, 68–69
  at start of school year, 34–37
Initial assessments *(see* Sizing-up
  assessment)
Instruction, 30
  (See also Delivering instruction;
    Educational objectives; Planning
    instruction)

Instructional decisions, 2–3, 46–48, 64
  (*See also,* Delivering instruction;
    Educational objectives; Planning
    instruction)
Instructional objectives (*see*
  Educational objectives)
Instructional package, 54–58
Instructional process:
  steps in, 31–32
  teachers' view of, 63–65, 133, 137
  (*See also* Delivering instruction;
    Planning instruction)
Interactive assessment (*see* Delivering
  instruction)
Interpreting test scores:
  achievement-ability comparison, 245
  criterion-referenced system, 194–199,
    257–258
  errors in, 252–253, 257–258
  grade equivalents, 239–241, 244–245
  norm-referenced system, 194–195,
    216–217, 231
  objective by objective, 255–256
  percentile bands, 246
  percentile rank, 238, 244–245
  raw score, 238
  stanine, 239, 241, 244–245
  in state-mandated tests, 255, 257
Interpretive exercise:
  advantages and disadvantages,
    100–102
  characteristics of, 100
  construction of, 101
  examples of, 96
Iowa Tests of Basic Skills, 14, 228, 232,
  247
Item difficulty, 234
Item discrimination, 234
Item writing (*see* Test items)

Judgment:
  in essay scoring, 119–121
  in grading, 190–193
  during instruction, 62–64
  in performance assessment, 138–140,
    147–148
  in planning instruction, 32, 34, 36–37,
    46–48

Key, for scoring, 118

Learning objectives (*see* Educational
  objectives)
Legal issues in grading, 118
Length of test, 88–89
Lesson plans:
  assessing textbook plans, 58
  criteria for judging, 58
  examples, 49, 55–57, 85–86
  higher-level behaviors, 53, 60
  means vs. ends, 60, 84
  model of, 49
  teacher characteristics, 60
  in textbooks, 54–59
  (*See also* Planning instruction)
Letter grades, 185, 214–217
Local norms, 237
Logical errors, 41
Lower-level behaviors, 10, 53

Management by objectives (MBO),
  197–198
Marking book, 207
Marking pupils (*see* Grading pupils)
Matching items:
  advantages and disadvantages, 97
  constructing, 107–108, 111–113
  examples, 97
  outcomes assessed, 97
Measurement, 4–5, 118
  (*See also* Scoring tests)
Mental Measurement Yearbooks, 236
Metropolitan Achievement Tests, 14, 228,
  241
Minimum competency tests, 257
  (*See also* State-mandated achievement
    tests)
Motivation of pupils, 190
Multiple-choice items:
  advantages and disadvantages, 96
  construction of, 104–108, 111, 113
  examples, 96
  and guessing, 96
  outcomes assessed, 96
Multiple grading system, 201

National achievement tests (*see* Standardized achievement tests)
"None of the above," 112
Norm group, 232
Norm-referenced comparison, 194–195, 199, 216 217, 231
Norm-referenced grading curve, 194–195
Normal curve equivalents, 244
Norms:
  development of, 234–235
  examples of, 241–250
  and grade equivalents, 239–241
  judging adequacy of, 235–236, 251–252
  local, 235
  percentile rank, 238–241
  in standardized test construction, 234–236
  stanines, 239–241
Numerical rating scales, 152–153, 160, 167

Objectives (*See* Educational objectives)
Objectivity, 66, 121–122, 190–192
  (*See also* Bias; Performance assessment; Scoring tests)
Observation:
  defined, 13–14
  improving, 42–45
  informal classroom, 35–36
  during instruction, 62–63, 66
  in performance assessment, 137
  planned vs. unplanned, 13–14, 135
Observational techniques:
  anecdotal record, 148–149
  checklist, 149–151
  portfolio, 161–170
  rating scale, 151–154
  rubric, 151, 154–155
Observer prejudgment (*See* Bias)
Official assessment:
  defined, 8, 82
  in grading, 184–185
  importance of, 82–84
  in judging school effectiveness, 254–255
  in relation to instruction, 82

Official assessment (*cont.*):
  standardized achievement tests, 228–230
  state-mandated achievement tests, 254
  teachers' reactions to, 83, 191
Options, 96, 111
Oral questioning, 69–72
  (*See also* Questioning)
Otis Lennon School Ability Test, 241

Parent-teacher conferences, 218–221
Peer review, 158, 160
Percentile bands, 245–246
Percentile norms, 238, 241
Performance assessment:
  advantages and disadvantages, 133–134, 170
  characteristics of, 134, 136, 139
  defined, 132
  in early childhood, 137–138, 159
  examples, 136–137, 140, 141, 148, 153, 154, 159, 160, 162, 167
  formal vs. informal, 135
  improving, 144–146, 151–152, 172–175
  methods of, 148–155, 162–169
  performance criteria for, 141–142, 146, 153–156, 165–166
  portfolios, 162–170
  purposes of, 139–140, 158, 161–163
  relation to instruction, 142, 161–165, 171
  relation to scoring essays, 147
  and reliability, 174–175
  of school performances, 133
  scoring, 147–148, 150–157
  setting for, 146–147, 166
  in special education, 137
  teacher use of, 133, 158, 161–164
  validity of, 170–174
Performance criteria, 140–146, 154
Performance objectives (*see* Educational objectives)
Performance standards, 194–196
  (*See also* Criterion-referenced comparison)
Planning instruction:
  vs. delivering instruction, 61–62

Planning instruction *(cont.)*:
  educational means vs. ends, 60, 84
  elementary vs. high school, 46
  examples, 55–57
  improving, 59–61
  instructional materials, 47–48
  instructional models, 48–49
  pupil characteristics in, 33
  pupil needs in, 33, 46
  and pupil readiness, 46
  purpose of, 32–33
  and sizing-up assessment, 46
  and teacher characteristics, 46–47
  textbooks, 47–48
  and time, 47
  (*See also* Educational objectives;
    Lesson plans)
Portfolio:
  advantages and disadvantages, 170
  defined, 162–163
  developing, 165–166
  examples, 44, 167, 169
  purposes, 163–165
  scoring, 166–169
Preparing pupils for assessment, 85–95
Premises, 97
Pretest, 44
Product assessment, 132–135
  (*See also* Performance assessment)
Psychomotor behaviors, 11–12, 133,
    136, 138
Published tests (*see* Standardized
    achievement tests)
Pupil needs (*see* Delivering instruction;
    Planning instruction)
Pupil-teacher conferences, 217–220
Purposes of assessment, 5–8

Questioning:
  higher- and lower-level, 70–71
  purposes, 69
  strategies of, 70–72
  types of, 69–71
Quizzes:
  in assigning grades, 208
  in monitoring instruction, 68

Rating scale:
  advantages and disadvantages, 151,
    152, 155

Rating scale *(cont.)*:
  defined, 151
  developing, 151–152
  examples, 153–154, 160
  scoring, 152–157
  types of, 151, 153
Raw score, 238
Readiness, 46, 55, 58, 59
Recall items (*see* Lower-level behaviors)
Records:
  anecdotal, 148
  school, 35
Relationship between assessment and
    instruction (*see* Validity)
Relative grading (*see* Norm-referenced
    grading curve)
Reliability:
  errors in scores, 20–22
  improving, 68
  of instructional assessment, 67
  meaning of, 20–21
  of paper-and-pencil classroom tests,
    90, 119–120, 122
  of performance assessment, 174–175
  and relation to validity, 21–22
  of sizing-up assessment, 41–42
  of standardized achievement tests,
    244–245, 253–254
  of state-mandated achievement tests,
    258
  and test length, 88–89
Report card examples, 162, 186–189
Report card grades (*see* Grading pupils)
Review test, 93
Reviewing items, 113
Rubric (*see* Scores)

Scholastic Aptitude Test (SAT), 14
School-based learning, 30
Score bands (*see* Percentile bands)
Scores:
  achievement-ability comparison, 245
  criterion-referenced, 195–197, 199
  grade equivalent, 239–241, 243
  norm-referenced, 194–195, 199
  objective by objective, 255
  percentile bands, 245–246
  percentile rank, 238, 243
  raw, 238

Scores (cont.):
    rubric, 151, 154–157, 162, 195–196
    stanine, 239, 243
Scoring tests:
    adjustments in, 198–199, 211–212
    analytic vs. holistic, 121
    distractions in, 119–120
    essay items, 119–122
    objective vs. subjective, 120–121
    rules, 121–122
    selection items, 118
    supply items, 119–122
Selection items, 13, 87, 96, 98–99
Self-assessment, 158, 160, 167
Self-fulfilling prophesy, 39
Sequential Tests of Educational Progress,
    228
Short-answer items:
    advantages and disadvantages, 97–98
    construction of, 104–105, 107, 108
    examples of, 98
    outcomes assessed, 98
    scoring, 118–119
Sizing-up assessment:
    accuracy of, 38
    characteristics of, 8, 38–39
    defined, 8–9
    effects, 37
    ethical aspects of, 37–38
    improving, 42–45
    and pupil descriptions, 24–26
    relation to instruction, 59
    and reliability problems, 41–43
    sources of information for, 35–36
    stability of, 38
    and validity problems, 40–41, 43
Social assessment, 7–9
Specific determiner, 112–113
SRA Achievement Series, 14, 228
Standardized achievement tests:
    administering, 14, 236–237, 252–254
    characteristics of, 228–229
    compared to other assessments, 229
    construction of, 232–235
    interpreting scores from, 241–250, 252
    norm-referenced nature of, 231
    norms, 235, 237–241, 251–252
    objectives assessed by, 232
    purpose, 228
    report forms, 242, 248, 249

Standardized achievement tests (cont):
    scores, 238–241
    teachers' perceptions of, 230–231
    validity of, 250–254
Standardized assessment instrument,
    14–15, 228
Stanford Achievement Tests, 14, 228
Stanford-Binet Intelligence Scale, 15
Stanine, 239
State-mandated achievement tests:
    characteristics of, 228, 254
    compared to other assessments, 229
    for curriculum evaluation, 254–256
    example, 258–260
    for pupil certification, 257–260
    scoring of, 255–257
    teachers' perceptions of, 230–231
    and test development, 254–255, 257
    types of, 254
Statewide standards, 257
Stem, 96
Subjectivity, 118, 120
Subtests, 232
Summative assessment, 82–83
Supply items, 12, 87, 96, 98–99

Taxonomy:
    affective, 10–11
    cognitive, 9–10, 71
    psychomotor, 11–12
Taxonomy of Educational Objectives,
    Cognitive Domain, 9–10, 71
Teacher-made vs. standardized tests,
    229, 232–236
Teachers' assessment responsibilities
    (see Ethical issues in assessment)
Teaching (see Delivering instruction)
Teaching as art, 68
Teaching to the test, 92
Test:
    defined, 4–5
    item, 95
    relation to assessment, 4–5
Test:
    (See also Classroom tests;
        Standardized achievement tests;
        State-mandated achievement tests)
Test administration:
    cheating, 116–117

Test administration *(cont.)*:
  physical setting, 115–116
  psychological setting, 116
Test anxiety, 116
Test battery, 231–232
Test form, 243
Test item construction problems:
  clues, 110–113
  item wording, 103–106
  lack of brevity, 106–108
  language level, 106
  more than one answer, 104–106
  narrowing desired response, 106–110
Test item types:
  comparison among, 99
  essay, 98
  interpretive exercise, 100–102
  matching, 97
  multiple-choice, 96
  short-answer, 97–98
  true-false, 97
Test items:
  ambiguity of, 104–105, 108–109
  analysis after testing, 119, 211–212
  clues, 110–113
  as communication, 103
  focusing pupils on, 106–109
  higher-level, 99–101
  language level of, 106
  and relation to instruction, 102–103
  reviewing, 113
  selecting, 86–88
  in standardized achievement tests,
    232–235
  trivializing behavior in, 102–103
  types, 96–101
  writing, 102–114
Test level, 243
Test manuals, 236, 250
Test-taking skills, 93–94

Testwiseness, 93–94
Textbook lesson plans (*see* Lesson
  plans; Planning instruction)
Textbook review lessons, 93
Textbook tests (*see* Classroom
  assessment)
True-false items:
  advantages and disadvantages, 97
  construction of, 105–106, 112–113
  examples, 97
  guessing, 97
  outcomes assessed, 97

Validity:
  and bias, 40, 233
  of classroom achievement tests, 84,
    86, 91
  of grading, 211–212
  improving instructional assessment,
    68–69
  improving performance assessment,
    172–175
  improving sizing-up assessment,
    42–45
  of instructional assessment, 66–67
  in interpreting assessments, 40–41,
    66, 92, 172–173, 252–254
  meaning of, 19–20
  of performance assessment, 170–171
  and reliability, 21–22
  of sizing-up assessment, 40–41
  of standardized achievement tests,
    250–254
  of state-mandated achievement tests,
    257

Wechsler Intelligence Scale for Children
  (WISC), 15